The
CATHOLIC SEXUAL ABUSE SCANDAL

Primer from the Pew—Unpacking Psychological,
Sociopolitical & Cultural Factors to Foster Change

JERRY J. PARESA

Editing, design, and distribution by Bublish, Inc.
Published by Fides et Spes Press.

ISBN: 978-1-64704-398-8 (paperback)
ISBN: 978-1-64704-397-1 (eBook)

Dedication

In loving memory of Pope St. John Paul II, whose motto was *"Totus Tuus"* (totally yours), who reminded us not to be afraid, and who inspired many vocations to the priesthood and religious life.

The abuse which has caused this crisis is by every standard wrong and rightly considered a crime by society; it is also an appalling sin in the eyes of God. To the victims and their families, wherever they may be, I express my profound sense of solidarity and concern…We must be confident that this time of trial will bring a purification of the entire Catholic community, a purification that is urgently needed if the Church is to preach more effectively the Gospel of Jesus Christ in all its liberating force.
Pope St. John Paul II, Address to US Cardinals, April 2002[1]

---

[1] Pope John Paul II, "Address of John Paul II to The Cardinals of the United States," April 23, 2002, Vatican City, Libreria Editrice Vaticana, https://www.vatican.va/content/john-paul-ii/en/speeches/2002/april/documents/hf_jp-ii_spe_20020423_usa-cardinals.html.

Table of Contents

Introduction

You all know very well, wherever you may be, the difficult period through which, in the mysterious design of God, the Church is now passing. Consider likewise and ponder on the sacred duty which is yours to stand by and to assist in her struggles, the Church which has bestowed upon you an office of such exalted dignity.
Haerent Animo, letter to Catholic clergy on
priestly sanctity, Pope Pius X, 1908[2]

During the last thirty-five years, few nonpolitical stories have been more impactful and have more consistently captured headlines than the Catholic clergy sexual abuse scandal. The news coverage has been at times a slow, constant trickle, largely due to the lag in cases being reported. Occasionally, stories involving high-profile Church personnel emerge. People of goodwill feel anger as they read harrowing stories of abuse, and empathize with all the victims. Non-Catholics watch their Catholic friends struggle for answers. While the press continues to cover

---

2   Pope Pius X, *Haerent Animo*, Apostolic Exhortation, Given in Rome, at St. Peter's, August 4, 1908, Papal Encyclicals Online, https://www.papalencyclicals.net/pius10/p10haer.htm.

the scandal, urging the Church toward greater transparency, a comprehensive and coherent analysis of the phenomenon has been wanting.

Now, decades into the crisis, the pain remains raw for many victims who have yet to find healing. For most onlookers, the situation is more similar to having US troops in Afghanistan for twenty years. Beyond the standard talking points, the topic has slowly faded from "top of mind" awareness, but most people have formed hardened opinions about the causes and the Church's response. If the sheer passage of time alone is a strategy by Church leaders to let the problem fade into a distant memory, it is faulty and short-sighted. The problem is enduring and the intervening years and experience in this crisis should prompt Church leaders to assess the problem honestly.

Two major studies on the crisis, both commissioned by the United States Catholic Conference of Bishops, were conducted by the John Jay College of Criminal Justice of the City University of New York. The first was published in 2004 and evaluated the scope of the problem between 1950 and 2002; it is hereafter referred to as the John Jay scope report. The second, hereafter referred to as the John Jay cause report, was published in 2011 and examined the causes for the period between 1950 and 2010. The authors of this second study observed in its executive summary that "no single 'cause' of sexual abuse…is identified as a result of our research."[3] Yet surely there are multiple causes, which arguably vary in degree of impact. The severity of this crisis demands that these potential causes be probed.

While the Church is no stranger to difficulty and persecution, this scandal has been largely self-inflicted, and She now buckles under the scourge of the sin and crimes of many of Her priests and leaders. This book serves to contribute to an understanding of the complex confluence of factors that make up this crisis, the response of the Church, and pathways toward solutions.

---

[3]   John Jay College Research Team, "The Causes and Context of Sexual Abuse of Minors by Catholic Priests in the United States, 1950–2010", (Study Report, May 2011), 2, http://votf.org/johnjay/John_Jay_Causes_and_Context_Report.pdf.

Some in Church leadership have tried to convince the public that they now have this under control by pursuing best practices like zero-tolerance policies, harsher and more expeditious penalties for offenders, and human development programs in the seminary. I am not convinced that these are sufficient, and most of the public is generally uninformed even of the steps taken so far. Church leaders, in large part, have been willfully slow to react and to disrupt the status quo, not because they view abuse indifferently, but because real change in such a large institution is hard. Real change for such a problem touches many other areas, and that makes it sinisterly complex. Its complexity makes it a uniquely "wicked problem."[4]

I am not writing this book as part of the Catholic Church's communication infrastructure or in any official capacity. Rather, I am a faithful Catholic writing in love and candor, in the spirit of canon 212 of the Code of Canon Law, which permits the expression of opinion for the good of the Church. My disappointment with the morally aberrant and criminal behavior involved in this crisis has prompted me to enumerate and examine some of the key proximate, contextual, and aggravating causes under one cover.

The problem must be viewed intelligibly and communicated clearly to people of goodwill and to faithful Catholics, many of whom have formed hardened conclusions and have come to see this situation as an impediment to their faith. The Church finds Herself in this situation because of apparent systemic failures, cultural cancers within the Church, poor handling, and weak and tardy communications. Only an honest appraisal can lead us to answers that will pave the way for concrete action. This crisis has also exacerbated the disillusionment that has deeply gripped society. I will address some disturbing societal trends that must be resisted—trends that have increasingly excluded God in exchange

---

[4]   Euphemia Wong, "What is a Wicked Problem and How Can You Solve It?", Interaction Design Foundation, retrieved 8/15/20, https://www.interaction-design.org/literature/article/wicked-problems-5-steps-to-help-you-tackle-wicked-problems-by-combining-systems-thinking-with-agile-methodology.

for a reliance on man's efforts. This leaves society vulnerable to moral relativism and totalitarian impulses that promise to deliver a utopia.

I am not writing this merely in the abstract, for I also had firsthand experience with abusive, inappropriate clergy behavior. The first instance involved an attempted inappropriate touching by a local diocesan parish pastor in the sacristy when I was fourteen years old. By then, I was already discerning the promptings of a call to the priesthood and, in many ways, I viewed this parish priest as a mentor. Yet, flawed in his character, his behavior violated my trust, and I could not view him the same way. The second instance occurred in Rome in 1988 when I was twenty years old, this time from a religious order priest attempting to inappropriately touch me while I was walking in front of him—in the presence of two other priests. Though I immediately rebuffed both instances before anything else could happen, I was pained by disappointment, knowing the ramifications for the victims and for the Church from this type of aberrant conduct. Though these experiences have personalized the crisis for me, I am not writing this book through the lens of a victim.

Though my victimhood was fairly benign compared to the traumatic experiences of others, every person reacts differently. I fully understand those who harbor anger or who feel a numbness from having been violated. I understand how faith and trust have been severely eroded and how families of victims were shaken to their core.

I can only speak through my own lens. At thirteen years of age, I had an experience of God—through no merit of my own. It was a profound and unmistakable knowledge of God's presence, and the imprint of that event has remained alive within me through the trials and tribulations of life. In discerning the call of God in that experience, I received clarification about my relationship with Him, which gave orientation to my life. As the events of my life continue to unfold, including reflections on those events from my birth to the experience of God at age thirteen, I continue to see His presence and providential hand at work. His presence was so pronounced that I did not lose my faith after those later unfortunate experiences, nor did I doubt that Christ's mission for His Church—through the same Spirit that touched me—was still alive and burning. I didn't go through the difficult mental pain and struggle of rising from the ashes. But that same Spirit that touched me is a Spirit of compassion, and I deeply empathize with all victims.

I am grateful to be a product of K–12 Catholic education. Following high school, I was in the inaugural class of seminarians in my diocese's newly opened House of Formation for undergraduate students, where I stayed for two years. During that time, I was honored to serve at Mass with Pope St. John Paul II on September 15, 1987, at the Los Angeles Coliseum. It was the feast of Our Lady of Sorrows. The Gospel reading for that occasion recounts that Simeon foretold the agony of Mary, Mother of Jesus. Simeon said, "You yourself a sword will pierce."[5] Both the victims of this crisis and the whole Church—the Mystical Body of Christ—endure a piercing over these scandals. Even after leaving the seminary, I served as a master of ceremonies for two bishops. While I wished to pen this book years earlier, I was delayed by a thirty-year career that included serving as a casino general manager and the chief executive officer of a complex organization.

As a college-level seminarian for my diocese, I gave celibacy very careful consideration. In the face of this pervasive sexual abuse crisis, I struggled to reconcile priestly mandatory celibacy with instances of abuse and unchaste clergy. This led me to question whether it was accurate that God must give the "gift" of celibacy to those He calls to the priesthood.

In 1988, prior to visiting Rome, I took a leave of absence from the seminary. The seminary rector encouraged me to see more of the world, and my spiritual director, in contrast, warned me that I might lose my innocence by leaving. There was a double irony in that situation: the rector later left active ministry, presumably to see more of the world, and my remaining in the Church structure was no guarantee against the loss of innocence, given the behavior of some clergy.

In 1993, long before the 2002 series of *Boston Globe* stories that gave this issue national attention, I wrote a letter to Pope St. John Paul II that referenced the grave improprieties and tragedies of this crisis. The letter was graciously acknowledged two months later by a reply from

---

[5] Luke 2:35, *The New American Bible*, Catholic Mission Edition, St. Jerome Press (Wichita, Kansas: Devore & Sons, Inc., 1987 and 1981).

the Vatican's Secretariat of State via the Apostolic Nunciature's Office in the United States.

The combination of experiences detailed above has given me insight into the topic, including the role of organizational culture. *Culture* typically refers to the spoken or unspoken beliefs, values, attitudes, customs, and behaviors of a group. It is succinctly summarized by the phrase "that's just the way we do things here." People in organizations are constantly evaluating situations in order to discern signs of the organization's culture—what the organization will tolerate and what it considers unacceptable. Most will quickly adapt to what they perceive and experience as a survival mechanism. And while culture initiatives in organizations may start at the top, there are also subcultures embedded so deep inside groups that the message may never trickle down to all levels without great effort.

Resolute and just action was taken by some bishops when knowledge of sexual abuse came to light in their diocese. But in many other instances, cultural factors permitted this abuse to persist or be covered up. This book will examine some of those prominent factors, including psychological pathology, candidate screening and formation, the pressure from the shortage of priests, the investment to shepherd a candidate through to ordination and beyond, clericalism, celibacy, the atmosphere of tolerating homosexual behaviors in the seminary and priesthood in many quarters, the pastoral theology around the bishop–priest relationship, a shortsighted effort to avoid scandal and preserve reputation, and both the rights of the clergy and canonical remedies under Canon (Church) Law.

The challenges created by this crisis are immense. Most prominent among these are the healing for those who have suffered from the grave sin against justice and faith at the hands of clergy, understanding the problem with clarity as well as the concrete actions needed to prevent the environment and culture which allowed this abuse to pervasively manifest itself, and creating the framework for effective service and evangelization in a post clergy-abuse world so that, as the Gospel is preached, "ears may hear."

St. Joseph, patron of the Universal Church, pray for us.

I

Hope on the Stormy Seas

Christianity has died many times and risen again;
for it had a god who knew the way out of the grave.[6]
G. K. Chesterton

Catholics are a Resurrection People. In baptism, by water and the Spirit, and in daily life, Catholics enter the Paschal Mystery of Christ's death and resurrection by dying to sin and rising to new life. But belief alone does not make redemption automatic. Redemption follows the grace of repentance, conversion, purification, and an obedience to God's will. In these difficult times, Jesus not only comforts, He also calls the Church to freely respond in trust to His invitation of renewal. To contrast the difference in roles between Christ who is comforter and

---

[6] Chesterton, G.K., *The Everlasting Man*, 1925, Part II, Chapter VI, retrieved 6/15/21, as quoted in https://www.worldinvisible.com/library/chesterton/everlasting/part2c6.htm.

Christ who challenges us, I will consider two passages from Mark's Gospel featuring a stormy sea.

The first is the Gospel passage that was proclaimed on May 21, 2019, at the installation mass of Archbishop Wilton Gregory as the seventh archbishop of Washington, DC. The now infamous and former cardinal Theodore McCarrick once held this seat. The reading proclaimed was Mark 4:35–41, "Jesus Calms the Storm." The narrative recounts that Jesus enters a boat with His disciples and instructs them to cross the Sea of Galilee to the other side. A violent squall comes upon them and high waves fill the boat with water. Panicking, the disciples awaken Jesus, who was sleeping at the stern of the boat. Jesus rebukes the wind and commands the sea to be still. Since Her earliest days, whenever She faced the headwinds of opposition and persecution, the Church has turned to this passage as a source of consolation and courage in the abiding presence of Jesus. Archbishop Gregory drew an analogy between his own trepidation in the face of the current storms in the Church and the fear of the apostles as the wind-blown waters of the sea swamped their small boat. Jesus was in the boat with them and ultimately calmed the water. This Gospel passage, once again timely, brings us hope and solace and reminds us that Jesus is indeed the Head of the Church. I would add that this fact reminds us that cults around personalities in the Church will frequently lead to disappointment.

But just a few chapters later in the Gospel of Mark there is another potent story involving turbulent waters on the same Sea of Galilee (Mark 6:45–52, "Jesus Walks on the Water"). The passage records Jesus walking on water during the fourth watch of the night as His disciples were "far out on the sea" and were "tossed about while rowing" into a wind that was against them. It speaks with equal force and relevance about the clergy sexual abuse crisis because it challenges the Church not only to see the Lord as comforter but also to be open to something new.

The passage records that Jesus *compelled* His disciples to enter the boat and cross to the other side of the Sea of Galilee to Bethsaida, a fishing village and border town near gentile territory. The story serves to transition the ministry of Jesus from Jewish territory to the gentile region of Tyre and Sidon. In this crossing of the sea, a symbol of openness to the gentiles, there is resistance by the disciples, which takes the form of strong headwinds. Despite the disciples' hesitation, Mark includes a curious sentence in the narrative: "He [Jesus] meant to pass them by"[7] as they wallowed on the sea, for Jesus understood His mission. Biblical scholars have understood the use of the phrase "pass by" to be a moment of epiphany. What is the epiphany here? Certainly, Jesus demonstrated power over nature in calming the wind and the sea, recapitulating in Himself the action of God creating from the chaos of the cosmos in the book of Genesis. But the passage notes that "their hearts were hardened."[8] Jesus exhorts them, "Do not be afraid."[9] One might take some poetic license to paraphrase His message to the disciples: "I am calling you to something new. Stop resisting and being defensive. Do not be afraid." Jesus doesn't just ride along as a calming companion. He challenges us to something new.

Some of the responses from Church leaders in this crisis have indeed been marked by resistance and defensiveness as a way of attempting to preserve their sense of autonomy and subsidiarity, the current world order, and the status quo. This second story from Mark's Gospel that brings us solace must also challenge us now, as a moment of grace, to cross the sea. The Church must see this crisis with clarity. Clergy sexual abuse is not a rogue expression of doctrinal heresy, nor a wave of sloth. This is a current-day expression of a history of misplaced and very injurious sexual expression by the clergy.

Tackling the deeper remedies that must be pursued will take loyalty, courage, and time. Speaking of a boat in the stormy seas, G. K. Chesterton wrote, "We men and women are all in the same boat, upon a stormy sea. We owe to each other a terrible and tragic loyalty."[10] One of

---

[7]   Mark 6:48, *The New American Bible*, Catholic Mission Edition, St. Jerome Press (Wichita, Kansas: Devore & Sons, Inc., 1987 and 1981).

[8]   Mark 6:52, *The New American Bible*, Catholic Mission Edition.

[9]   Mark 6:50, *The New American Bible*, Catholic Mission Edition.

[10]   G. K. Chesterton., *The Collected Works of G.K. Chesterton Volume 28: The Illustrated London News, 1908-1910*, as quoted in https://www.chesterton.org/lecture-91/, retrieved 6/15/21.

the seven gifts of the Holy Spirit is *fortitude,* which is defined as courage in the face of pain and adversity. That is loyalty.

There is a charming and gentle anecdotal story ascribed to Pope John Paul I during his brief thirty-three day pontificate. Speaking to a little boy, he asked, "When you are sick, does your mother love you and make you well?"

The boy replied, "Yes."

The pope then questioned, "And when she is ill, do you love her and make her well?"

"Yes," said the boy.

The pope continued, "So it is with the Church. When you are sick, She loves you and makes you well. When She is sick, love Her and make Her well."

Our help is in the Name of the Lord.

II

An Evil and Overwhelming Problem

What makes the crisis of clergy sexual abuse so persistently overwhelming? As I probed this crisis, I found a helpful paradigm in an article by Euphemia Wong titled, "What Is a Wicked Problem and How Can You Solve It?" The article contrasts the differences among puzzles, problems, and what Wong calls *wicked problems*.

Consider putting together a puzzle. It has only one right solution and its designer gives us all the relevant pieces—and only those pieces—needed to solve it. Problems, by contrast, can have multiple right solutions or no solution at all. Often, one must sift through useless information as well as insufficient relevant information in an attempt to discern whether a solution exists.

Then there are wicked problems. The qualifying word *wicked* is not intended to be understood in the narrow, moral sense, though it may be applied that way in some cases and does apply in the clergy sexual abuse scandal. Rather, it describes the sinister complexity of a problem that has deleterious consequences for people and society and that cries out for a solution. The article defines this type of problem as "a social or cultural problem that's difficult or impossible to solve—normally because of its complex and interconnected nature."[11] These problems often "lack clarity in both their aims and solutions and are subject to real-world constraints which hinder risk-free attempts to find a solution."[12] Examples of persistent societal wicked problems are homelessness, poverty, racism, failures in the education system, and cover-ups in large institutions. Because of the interdependent factors of these problems, solutions must be considered carefully because they can have unexpected or unintended consequences.

As I probe elements of this scandal, keep the following characteristics of wicked problems, pulled from Wong's article, in mind:

- Every wicked problem is essentially unique.
- There is no definitive formula for a wicked problem.
- Wicked problems have no stopping rule; there's no way to know whether your solution is final.
- Solutions to wicked problems are not true or false; they can be only good or bad.
- You cannot immediately test a solution to a wicked problem.
- Every solution to a wicked problem is a "one-shot operation" because there is no opportunity to learn by trial and error—every attempt counts significantly.
- Wicked problems do not have a set number of potential solutions.
- Every wicked problem can be considered a symptom of another problem.
- There is always more than one explanation for a wicked problem because the explanations vary greatly depending on the individual's perspective.[13]

---

[11] Euphemia Wong, "What is a Wicked Problem and How Can You Solve It?", Interaction Design Foundation, retrieved 8/15/20, https://www.interaction-design.org/literature/article/wicked-problems-5-steps-to-help-you-tackle-wicked-problems-by-combining-systems-thinking-with-agile-methodology.

[12] Wong, "What is a Wicked Problem?"

[13] Wong, "What is a Wicked Problem?"

I believe the clergy sexual abuse crisis possesses most, if not all, of the elements of a wicked problem as defined—and also "wicked" in the moral sense. Such classification will not be immune from criticism. Some will respond by saying, "Let's not make this more complicated than it is." They will reflexively, and understandably, retort that the behavior is criminal and its solution is fundamentally black-and-white. Likewise, any cover-up is criminal and straightforward, and solutions lie in the investigation of civil authorities, prosecution of the criminals, and allowing priests to be married.

Transparency and accountability all the way through to the highest levels of leadership are required. Justice demands this.

One cannot discount the reality that there will always be weeds among us, including those sown by the Evil One, and that mankind suffers from concupiscence and pathology. There is no quick solution to solving weakened human nature, save only for a reliance on the grace of God and responding with justice when harm occurs.

But a simplistic approach, like merely labeling all offenders as "pedophile priests," will never be sufficient in understanding the causes and cultural facets of this persistent wicked problem. Only a thoughtful examination can aid us in crafting meaningful solutions that will be able to take hold in a large and complex institution like the Church.

While driving one day I heard a radio show commentator, whose name I cannot recall, offer this classic and always applicable insight, though he was speaking on a different subject: "When things go wrong, I learn the most." Because understanding a problem is critical in the search for a solution, I will cite a quotation used by a speaker on the website about wicked problems: "If I had an hour to solve a problem, I would spend 55 minutes thinking about the problem and 5 minutes thinking about solutions."[14]

This book spends the necessary "fifty-five minutes" on key facets of the problem in the hope that strong candidates for solutions may unveil themselves.

---

[14] Wong, "What is a Wicked Problem?" (Speech on website was transcribed; speaker was unidentified).

The Scope, the Construct of Causes, and the Two-Tiered Solution

So, how did we get here? What went so terribly wrong? How did the Church, who speaks to all people of goodwill about the dignity of the human person, find Herself in the predicament of tolerating an environment that caused harrowing harm to those She is meant to protect?

The Scope

A 2013 article written at the end of Pope Benedict XVI's pontificate reflects on the scope of the problem, stating,

> According to the U.S. Conference of Catholic Bishops' Office of Child and Youth Protection and independent studies commissioned by the bishops, in the United States, there have been:
>
> - More than 6,100 accused priests since 1950.
> - More than 16,000 victims identified to date...

- $2.5 billion in settlements and therapy bills for victims, attorney fees and costs to care for priests pulled out of ministry from 2004 to 2011."[15]

Some now estimate that 6,800 priests have been accused. Former priest and canon lawyer Thomas Doyle, who coauthored a confidential memo to the US Catholic Conference of Bishops on this matter in 1985, estimates that the crisis implicates some 15,000 priests. Additionally, but in more limited numbers, there were bishops, deacons, and other Church personnel directly responsible for abuse as well.

According to the 2011 John Jay cause report,[16] of the 10,667 reported incidents of abuse, 80.5 percent (8,587) had taken place by 1985, but only 9.44 percent of those (810) had been reported to a diocese by then. In 2002 alone, another 3,399 cases were reported, which was the same year the *Boston Globe* began a series of articles that focused national attention on the problem. While some worried that the media spotlight would lead to fabricated cases in pursuit of perceived deep Church pockets, this heightened attention could just as easily have afforded courage to legitimate victims to come forward. By 2011, according to the same study, only 3 percent of abusive priests had been criminally convicted and only 2 percent received a prison sentence.[17]

The Construct of Causes

In proffering a list of factors for this most recent era of clergy sexual abuse, I found some have a more direct and immediate role (proximate causes)

---

[15] Emma Beck, Eliza Collins, and Cathy Lynn Grossman, "Pope Benedict XVI Leaves a Mixed Legacy on Clergy Sexual Abuse," *National Catholic Reporter*, Feb. 13, 2013, par. 7, retrieved 6/4/21, https://www.ncronline.org/news/accountability/pope-benedict-xvi-leaves-mixed-legacy-clergy-sexual-abuse.

[16] John Jay College Research Team, "The Causes and Context of Sexual Abuse of Minors by Catholic Priests in the United States, 1950–2010" (Study Report, May 2011), 9, http://votf.org/johnjay/John_Jay_Causes_and_Context_Report.pdf.

[17] "The Causes and Context of Sexual Abuse of Minors by Catholic Priests in the United States, 1950–2010" (May 2011), 10.

while others are more broadly contributive (contextual and aggravating causes). Gleaning insight from Church history and this most recent manifestation, I will speak to features of this persistent problem, presenting factors that are already manifest in chronicled stories and reports.

1. Proximate Causes

   A. Personality disorders manifested pre- and post-ordination and poor understanding of them
   B. The increase in homosexual persons in the seminary and priesthood
   C. Ineffective, and sometimes compromised, bishops
   D. Clericalism tied to a sense of arrogance and immunity by perpetrators and Church leaders; abuse of power
   E. Gaps in key areas of candidate screening and priestly formation

2. Contextual Causes

   A. Mandatory celibacy
   B. Shortage of priests and cost of training ("sunk costs")
   C. The sexual revolution and changing norms in society
   D. Pastoral theology relating to the relationship between bishop and priest
   E. Challenges in the application of Canon Law
   F. Alcohol abuse and substance abuse
   G. Culture in subsets of the clergy (fraternity)

3. Aggravating Causes

   A. Shortsighted tactics to avoid scandal
   B. Failure to contact and cooperate with civil authorities
   C. The transfer of clerics and lack of transparency
   D. On-the-fly litigation strategies
   E. Poor crisis communication

The Two-Tiered Solution

While watching the Catholic Eternal Word Television Network in 2019, I listened as a bishop was interviewed on the clergy abuse crisis. He rightly suggested that if more people (presumably those responsible for the present crisis) had availed themselves of the confessional and had not covered up these criminal behaviors, the situation would be much better. Interior conversion—a return to the values of the Gospel—has aided the Church with reform of abuses in the past. Even before the Protestant Reformation, some leaders called for evangelical piety in response to superstitions that had crept into popular belief.

In a speech she gave on the crisis to the US Conference of Catholic Bishops on June 13, 2002, Margaret O'Brien Steinfels quoted from the 1937 book, *The Splendor of the Church*, written by the late French theologian Henri de Lubac. Those words are worth repeating here because they illustrate a starting point for interior conversion:

> We are all men [...] and there is none of us but is aware of his own wretchedness and incapacity; for after all we keep on having our noses rubbed in our own limitations. We have all, at some time or other, caught ourselves red-handed...trying to serve a holy cause by dubious means...so that there are scanty grounds for making exceptional cases for ourselves; and none at all for the withdrawal implied in a grimly-judging eye. If we behave in that way, we fall into an illusion like that of the misanthrope, who takes a dislike to humankind, for all the world as if he himself were not part of it...[18]

---

[18] Margaret O'Brien Steinfels, "The Present Crisis through the Lens of the Laity," June 13, 2002, USCCB meeting in Dallas, Texas, https://www.usccb.org/issues-and-action/child-and-youth-protection/upload/The-Present-Crisis-through-the-Lens-of-the-Laity.pdf.

De Lubac's message does not mean that Christians must cease to discern sinful behavior or to dispense with justice when the circumstances demand it. Rather, his words appropriately orient the Christian to two important truths:

1. His words remind the Christian of Christ's words in the Gospel of Matthew: "Why do you notice the splinter in your brother's eye, but you do not perceive the wooden beam in your own eye?"[19]
2. His words serve to bring the Christian to authentic empathy when it is realized that all fall short of the glory of God and require His forgiveness. The great equalizer is sin resulting from our fallen nature. There are many wounded souls in this tragic crisis, not the least of whom are the victims.

Indeed, if Christians are to preach the Gospel always, using words only if necessary, then their witness must be based in behavior. The authentically lived Christian life is not easy and will challenge human proclivities at every turn. Therefore, effective evangelization can only be rooted in interior reform and daily conversion—precisely St. Paul's meaning when he wrote, "I have been crucified with Christ."[20]

But is interior reform enough? The late Archbishop John Quinn of San Francisco delivered a lecture on June 29, 1996, at Campion Hall, Oxford, regarding the papacy and collegiality. Reflecting on ecumenical dialogue and being open to a new situation, he made some telling comments on reform that speak squarely to the current topic:

> He [the late Cardinal—theologian Yves Congar] goes on to observe the lesson of history that personal holiness of itself is not sufficient to bring about a change and that great holiness has existed in the very midst of situations that cried out for change.

---

[19] Matthew 7:3, *The New American Bible*, Catholic Mission Edition, St. Jerome Press (Wichita, Kansas: Devore & Sons, Inc., 1987 and 1981).

[20] Galatians 2:20, *The New American Bible*.

But he comes to a fundamental and inescapable challenge when he raises the question of why reform-minded men and women of the Middle Ages in fact missed the rendezvous with opportunity. Why did so little happen when there was such a general thirst for reform? Among other things, he cites their penchant for focusing on this or that specific abuse [...]

Most of those who wanted reform, he said, were prisoners of the system, incapable of reforming the structures themselves through a recovery of the original vision, incapable of asking the new questions raised by a new situation. Reform meant to them simply putting the existing structures in order. The further, deeper, long-term questions were never asked. Their vision stopped at the water's edge. The moment passed, and a wounded Church suffered incomparable tragedy.[21]

Therefore, it seems to me that the important obligations of transparency and going to confession alone won't get the Church to the goal of understanding and addressing the root causes of the scandal. It will take a realignment marked by both interior reform and significant, concrete steps, only some of which are already underway.

More recently, this theme was echoed by Pope Francis in his homily at St. Peter's Basilica on October 6, 2019, when he said,

"...if we spend our days content that 'this is the way things have always been done,' then the gift vanishes, smothered by the ashes of fear and concern for defending the status quo. [...] Prudence is not indecision; it is not a defensive attitude. It is the virtue of the pastor who, in order to serve with wisdom, is able to discern, to be receptive to the newness of the Spirit. Rekindling our gift in the fire of the Spirit is the opposite of letting things take their course without doing anything.

---

[21] Archbishop John R. Quinn, "The Claims of the Primacy and the Costly Call to Unity," (Visiting Fellow, Campion Hall, Oxford, June 29, 1996), pars. 19-21, http://www.usao.edu/~facshaferi/QUINN.HTML, retrieved Nov. 5, 2006.

Fidelity to the newness of the Spirit is a grace that we must ask for in prayer"[22]

Pursuing concrete actions of reform, which this crisis demands, is the very invitation of Jesus to cross the sea with trust.

---

[22] Pope Francis, "Homily of Pope Francis: Holy Mass for the Opening of the Synod of Bishops for the Pan-Amazon Region," October 6, 2019, Papal Chapel, Saint Peter's Basilica, Libreria Editrice Vaticana, https://www.vatican.va/content/francesco/en/homilies/2019/documents/papa-francesco_20191006_omelia-sino-do-amazzonia.html.

IV

Crisis Communication: Tone at the Top

I will begin with a monumental aggravating factor in the clergy sexual abuse scandal: the lack of effective communication. The failure to provide a unified, authentic and timely message on this scandal—to victims, the faithful and people of good will—was a significant setback. The Church has been no stranger to scandal over the course of its two-thousand-year history. It is a Church composed of both saints and sinners. With this long-term perspective, the Church tends not to be susceptible or sympathetic to sensationalism. As a large institution, it doesn't have an effective unified command when it comes to swift channels of communication. It is generally more deliberative and methodical. It tends to prudently weigh competing values in order to avoid distortion and misalignment. Yet it is well known that any organization's reputation can be won or lost during moments of crisis.

Though the sexual abuse scandal itself is much weightier and cannot be reduced to an examination of poor messaging, the initially slow and off-message response by Church officials is a case study in crisis communication.

Crisis Communication

Typical crisis communication occurs in response to an event that is usually relatively finite in time, such as the span of a day or a week. Crisis communication often refers to initial messaging as "holding messages," which are intended to provide some factual information even in the "fog of war" when all the facts are still emerging. Those in the media understand that the relevant authorities may not initially have all the answers. In today's environment, the media seeks to understand what happened, why it happened, what the response is, and how it can be prevented in the future.

While the media's questions persisted, this scandal occurred over several decades, with both slow trickles and periodic watershed moments involving high-profile cases, culminating with the national coverage by the *Boston Globe* beginning in early 2002. As media attention became more aggressive, Church leaders realized they wouldn't be able to buy the time needed to figure this out on their own. They were forced into messaging because it was no longer avoidable.

The Church's messaging was tardy, inconsistent, and, to this day, incomplete. This reality continues to hurt the Church. Coverage by the *Boston Globe* provided an opportunity to lay it all out with some clarity. That moment passed, and the underlying causes of the crisis continue to appear largely unaddressed.

When the clergy sexual abuse situation reached an apex in the United States around 2002, a Catholic News Service article served to contrast the pope's remarks with those of some in the Vatican Curia. Describing Pope St. John Paul II's words at the end of a nineteen-page Holy Thursday letter to all priests, the article notes that "the perpetrators of such scandals have betrayed the priesthood and cast a 'shadow of suspicion' over the many good priests in the world. The pope said the church was concerned for the victims of such abuse and wants to handle each case 'in truth and justice.'"[23]

On the same day as the release of the pope's letter, the Prefect of the Congregation for the Clergy, the late Cardinal Darío Castrillón Hoyos, spoke at a press conference.

> The same Catholic News Service article notes that he "listened and took notes as journalists asked more than a dozen questions about the Vatican's handling of sex abuse cases. In response, the cardinal read a two-page prepared statement—interspersed with a few pointed asides—detailing past and present steps taken by the Church to deal with the problem, most of them having to do with Canon Law. Cardinal Castrillón prefaced his remarks by saying it was interesting to note that many of the journalists' questions were posed in English—a fact that he said 'already says something about the problem and gives it an outline.' He said the problem of clerical sex abuse had developed in a culture of 'pan-sexuality and sexual licentiousness.'"[24]

Based on countless similar clergy sexual abuse cases worldwide, scandal and sexual licentiousness are not problems unique to the US or to English-speaking countries. But it was clear that among some in the Curia, there was a bias toward certain English-speaking countries. Impugning the motives of those who ask questions is not a recommended crisis communication tactic.

After acknowledging an unnamed US study that estimated a low percentage of clergy with "'tendencies' toward such abuse," Cardinal Castrillón then stated, "'I would like to know the statistics from other groups and the penalties the others have received and the money the

---

[23] Catholic News Service, "Pope Says Clergy Abusers Betray Priesthood in Letter," Catholic News Service (2002), retrieved April 2, 2002.
[24] Catholic News Service, "Pope Says."

others have paid to the victims,' departing from his prepared statement."[25] Deflecting attention away from the Church's own problem is also not a helpful tactic, and clergy are rightly held to a higher standard.

In addressing some shortcomings in Canon Law, the Church had, by then, lengthened its statutes of limitations for such crimes from five years to ten, "a period that begins after the alleged victim's 18th birthday; it also raised the church's legal definition of a minor from 16 to 18 in such cases."[26] Yet Cardinal Castrillón "…interrupted his prepared remarks to say: 'I would like to see in what other legislation in the world this has been done.'"[27] Boasting about doing the right thing, or expressing agitation in doing so when compared to others, misses the mark.

The cardinal went on to say, "The laws of the church are serious and severe and have been drawn up in a tradition…of dealing with internal matters in an internal way."[28] This statement lacked all situational awareness. Yes, the Church has had to create such laws to address issues throughout its history, but its "internal way" has been an aggravating factor in the problem all along.

The most reasonable off-the-cuff remark Cardinal Castrillón Hoyos made was summarized by the article writer in this fashion: "The cardinal said the church expects its ministers to be treated like other citizens by civil authorities—without advantages, but without disadvantages, either."[29] Yes, there should be a presumption of innocence and there should be legal due process. But justice is also required when the cases of those credibly accused have been adjudicated.

On June 4, 2002, Stephen Weeke, a reporter assigned to the story, chronicled the bias by the Vatican Curia. Reacting to a nine-page article published in *La Civiltà Cattolica*, a twice-monthly Italian magazine produced by Jesuit priests, Weeke writes,

---

[25]   Catholic News Service, "Pope Says."
[26]   Catholic News Service, "Pope Says."
[27]   Catholic News Service, "Pope Says."
[28]   Catholic News Service, "Pope Says."
[29]   Catholic News Service, "Pope Says."

The article goes after American journalists' handling of the current child sex abuse scandal engulfing the Catholic Church in America. To put the importance of this kind of article in context we need to remember that this isn't just a case of one individual Jesuit priest speaking his mind: all the articles in this publication are pre-approved by the Vatican before they get published. The problem with this is that most people in the world don't really understand how the Vatican "machine" works. When they hear about these statements they think this stuff is coming straight from the pope. It's not. What it reflects is what the 'Curia' is thinking, that's the administrative bureaucracy that runs the church for the pope, and has done so for centuries. [...] So the article is an interesting look at what the Curia is thinking these days [...] instead of confronting the issue head on, a church mouthpiece appears to have chosen to focus on the placement of satellite trucks in front of the Vatican rather than on why the television equipment was put there in the first place.[30]

One or both of the following seem to be true: authorities in the Vatican were truly unaware of the magnitude of the problem and believed this was being fueled by anti-Catholic bigotry, or they were truly ill-prepared for crisis communication. By this point in time, there had been ample attention to clergy sexual abuse. I suspect it was the latter.

This "tone at the top" put bishops across the globe, and in the United States, in a real quagmire. The very authorities they needed to turn to for assistance in handling the disposition of accused priests through Canon Law seemed to need to overcome bias themselves and to seriously acknowledge the scope and magnitude of the problem and its pastorally devastating effects.

---

[30] Stephen Weeke, "Vatican Takes Aim at American Press," NBC News, June 3, 2002, retrieved on 6/25/21, https://www.nbcnews.com/id/wbna3071438.

Early Messaging

Much of the early messaging by Church leaders, while attempting to be sensitive to the victims, was often interspersed with themes of defensiveness and a deflection of responsibility:

- We are a Church made of saints and sinners.
- It happens in all sectors of society.
- Only 3–5 percent of priests were implicated.
- This all happened decades ago (as if the underlying issues are no longer there).
- It is the anti-Catholic media that gives attention to these cases, disproportionate to other organizations.
- It is the United States' white Anglo-Saxon Protestant bigotry against Catholics, currents of which have episodically existed since the country's colonial period.
- It is the United States culture's obsession with sex.
- Many victims are only looking for a settlement.

These themes combined with revelations about abusive clergy being moved from parish to parish, or from diocese to diocese, and given treatment and readmitted into active ministry made for an unpalatable and toxic cocktail that further eroded credibility.

Preferred Messaging

Any combination of the messages below would have worked much better. I would argue that these messages continue to be applicable today and are worth repeating whenever the opportunity presents itself:

- We are committed to the protection of children and young people.
- Even though all human persons fall short, these crimes are intolerable and incompatible with the Gospel and the Christian life.

- This is a seminal moment of reform and purification in the Church, and we will work with experts and leaders to get to the bottom of it.
- We demand justice for the victims, for whom we are praying and offering support.
- We're fully cooperating with law enforcement at every step.
- We are addressing the inadequacies in Church Law to handle these cases.
- We've established reporting mechanisms to respond to cases swiftly and pastorally.
- Because predators often "groom" victims and seek out the vulnerable, we ask for the partnership of parents and guardians of children to be vigilant with us and report anything that is unusual or of concern.
- Please support our good priests who feel the weight of this challenging time.

To their credit, many bishops did communicate these messages early in the crisis.

Communication Lessons Learned

There is some evidence of a gradual communications shift at the Vatican during Pope Benedict XVI's tenure, as the Vatican better understood it was now in "damage control." As the Holy See issued changes in procedures to handle clergy sexual abuse cases, they were published in multiple languages and made available on the Vatican's website. Quoting P. Federico Lombardi, Director of the Vatican press agency, "It is right for there to be transparency about the laws that are in place to combat these crimes, and it is appropriate that those laws be presented in their entirety to enable anyone who needs information on the topic to have full access to them."[31] Some bishops also made similar information available on their diocesan websites.

In hindsight, it appears the Vatican has made progress on this front. Consider the following coverage in 2019 by Greg Erlandson of the Catholic News Service:

> In a remarkably frank and detailed speech, the Vatican official heading the department charged with reviewing the clergy sexual abuse allegations [Msgr. John Kennedy] told an assembly of Catholic journalists that his investigators and the press "share the same goal, which is the protection of minors, and we have the same wish to leave the world a little better than how we found it." [...]
>
> "I can honestly tell you that, when reading cases involving sexual abuse by clerics, you never get used to it, and you can feel your heart and soul hurting." [...] "There are times when I am pouring over cases that I want to get up and scream, that I want to pack up my things and leave the office and not come back." [...]
>
> "What of the father, mother or siblings of the child who have to look at that child and live through this? What can they say? Everything has been taken from them. You believe me when I am telling you these things. Can you imagine what it might be like not to be believed by church authorities? What would it be like to remain silent because a person did not have the courage to come forward and name their abuser?" [...]
>
> "In all honesty, this work has changed me and all who work with me." [...] "It has taken away another part of my innocence and has overshadowed me with a sense of sadness."[32]

---

31 Davide Cito, "The New Delicta Graviora Laws," *Ave Maria International Law Journal*, Vol. 1, Issue 1, ISSN no. 2375-2173 (Fall 2011): 90–116, 93, https://ave-marialaw-international-law-journal.avemarialaw.edu/Content/iljarticles/2011. Cito.DelictaGraviora.final.pdf.

32 Greg Erlandson, "Vatican Official Praises Catholic Media for Coverage of sex Abuse Crisis," Catholic News Service (June 20, 2019), retrieved 7/29/2020, pars. 1, 3, 11, 22, https://www.catholicregister.org/faith/item/29772-vatican-official-praises-catholic-media-for-coverage-of-sex-abuse-crisis.

This example of communication is based on truth, transparency, openness, and empathy. I pray that it continues. In fairness, all three recent popes who have handled the burden of this crisis have been deeply pained by the scandal and have expressed deep sorrow for the victims. But this chapter has shown an evolution in the Church's messaging as the magnitude of the crisis has borne down on the Church. The Church did not get out in front of this crisis effectively and honestly, and this has retarded the public's understanding of the problem, the solutions, and the road back to credibility.

V

Living the Truth in Love

To defend the truth, to articulate it with humility and conviction, and
to bear witness to it in life are therefore exacting and indispensable forms
of charity. Charity, in fact, "rejoices in the truth" (1 Cor. 13:6).
Caritas In Veritate, Pope Benedict XVI, June 29, 2009[33]

Solutions to the clergy sexual abuse problem will be the fruit of Christian love and justice. But it must begin with truth, which is the antecedent to love's willful expression. Truth is the only road to clarity about this crisis, and truth must compel Church leaders to act justly and consistently in regard to the propositions listed:

[33] Pope Benedict XVI, Encyclical Letter *Caritas in Veritate*, #1, Given in Rome, At Saint Peter's, June 29, 2009, #1, https://www.vatican.va/content/benedict-xvi/en/encyclicals/documents/hf_ben-xvi_enc_20090629_caritas-in-veritate.html.

- Truth responds compassionately to the harm, palpable hurt, and betrayal of victims and their families.
- Truth acknowledges the crimes and the grave sin involved in this crisis.
- Truth recognizes systemic cultural and moral defects within the Church and resolves to address them effectively.
- Truth concedes that the witness to the Gospel has been compromised by the behavior of many Church leaders in handling these cases.
- Truth is wedded with accountability, for "when one has had a great deal given on trust, even more will be expected" (Luke 12:48).
- Truth must communicate the problem and its causes with humility and sincerity and, in love, resolve to enact reform and seek justice that aims to heal and restore.

In this chapter, I will look at this criminal behavior truthfully and in relation to sin and scandal.

Clergy Sexual Abuse as Sin

The *Catechism of the Catholic Church* defines sin as "an offense against reason, truth, and right conscience; it is a failure in genuine love for God and neighbor caused by a perverse attachment to certain goods. It wounds the nature of man and injures human solidarity. It has been defined as 'an utterance, a deed, or a desire contrary to the eternal law.'"[34] Consistent with this definition, the crimes of clergy sexual abuse, which included cover-ups and abuse of power, in the objective sense, qualify as grave sins in every regard.

---

[34] Libreria Editrice Vaticana, *Catechism of the Catholic Church*, 2nd ed (Citta del Vaticana: Libreria Editrice Vaticana, 1997), 453, #1849.

Clergy Sexual Abuse as Scandal

St. Paul reminds us that "all have sinned and are deprived of the glory of God."[35] He recounts his own struggles when he says, "For I do not do the good I want, but I do the evil I do not want."[36] But personal sin can also be a source of scandal.

In the *Catechism of the Catholic Church*, the concept of scandal appropriately comes under the heading of "Respect for the Dignity of Persons." Therefore, scandal is not simply a bad or an embarrassing incident that disgraces reputation. Rather, it is first and foremost a harm against the dignity of persons that has moral and often legal consequences. As such, prioritizing the protecting of reputation before healing the harm and implementing the needed reform is ineffective and replete with danger. The Catechism defines scandal as

> an attitude or behavior which leads another to do evil. The person who gives scandal becomes his neighbor's tempter. He damages virtue and integrity; he may even draw his brother into spiritual death. Scandal is a grave offense if by deed or omission another is deliberately led into a grave offense. Scandal takes on a particular gravity by reason of the authority of those who cause it or the weakness of those who are scandalized. Scandal is grave when given by those who by nature or office are obliged to teach and educate others. Jesus reproaches the scribes and Pharisees on this account: he likens them to wolves in sheep's clothing.[37]

The abused in this serious crisis need healing and restoration. Victims are left with confusion, anger, despair, loss of faith, and "spiritual death," all of which are particularly aggravated when leaders do not listen and when the violator remains in active ministry or escapes justice. Tragically, some victims have even committed suicide.

---

[35] Romans 3:23, *The New American Bible*, Catholic Mission Edition, St. Jerome Press (Wichita, Kansas: Devore & Sons, Inc., 1987 and 1981).

[36] Romans 7:19, *The New American Bible*.

[37] Libreria Editrice Vaticana, *Catechism*, 551, #2284-85.

The clergy sexual abuse phenomenon is a tragic crisis of sin and scandal; it is a physical offense and sin against the human dignity of the victim, and it simultaneously undermines authority in an important societal institution and impairs and muddles the good influence of the pilgrim Church in the world, as this pernicious sin instead gives witness to behavior that is antithetical to both preaching and belief. The Church becomes like a pearl that has lost its luster, as society now focuses only on what She singularly has in common with human institutions.

In the Judeo-Christian Catholic tradition, sin is not a private matter. Popular thinking evaluates behavior by whether it "feels good" or not, or whether it is likely to cause feelings of guilt or not. Christians do not use that subjective measurement when determining whether behavior is sinful. Sinful behavior injures all of us. Because man is a social being, even sin that is not public has a social dimension because it diminishes the Christian's capacity to love God, themselves, and others in truth, as Christ has loved them.

A Grave Sin Against the Faith *(Delicta maiora contra fidem)*

Embedded in the story of the fall of Adam and Eve is a clear message: the actions of persons have consequences. Clergy sexual abuse is not only a crime and a moral sin *(contra mores)*, it is also a sin against the faith *(contra fidem)*.

In addition to the abovementioned harmful consequences for victims, the sin and the scandal also undermine the faith of victims' families and even of those who are not direct victims. In June 2002, the President of the United States Catholic Conference of Bishops, Bishop Wilton D. Gregory, gave a speech (later reprinted by the Associated Press) to the assembled bishops, wishing to address the crisis candidly. Curiously, he remarked, "This crisis is not about a lack of faith in God. In fact, those Catholics who live their faith actively day by day will tell you that their faith in God is not in jeopardy.... What we are facing is not a breakdown in belief...."[38] In what was otherwise a contrite and comprehensive, albeit tardy, speech on the crisis, I think his observation about the impact on faith was shielded from what was taking place. Because one cannot see God, people experience Him through perceptible signs. When those signs that are meant to be trusted instead become a source of injury, understandable disillusionment will follow.

A Gallup Poll article published in April 2018 notes the following data-driven observations: "U.S. church membership was 70% or higher from 1937 through 1976," and only fell "modestly to an average of 68% in the 1970s through the 1990s. The past 20 years has seen an acceleration in the drop-off, with a 20-percentage-point decline since 1999 and more than half of that change occurring since the start of the current decade. The decline in church membership mostly reflects the fact that fewer Americans than in the past now have any religious affiliation." That figure "has more than doubled, from 8% to 19%."[39] Also in 2018, Gallup noted that "from 2014 to 2017, an average of 39% of Catholics reported attending church in the past seven days."[40] The relationship of this drop-off to the timing of the apex of this crisis should be noted. While there were several articles on the clergy sexual abuse crisis in the 1980s and 1990s—including a *New York Times* article in 1986 by Jonathan Friendly—the issue reached widespread visibility through a series of articles and editorials in the *Boston Globe* in early 2002. Societal disillusionment in institutions abounds, and its connection to the clergy scandal is unmistakable.

---

[38] Bishop Wilton D. Gregory, "Statement by President of the U.S. Catholic Bishops on Sexual Abuse," USCCB Conference in Dallas, Texas, (June 13, 2002), 1, https://www.usccb.org/issues-and-action/child-and-youth-protection/upload/Statement-by-President-of-the-U.pdf.

[39] Jeffrey M. Jones, "U.S. Church Membership Down Sharply in Past Two Decades," Gallup (April 18, 2019), https://news.gallup.com/poll/248837/church-membership-down-sharply-past-two-decades.aspx.

[40] Lydia Saad, "Catholics' Church Attendance Resumes Downward Slide," Gallup (April 9, 2018), http://news.gallup.com/poll/23226/church-attendance-among-catholics-resumes-downward-slide.aspx.

The Victims

The victims are innumerable, with estimates of direct victims as high as fifteen thousand. They have suffered principally at the hands of priests and prelates, as well as some deacons and others involved in ancillary activities in the Church. Whatever form clergy sexual abuse takes, depraved and painful as every instance is, many cases come to light only long after the fact. It is reasonable to conjecture that some may never come to light. Statistics about the low reporting by abuse victims support this conclusion. Some case reporting is likely to trickle in long after initial corrective measures are established, and, until a new culture is put into place, new cases will inevitably arise.

There are also innumerable collateral victims, those within the fold of the Mystical Body of Christ and in society at large. The Church finds Her voice impaired by the scandal. Catholics, flooded with a range of emotions, are left bewildered. Some are using the scandal as a pretext to leave the Church while those still in the pews are hoping for answers, healing, and reform. Then there are the just and righteous clergy, who carry the weight of hurt and betrayal and who contend with navigating ministry in this new, regulated environment where no words can seem to bring consolation. Even the Church's separated Christian brothers and sisters have been hurt by this, for it undermines the Gospel wherever it is preached, and it ultimately impedes ecumenical dialogue. Sin injures human solidarity. It injures Christian unity. It also mires the Church down in internal reflection and crisis administration, diminishing the effectiveness of Her mission to engage, "with maternal solicitude," all people, "whether they be believers or not."[41]

---

[41] Pope St. Paul VI, Second Vatican Ecumenical Council Decree *Christus Dominus*, #13, October 28, 1965, https://www.vatican.va/archive/hist_councils/ii_vatican_council/documents/vat-ii_decree_19651028_christus-dominus_en.html.

This book attempts to examine this crisis in truth, to advance understanding and thereby focus on pathways for solutions. This maxim attributed to Johann Wolfgang von Goethe captures my effort: "It is easier to perceive error than to find truth, for the former lies on the surface and is easily seen, while the latter lies in the depth, where few are willing to search for it."[42]

---

[42] Johann Wolfgang von Goethe, retrieved 6/20/21, cited in https://www.inspiringquotes.us/author/5643-johann-wolfgang-von-goethe/page:6.

VI

A Cocktail of Combustible Factors

In keeping with the themes of truth and the unique nature of a *wicked problem*, I want to survey many of the factors involved in this crisis. The clergy sexual abuse phenomenon is unique, but not because all its features are unique. Rather, it derives from a particular confluence of characteristics and their interdependent complexities. Analyzing the root causes of sexual abuse in a general sense is already challenging, but even more so because it manifests itself amid a combination of factors in the Catholic Church. I will begin by differentiating between what is not unique to the Catholic clergy sexual abuse crisis and then transition to those characteristics that *are* unique.

Nonunique Factors

Sexual Assault and Sexual Abuse in Societal Institutions

The sexual abuse of adults and minors occurs in all sectors of society and is not unique to the Catholic Church. It can be argued that it should never happen in an organization that is meant to be the haven of Godliness. Yet, the Church shares components found in other institutions and is inhabited by both saints and sinful humans. There will be sin—even when steps to mitigate and minimize risk are in place.

Sadly, cases of sexual assault and sexual abuse have been chronicled—at the hands of both male and female predators—in schools, in the US military, in human sex trafficking, in the Boy Scouts, in Hollywood, in the infamous McMartin Preschool molestation case in the 1980s, in Congress, and in homes across America.

As a specific example, consider the May 2, 2019, *New York Times* article on the US military, which reported an estimated "20,500 instances of 'unwanted sexual contact' in the 2018 fiscal year," up "38 percent from the previous survey in 2016." The 2018 survey "indicates that alcohol use remains a stubborn contributing factor, and was involved in 62 percent of assaults on women."[43]

Some may see this modern-day clergy crisis as something new in the Church, but, regrettably, it is not unique in the Church's long history. The Church has seen episodic outbreaks of this nature in the past, but today society has rightly shone light on these crimes against the dignity of victims.

Sexual Assault in Other Religious Institutions

As enumerated above, sexual abuse can be found in many institutions and in society at large. Regarding religious institutions, sexual assault and even the sexual abuse of minors is not unique to the Catholic Church.

In June 2019, when the US bishops met in Baltimore to further address sexual abuse, there was also a Southern Baptist convention underway in Birmingham, Alabama, that was addressing the same concern. As covered by National Public Radio, the convention featured a female Baptist speaker who was an abuse survivor when she was a teenager. The story provided a transcript of an archived sound recording made by the

---

[43]   David Philipps, "'This Is Unacceptable': Military Reports a Surge of Sexual Assaults in the Ranks," *New York Times*, (May 2, 2019), par. 2, https://www.nytimes.com/2019/05/02/us/military-sexual-assault.html.

victim. It reads: "He wrapped the ball around the pole to the point that I was tied to the pole. He said, 'Susan, will you answer God's call? And will you help me in my ministry?' And I said yes. And he leaned over, and he kissed me."[44]

Religious leaders of other traditions have leveraged their position of authority to initiate unwanted advances and sexual abuse even of minors. The John Jay cause report cites a book by Philip Jenkins, "in which he reported that 10 percent of Protestant clergy have been involved in sexual misconduct, of whom about 2 or 3 percent are child sexual abusers."[45] Gleaning information from insurance carriers, the same report also mentions that "the insurers estimate that Protestant churches receive upwards of 260 reports annually of sexual abuse by clergy, church staff, volunteers, or congregation members from persons eighteen years of age or younger."[46]

In a November 27, 2019, article titled "Sex Abuse in the Orthodox Church? POKVOR.org Sheds Light on a Dark Secret," Irene Archos writes the following:

> Sex abuse in the Orthodox Church? Nah. That doesn't happen here. Our priests don't have to be celibate, so they don't have to grapple with urges. Our choir boys do not get abused by clergy in cloak rooms. That happens in the Catholic Church....But what is the truth about sex abuse in the Orthodox Church?...
>
> Imagine yourself a devout Orthodox Christian attending your local parish in California. You respect the priest; you know the people there; most likely you have more than one intimate connection with those in the parish either as god-parents, friends, or study mates. Then one Sunday morning, you walk in to find families with children you have known

---

[44] NPR, "Southern Baptist Convention and Sexual Abuse," June 14, 2019, par. 2, https://www.npr.org/2019/06/14/732628096/southern-baptist-convention-and-sexual-abuse.

[45] John Jay College Research Team, "The Causes and Context of Sexual Abuse of Minors by Catholic Priests in the United States, 1950–2010" (Study Report, May 2011), 20, http://votf.org/johnjay/John_Jay_Causes_and_Context_Report.pdf.

[46] John Jay College Research Team, "The Causes and Context," 20.

for years have disappeared. And then you hear the shocking news: four children have been allegedly sexually abused by a catechumen in the parish. The parents of the children bring a suit against the Orthodox Church of America for their knowledge of the status of a layman…as a sex offender. But the Bishop refuses to compensate the victims; he refuses to admit of any wrongdoing on the church's part. The parish council agrees to pay for the therapy for the children, but he dismantles the program.

As the sad tale unfolds, you witness your family disintegrate. You start to question the very foundations of your faith.[47]

In this example, it was not the cleric who committed the sexual abuse, but its effect on the community's solidarity and faith was shattering, and the leadership, according to the article, appears to have been nonresponsive to the impact.

Underreporting and Low Conviction Rate of Abuse Cases

While clergy were thought to be beyond reproach, and internal investigations and slow Church response hampered the progress of many cases, the actual reporting on sexual assault and abuse remains stubbornly low in society at large. The Darkness to Light website's document "Child Sexual Abuse Statistics" states that while "it is estimated that only 4 to 8% of child sexual abuse reports are fabricated, arrests are made in only 29% of child sexual abuse cases and are 32% more likely to be made in incidents involving older children. For children under six, only 19% of sexual abuse incidents result in arrest."[48] For example, in the case of rape or attempted rape, only 31 percent are reported to police, some 5.7

---

47 Irene Archos, "Sex Abuse in the Orthodox Church? POKVOR.org Sheds Light on a Dark Secret," November 27, 2019, par. 1-2, https://greekamericangirl.com/sex-abuse-in-the-orthodox-church/.

48 Darkness to Light, "Child Sexual Abuse Statistics" (Issue Brief and Statistical Report, 6/1/2021), 8, https://www.d2l.org/wp-content/uploads/2017/01/all_statistics_20150619.pdf.

percent lead to an arrest, and less than 1 percent lead to conviction and incarceration.[49]

Sexual Assault and Sexual Abuse Not Unique to Celibate Men

Sexually assaulting adults or sexually abusing minors is not behavior that is unique to celibate, unmarried men. Perpetrators can be male or female, of heterosexual or homosexual orientation (or a confused orientation), and married or unmarried.

The literature is sparse on the comparative prevalence of married and unmarried sexual assault perpetrators. Perhaps more study is needed. The US Air Force commissioned a study that resulted in a 2015 report by the Rand Corporation titled "A Review of the Literature on Sexual Assault Perpetrator Characteristics and Behaviors." The report referenced a study that looked at Navy recruits and their experiences with sexual assault: "Thirteen percent of the more than 5,000 men surveyed reported having perpetrated sexual assault since reaching 14 years of age. The only significant factor associated with sexual assault perpetration was marital status; men who were married were least likely to report having perpetrated sexual assault (Stander et al., 2008)."[50] This study appears to be based on self-reporting, but "least likely to report" does not mean that married men don't perpetrate sexual assault.

While not all of the reported clergy sexual abuse cases of minors involved diagnosed pedophilia, other, more general data suggests that perpetrators diagnosed with pedophilia are both married and unmarried and that they often suffer from a confused sexual identity, sometimes beginning at the time of their own puberty.

---

[49] Andrew Van Dam, "Less Than 1% of Rapes Lead to Felony Convictions: At Least 89% of Victims Face Emotional and Physical Consequences," *Washington Post*, Oct. 6, 2018, https://www.washingtonpost.com/business/2018/10/06/less-than-percent-rapes-lead-felony-convictions-least-percent-victims-face-emotional-physical-consequences/.

[50] Rand Corporation, "A Review of the Literature on Sexual Assault Perpetrator Characteristics and Behaviors," 2015, 26, https://www.rand.org/content/dam/rand/pubs/research_reports/RR1000/RR1082/RAND_RR1082.pdf.

The second study commissioned by the Church in order to reflect on the causes and context of the crisis notes that "an exclusively male priesthood and the commitment to celibate chastity were invariant during the increase, peak, and decrease in abuse incidents, and thus are not causes of the 'crisis.'"[51] Celibacy was a "constant," a controlled factor, throughout the phenomena.

But the Church has long recognized the difficulty of living as a celibate. In describing the celibate life of those not properly prepared for or disposed to it, a Church document published in 1961 titled *Religiosorum Institutio* states that "...religious celibacy [for such persons] would be a continual act of heroism and a trying martyrdom."[52] But the difficulty of such a life choice alone does not necessarily lead to sexual assault or abuse of minors. There are countless examples of priests throughout history who have lived their commitment faithfully. But for priests with psychological and developmental issues, or those unable to keep the commitment and who end up living a double life, celibacy can be a serious contributing factor to this behavior.

While married men may be statistically less likely to sexually assault adults or sexually abuse children, married men do commit these offenses. I believe celibacy is best understood as being among the more influential contextual factors and not as being a proximate cause of the crisis.

Abuse of Power

The Catholic clergy sexual abuse scandal exposed an abuse of power on several distinct levels. First, the perpetrators abused their respected authority and their relationships with the victims. Second, the response by some Church leaders was marked at times by intimidation, deception,

---

[51] John Jay College Research Team, "The Causes and Context of Sexual Abuse of Minors by Catholic Priests in the United States, 1950–2010" (Study Report: May 2011), 3, http://votf.org/johnjay/John_Jay_Causes_and_Context_Report.pdf.

[52] Sacred Congregation for Religious, "*Religiosorum Institutio*: Instruction on the Careful Selection and Training of Candidates for the States of Perfection and Sacred Orders," February 2, 1961, #30, https://www.ewtn.com/catholicism/library/religiosorum-institutio-2007.

and cover-up attempts. It could be characterized as a culture of impunity. Even so, this behavior is not unique to the Catholic Church. In any institution, people in positions of authority often engage in risky, immoral, and illegal behavior.

Consider the myriad of defrocked politicians. People in positions of authority are often very intelligent and should know better than to engage in inappropriate behavior and risk getting caught. The result of being caught is highly predictable and would ordinarily be perceived by the risk-taker. It raises the timeless question of why intelligent and otherwise successful people still engage in risky behaviors. A *Seattle Times* article published on March 11, 2008, observing such cases as former New York Governor Eliot Spitzer and former New Jersey Governor James McGreevey, states,

> For psychologists and political analysts who found themselves dissecting the Spitzer story, it was a question of the chicken or the egg: In such situations, does the risky behavior precede the powerful job? Or does something about being in power cause the behavior?…
>
> "The problem is we don't know when this behavior started for this person," said [Steven] Cohen, a professor of public administration at Columbia University. "Politicians are like the rest of us. The fact that they're flawed and do stupid things shouldn't surprise us."[53]

Steven Cohen's question about when this behavior begins is especially critical to the discussion of sexual assault and abuse and cannot be overlooked. Numerous studies point out that one of the highest and most consistent predictors of sexual assault or abuse is the perpetrator's similar past behavior. Studies indicate that this past behavior is a more reliable predictor than even the perpetrator themselves having been previously

---

[53] Jocelyn Noveck, "Why Do Smart People Do Risky Things?" *Seattle Times*, March 11, 2008, pars. 3, 8, https://www.seattletimes.com/seattle-news/politics/why-do-smart-people-do-risky-things/.

abused. Research has shown only mixed, nonconclusive findings on the propensity to assault if one has been sexually assaulted in the past.

What might impede rationality and lead one to act so grievously? In his November 2, 2016, article, "Intelligence and Stupid Behavior," Steven Greenspan, PhD, cites some of the noncognitive contributors to irrational behavior as profound arrogance, a sense of immunity, a lack of social risk-awareness, and a fixation on one's individual wants or needs. These behaviors are often driven by deeply held beliefs and exacerbated by alcohol, by a biological state of disequilibrium, or both.[54] Clearly, most, if not all, of these conditions are at play in the clergy sexual abuse of minors.

Cover-ups and Scandal Avoidance

Covering up behavior and scandal is also not unique to the Catholic Church, though throughout its history, the Church has been very sensitive to scandal avoidance because of its extreme harm to faith. But that avoidance must never serve as a pretext to willful cover-up.

Generally, people act in their own self-interest and often cover up the actions of their own group, be it a family or an institution. Victims of domestic violence often will not cooperate in the prosecution against their spouse. Police organizations have internal investigation units. Congress has its own ethics committee.

Every organization would like its problems to go away quietly. And on occasion, isolated problems can be handled without much rippling in the water. But pervasive problems, problems that reflect a defection in an organization's culture and systems, and subsequent attempts at cover-up, are bound to see the light of day—as they should. These characteristics reflect profound arrogance, a sense of immunity, and a culture with a low social risk-awareness. In the Church, these can be features of what

---

[54]   Steven Greenspan, "Intelligence and Stupid Behavior," *Psychology Today,* posted November 2, 2016, https://www.psychologytoday.com/us/blog/ incompetence/201611/intelligence-and-stupid-behavior.

has been coined *clericalism*, but they exist under other names and in other institutions as well.

In a 2015 article titled "Cultures of Impunity," Paul Starr sums up the culture of institutional cover-up succinctly:

> From churches and the military to college campuses, sexual assault has long been hushed up. Often, it's not just the original crimes but the cover-ups that raise questions about the institutions and implicate their leadership....
>
> On the one hand, when individuals violate criminal laws, we expect them to be held accountable....
>
> On the other hand, it is sometimes all too easy to focus on bad actors and avoid the larger institutional implications of long-standing patterns of abuse. A culture of impunity is likely to develop only if leaders or organizations have turned a blind eye to malfeasance or actively concealed it....
>
> But how to get that accountability as well as sustained institutional change is extremely difficult....
>
> In cases of sexual assault, religious, military, and university leaders may believe that they are serving a higher purpose by preventing their institutions from being tarnished, their subordinates or students from being disgraced at a young age, and their communities from being subjected to ugly public proceedings....
>
> This calculus doesn't include the deep effects of a culture of impunity on either the victims or the perpetrators. Those who suffer abuse suffer again when their voices are not heard. Those who commit abuse come to believe in their own privilege and entitlement....
>
> The specter of collateral damage and the protection of the powerful are a big part, but only part, of the story behind cultures of impunity. Another reason for failures to prosecute lies in public deference to authority and what might be thought of as motivated blindness.[55]

---

[55] Paul Starr, "Cultures of Impunity," The American Prospect, July 24, 2015, pars. 2, 5-7, 9-10, 13, retrieved on 6/25/21, https://prospect.org/labor/cultures-impunity/.

Whenever Church leaders opted to handle sexual abuse cases without transparency, it was symptomatic of a culture of impunity, and this often resulted in a miscarriage of justice for the victims and the whole community.

Alcohol and Substance Abuse

Studies have consistently shown that alcohol is often a contextual factor in sexual assault. Whether it reduces inhibitions or skews perceptions about sexual interest cues from the victim, alcohol use is frequently part of the equation. Alcohol use is certainly not unique to the Catholic Church.

Despite St. Paul's warnings about drunkenness, more than a few priests have been treated for alcohol abuse. Any behavior can become a compulsion. It was my experience that many social gatherings of priests involved alcohol, including hard liquor. Some even spoke as though they glamorized it. I suppose that for those priests who see religious celibacy as "an act of heroism and a trying martyrdom,"[56] alcohol can become an attachment and a problem. Consistent with broader studies and findings on the issue, alcohol use appears in clergy sexual abuse cases—including as the most frequently appearing enticement in the nearly 21 percent of cases where a gift or enticement was offered to the victim.[57] Alcohol can impair one's use of their highest faculty—the mind—and separate one from reality.

Predatory Behavior: "Sizing up" and "Grooming"
the Environment and Victims

Predators are often cunning and sophisticated, and this is not unique to the Catholic clergy abuse scandal. *Grooming*, both of victims and of the environment, has been defined as "a predatory act of maneuvering

---

[56] Sacred Congregation for Religious, "*Religiosorum Institutio*," #30.

[57] John Jay College of Criminal Justice, "The Nature and Scope of Sexual Abuse of Minors by Catholic Priests and Deacons in the United States: 1950–2002" (Study Report, February 2004), 76, https://www.bishop-accountability.org/reports/2004_02_27_JohnJay_revised/2004_02_27_John_Jay_Main_Report_Optimized.pdf.

another individual into a position that makes them more isolated, dependent, likely to trust, and more vulnerable to abusive behavior."[58]

To illustrate, a nonexhaustive list of such behaviors includes the following: "Special attention, outings and gifts; isolating the child from others; filling the minor's unmet needs; filling needs and roles within the family; treating the child as if he or she were older; gradually crossing physical boundaries, and becoming increasingly more intimate/sexual; and use of secrecy, blame, and threats to maintain control."[59]

Moving forward, the Church is counting on a partnership with parents to help identify these situations by exercising prudent oversight, being attuned to signs and patterns like those listed above, and becoming aware of factors in the home life that may affect a child's development and vulnerability.

Cultures of Fraternity

Broadly speaking, a fraternity is a group of associated or formally organized people sharing a common profession (i.e., a guild), interest, or religious or secular aim. Psychologists recognize that "joining groups satisfies our need to belong, gain information and understanding through social comparison, define our sense of self and social identity, and achieve goals that might elude us if we worked alone. Across individuals, societies, and even eras, humans consistently seek inclusion over exclusion, membership over isolation, and acceptance over rejection."[60]

This need to belong is not unique to those in the Catholic Church. Police officers, doctors, members of Congress, and many others view

---

[58] Paul Ashton, "Grooming: Psychological, Physical and Community," National Catholic Services LLC, 6/15/2021, 1, https://d2y1pz2y630308.cloudfront. net/20307/documents/2019/10/2019_10%20VIRTUS%20Monthly%20 Bulletin.pdf.

[59] Darkness to Light, "Child Sexual Abuse Statistics," 3.

[60] Forsyth, D. R. (2021). The psychology of groups. In R. Biswas-Diener & E. Diener (Eds), *Noba Textbook Series: Psychology*. Champaign, IL: DEF publishers, pars 1, 5, Retrieved from http://noba.to/trfxbkhm or https://nobaproject.com/ modules/the-psychology-of-groups.

themselves as part of a unique, small, and sometimes elite club. They often have their own worldview and their own language, and, among themselves, they let their hair down. They often compare and share similar educational and professional experiences, roles, and aims. Such groups also share in other dynamics such as cliques, gossip, back-stabbing, and vying for respect and position.

There can also be organized or informal fraternal groups or associations with malevolent purposes that are founded on a shared attachment to certain behaviors or interests. Such groups may participate in, or facilitate, certain behaviors and shield each other from outside scrutiny. The survival of their group might well have to rely upon "honor among thieves." There are pockets of clergy and leaders in the Church who exhibited these behaviors in the clergy sexual abuse crisis.

There is another fraternal dynamic worth mentioning here. In his article about the Civil Rights Movement and individual attitudes of various leaders in the South, James Sellers points to a group dynamic that transcends any particular situation. Sellers contrasts officials of segregated Southern cities who in private conversations described themselves as not being "a die-hard, metaphysical segregationist," yet when placed in a group setting, like a city commission, whistled a different tune. Sellers writes, "The individual sense of morality quickly evaporates and a group code appears. The more official the group he joins, the more this reversal is likely. What we have here is a form of the problem of 'moral man and immoral society.' Men will uphold and sanctify injustices when they operate as groups, injustices they often will not countenance as individuals."[61] This article's observation helps to explain the power of cliques and subcultures and the lack of courage by some to stand by their convictions or report their knowledge of wrongdoing.

Among the Catholic clergy, it is helpful to distinguish between clericalism and a clerical culture. To the extent that a clerical culture fosters and supports qualities becoming to their state in life, it is not necessarily bad. Such a culture for the clergy would involve opportunities for prayer,

---

[61] James Sellers, "A Fuller Definition of Civil Rights," *New Theology No. 1* (NY: Macmillan Co., 1964, 1967), 228–229.

self-reflection, education, mentorship, shared ministerial experiences, a life moderated to support celibacy, and genuine friendships that enhance ongoing, healthy human development.[62]

The debate about what constitutes a healthy clerical culture has led to various models for seminary training. Katarina Schuth, OSF, author of *Seminaries, Theologates, and the Future of Church Ministry*, states that "common to all models is the intention to promote authentic discipleship, healthy community life, and leadership potential."[63] The "self-contained" model is described as "a place set apart where energies and resources are focused on priestly formation and identity and, with few exceptions, only candidates for the priesthood are enrolled. Contacts with the world beyond the seminary are kept to a minimum, with pastoral placements being carefully constructed and restricted."[64] By contrast, the "interconnected" model is described as "a place that provides a formational climate closely reflecting the reality of contemporary ministry. It develops faith partnerships with members of the larger community and promotes collaboration. In their programs, the schools...educate seminarians and lay students who will be ministering together after they complete their courses."[65] Viewpoints vary on which model strikes the right balance, one that "promotes a realistic and distinct priestly identity."[66] The self-contained model is the most prevalent. Although inextricably connected to many aspects of clerical culture, clericalism often loses sight that the priest, in the example of Christ, "has come to serve and not to be served."[67]

In addition to the factors discussed above—those that are not unique to the Church but that are in play—I now turn to factors unique to the clergy sexual abuse crisis, which add fuller context and deeper dimension to its character.

---

[62] Katarina Schuth, *Seminaries, Theologates, and the Future of Church Ministry* (Collegeville, Minnesota: The Liturgical Press, 1999), 127.

[63] Schuth, *Seminaries,* 127.

[64] Schuth, 127.

[65] Schuth, 128.

[66] Schuth, 129.

[67] Matthew 20:28, *The New American Bible.*

Unique Factors

The Overall Demographics of Catholic Clergy

In its present composition, the Catholic clergy has some unique character-istics. Beyond the relatively small number of predators who were married permanent deacons or staff and volunteers in parishes, priest-predators came from among all celibate males. Moreover, there has been an in-crease in what some have termed "the gaying of the priesthood"[68] from the 1950s onward. Estimates about the number of priests with a homo-sexual orientation vary from 16 percent to as high as 50 percent, with a notable uptick in the 1970s. I propose that this uptick corresponded with two events in the 1970s: the mass exodus of clergy once manda-tory celibacy was not relaxed following the Second Vatican Ecumenical Council (1962–1965), and the removal of homosexuality as a paraphilia (an unusual sexual interest) by the psychiatric community in 1973.

Consider the observation of sociologist Fr. Paul Sullins, PhD, a married priest working for the Ruth Institute at the Catholic University of America. In the abstract of Sullins's forty-seven-page work titled "Is Catholic Clergy Abuse Related to Homosexual Priests?" he writes, "Prior to the 1950s the proportion of homosexual men in the priesthood was about the same as in the general population. By the 1980s homo-sexual men made up over 16 percent of the presbyterate, which is over 8 times that of the general population."[69]

The executive summary of the John Jay cause report, commissioned by the Church on the crisis, includes the following sentence: "Priests who had same-sex sexual experiences either before seminary or in the seminary were more likely to have sexual behavior after ordination [as

---

[68] Ross Benes, "How the Catholic Priesthood Became an Unlikely Haven for Many Gay Men," Slate, April 20, 2017, par. 5, https://slate.com/human-interest/2017/04/how-the-catholic-priesthood-became-a-haven-for-many-gay-men.html.

[69] Paul Sullins, abstract to "Is Catholic Clergy Sex Abuse Related to Homosexual Priests?" (Study Report: Abstract posted Feb. 16, 2019; Report posted Dec. 11, 2018 and revised May 28, 2021), https://papers.ssrn.com/sol3/papers.cfm?abstract_id=3276082, retrieved 6/21/21.

were heterosexual priests], but this behavior was most likely with adults. These men were not significantly more likely to abuse minors." I will thoroughly probe this finding in chapters VII and VIII as I explore the spectrum of motivations for abuse.

As for age, there has been a gradual "graying" of the priesthood as well. In 1970, the median age was thirty-five. By 2009, the median age was sixty-three.[70] An aging population is not unique to Catholic clergy. The average age of doctors, for example, has steadily risen. But because the clergy sexual abuse cases have decreased, one might wonder whether—in addition to implemented preventive measures, greater vigilance and fewer priests—the clergy's advanced age might also be a factor. Many priests are chaste by leading virtuous lives. Others may be chaste by aging. According to the John Jay cause report, the largest group of priest-abusers, accounting for 40 percent of the cases, were between the ages of thirty and thirty-nine. This fact may afford added light to New Testament wisdom found in the Greek word *presbyteros*, which is translated as "elders" or "fathers" or "old men."

The Predominant Gender and Age of Victims

One cannot read the John Jay scope report commissioned by the United States Catholic Conference of Bishops without one very significant statistic standing out: approximately 81 percent of the victims were male.[71] Consider this fact in contrast to the general statistics about child abuse: by the age of eighteen, one in seven girls and one in twenty-five boys will have been sexually abused.[72]

Moreover, the vast majority of the clergy sexual abuse victims fell into one of two age groups: eleven to fourteen or fifteen to seventeen.[73] There are terms that cover this motivation for behavior: hebephilia,

---

[70] Center for Applied Research in the Apostolate, Frequently Requested Church Statistics, Georgetown, https://cara.georgetown.edu/frequently-requested-church-statistics/.
[71] John Jay College of Criminal Justice, "The Nature and Scope," 9.
[72] Darkness to Light, "Child Sexual Abuse Statistics," 1.
[73] John Jay College of Criminal Justice, "The Nature and Scope," 54.

ephebophilia, and pederasty—none of which are officially classified as clinical sexual paraphilias.

Additional Unique Factors

I will only briefly enumerate the following additional unique factors here, as I cover most of them in greater detail in subsequent chapters.

Clericalism

While arrogance in someone holding office is not unique, the idea of clericalism, or the superiority of the clergy, has found some basis, albeit unbalanced, in the Church's theology on the priesthood. It is rare to find a comparable profession that has a supporting theology.

Shortage of Priests

The shortage of priests has accelerated over the last few decades. Parishes have had to close, and priests have been imported from developing countries with an abundant flow of clergy. This situation has put bishops under tremendous pressure to retain priests.

Church–State Jurisprudence

Unlike a localized, domestic entity or company, the Church is an international society, with its hierarchical leader domiciled overseas in a city–state. American church–state jurisprudence also comes into play. Through cooperation, there is concurrent jurisdiction of Church and state, each according to its area of competence, over those accused of these sexual abuse crimes.

Bishop–Priest Relationship

Priests, who act as coworkers in the fullness of the bishop's ministerial priesthood, have a special relationship with their bishop, who is the spiritual father of his diocese and ultimately chooses, mentors, and shepherds his priests. Numerous Church documents speak of this relationship in very nurturing terms. It is not a relationship that is severed easily or without good cause.

The Character of Holy Orders

According to Catholic theology, the sacrament of Sacred Orders, like Baptism and Confirmation, creates an ontological change in the recipient. It is a mark on the soul, a change in character. Hence, once ordained, a priest will remain so forever, though he may be temporarily or permanently barred from licitly and publicly exercising that priesthood. Despite the colloquial expression used in reference to abusive priests, "just remove him from the priesthood," a priest cannot be removed or dismissed from his priesthood. Church Law provides for due judicial review and process in the steps to removing a priest from his ecclesial office or "clerical state."

Consider how a cynical outsider may view the priesthood: a particular nonhereditary caste of Catholic Christians, relatively few in number, whose all-male, celibate, two-tiered fraternity (bishop and priest) is comprised of relatively well-educated men who are ontologically distinct by virtue of a sacrament, who alone can act in the person of Christ, whose authority forms part of the governing hierarchy of the Church, and who can perform acts that not even the angels of God can do—even if they are not in a state of grace. They live in relative isolation and act with relative independence, and the sublime dignity of their office commands unquestioned reverence and deferential treatment.

One doesn't need a wild imagination to discern how a culture of this description can go askew. When described in this manner, one might think it is similar to a description of cult leaders. If it was not designed by the will of Christ, and if it were not for the witness of countless priests properly disposed and orientated to Christ who more closely measure up to the ideal, we might be justified in being quite wary of such an institution. Here, I am reminded of the observation of St. Anthony Mary Claret: "Virtue, then, is so necessary to the priest, that even evil men expect priests to be good."[74]

Transparency and the Media

Lastly—though investigative journalism, the media, and social media are taken for granted—this episode of clergy sexual abuse was exposed and heightened by media reporting. In a 1985 report to the United States Catholic Conference of Bishops, advisors warned the national episcopate that the clergy sexual abuse problems "now carry consequences never before experienced."[75]

As shown throughout this chapter, there is a confluence of unique and not-so-unique factors involved in the clergy sexual abuse scandal. Some of the issues can be resolved by enacting best practices of mitigation to minimize risk and by evaluating and changing processes and laws where necessary. Still others will force the Church to examine more deeply the historical lexicon linked to the priesthood, modes of ministry, and the selection, screening, and formation of candidates.

---

[74] *The Autobiography of St. Anthony Mary Claret* (Rockford, Illinois: TAN Books and Publishers, 1945, 1985), 39.

[75] F. Ray Mouton and Thomas P. Doyle, "The Problem of Sexual Molestation by Roman Catholic Clergy: Meeting the Problem in a Comprehensive and Responsible Manner" (final draft, June 8–9, 1985), 3, retrieved 6/25/2021, https://www.bishop-accountability.org/reports/1985_06_09_Doyle_Manual/DoyleManual_NCR_combined.pdf.

VII

A Look at the Clinical Side of Child Sexual Abuse

In this chapter, I will embark on the necessary examination of the clinical side of child sexual abuse. This analysis may appear to some as a dispassionate and systematic review of clinical information. Disgust, anger, and other high emotions around this subject are justified and understandable. Suffice it to say at the onset that child sexual abuse is unequivocally criminal and immoral regardless of the motivation of the perpetrator. In pursuing these insights, I encourage the reader to suspend any assumptions and apply critical thinking.

To truthfully understand the causes of abuse in these cases and to candidly find starting points for leaders to address institutional change, it is important to explore the existing framework in this field of science and probe two distinct, key topics: whether the specific diagnosis of pedophilia applies to all the abuse cases and notable human development characteristics in the clergy.

Key Questions

Question 1: Are All the Clergy Cases Classified as Pedophilia?

The first key question asks whether it is accurate to classify *all* the reported instances of clergy sexual abuse of minors as pedophilia. Pedophilia is a very specific psychiatric diagnosis—one of eight recognized paraphilias. To be clear, all instances in the clergy abuse of minors constitute some form of child sexual abuse, but the motivations are different across the spectrum of cases; therefore, distinguishing these motivations is required to address the problem comprehensively. Pedophilia has been the umbrella term used by many in the media, in pundit reports, by some who have innocently confused all child sexual abuse as pedophilia under the law, and by some with a specific social or political agenda in relation to the role of homosexual behavior in the majority of the cases.

Question 2: What are the Human Development Characteristics of Perpetrators in Clergy Cases?

The second area will be an exploration of the available data on the human development characteristics of the clergy during this crisis in order to discern any insights related to the causes of the sexual abuse of minors by the clergy.

The State of Affairs in Mental Health Science

In setting the stage for the narrow discussion of the clergy sexual abuse of minors, it is critical to open with a general overview of the state of affairs in the mental health field. There are many stakeholders who seek a certain reliance on this science: the legal system, lawmakers, patients and their families—indeed, all of society. Arguably, there are three pillars that intersect in this portrait of the science of mental health today:

1. The progress of the science itself

2. The implications for society based on the interpretation of the science

3. The external pressures of stakeholders in society that attempt to influence the science

The progress of the science

On September 25, 2003, the American Psychiatric Association released a statement affirming the "irrefutable evidence that mental and behavioral disorders exact devastating emotional and financial tolls on individuals, families, communities and our Nation."[76] It is estimated to have billions of dollars of impact annually in the United States and ranks only second to heart disease as a societal burden.

Despite the clinical insights gained over decades of study into sexual abuse, it remains a relatively dark and opaque world, one that science has not completely figured out. Because child sexual abuse is so horrific, society rightly responds with fear and scandal, and politicians and the courts react. In the introduction of a well-known 1964 manual titled *Pedophilia and Exhibitionism*, the authors quote Manfred Guttmacher and Henry Weihofen[77] when they write that "there is doubtless no subject on which we can obtain more definite opinions and less definite knowledge."[78] As this science emerges from its nascent state, there are still mysteries surrounding it that would be admitted by any honest clinician.

As recent as 2003, the American Psychiatric Association acknowledged those who "express their impatience with the pace of science,

---

[76] American Psychiatric Association, "American Psychiatric Association Statement on Diagnosis and Treatment of Mental Disorders," September 25, 2003, Release No. 03-39, par. 8.

[77] Manfred Guttmacher and Henry Weihofen, "Sex Offenses," The Journal of Criminal Law, Criminology, and Police Science, Vol. 43, No. 2 (Jul.-Aug., 1952).

[78] J.W. Mohr, R.E. Turner, and M.B. Jerry, *Pedophilia and Exhibitionism* (Toronto, Canada: University of Toronto Press, 1964), Introduction.

[noting] that the human brain is the most complex and challenging object of study in the history of human science."[79]

The implications for society in interpreting the data

Those in the field of mental health are pressured to portray credibility, integrity, and provide value to the legal system and to the overall epidemic of mental health in society. They attempt to balance objective science with a reduction of stigma about mental health disorders so that more people will avail themselves of mental health care.

When considering the evolution of how some disorders were progressively reclassified over the decades (e.g., from sociopathic personality disorder to sexual deviation to paraphilia), some in the field resist any role in the "'cracking of the moral whip' and making psychiatrists into 'the guardians of cultural values.'"[80] The findings of science can have real impact on people. For example, "diagnoses can be used to imprison and/or commit an individual based on their future likely danger to society."[81]

While psychology studies human conduct (e.g., how man actually acts) and seeks to understand what motivates behavior, it is beyond its purview to provide us with answers on how man ought to behave, or whether such behavior fulfills the supreme good for man.

The external pressures of stakeholders on the science

Social force is also exerted in the other direction, attempting to influence scientific outcomes. The diagnoses of certain conditions are, at least to some extent, "dependent on cultural views of acceptability. [...and]

---

[79] American Psychiatric Association, "American Psychiatric Association Statement on Diagnosis and Treatment of Mental Disorders," par. 3.

[80] Michelle A. McManus, Paul Hargreaves, Lee Rainbow, Laurence J. Alison, *Paraphilias: definition, diagnosis and treatment*, September 2, 2013, par. 7 https://www.ncbi.nlm.nih.gov/pmc/articles/PMC3769077/, or https://facultyopinions.com/prime/reports/m/5/36.

[81] McManus, Hargreaves, Rainbow, Alison, *Paraphilias,* par. 2.

the malleability of sexual norms across time and cultures."[82] If certain conditions or behaviors drop off the list of disorders, on what basis do others remain? What conditions must exist for other disorders to drop off the list? I will address this dynamic and its potential negative impact on society in greater detail later in this chapter.

Sexual Assault and Sexual Abuse

The criminal act of sexual assault occurs in many forms, with diverse characteristics and in a variety of contexts. Behavioral scientists often use the term "sexual violence" to emphasize and capture all such harmful and traumatic acts, including those not codified in law. The victim can be either an adult or a minor. Since the clergy sexual abuse scandal is focused primarily on the abuse of minors, I will be examining some clinical information and defining some specific terminology in this field.

"Sexual Abuse" Defined

In legal parlance, sexual abuse is a subset of sexual assault that typically refers to acts against minors. Additionally, it has aggravating elements like an age differential, the abuse of power or authority, and betrayal of trust. Because of these factors, sexual abuse can also apply to acts against other vulnerable members of society, such as the elderly, the handicapped, the mentally impaired, and patients at the hands of their doctor.

"Minor" Defined

A minor is someone who has not reached the "age of majority," or the "age of consent," which represents what society has defined as the line between childhood and adulthood. This line is typically the age of eighteen in American jurisprudence. Canon 97 of the 1983 Code of Canon Law (current Church Law) provides a similar description: "A person who

---

[82] McManus, Hargreaves, Rainbow, Alison, *Paraphilias,* pars. 1-2.

has completed the eighteenth year of age is an adult; below this age, a person is a minor."[83] Prior to a very recent change, the term *minor* is used again in canon 1395 in relation to violations against clerical chastity. In that instance, the victim age of sixteen is used as a component of the offense, and this point will be revisited in chapter XVII.

Studies and Key Data

In the wake of the recent scandal, both Church leaders and professionals from the relevant sciences have grappled with the phenomenon of child sexual abuse generally, and the clergy sexual abuse of minors specifically. Scientific studies and surveys have been commissioned and reviewed, and past literature and studies have been scoured over. Although many past studies on child sexual abuse have been conducted, variances in methodology and in the definition of the term "sexual abuse"[84] have created some challenges in discerning consistent findings.

Sadly, according to the Darkness to Light website, which provides helpful support information on sexual abuse, the statistics reflect that one

---

[83] James A. Coriden, Thomas J. Green, and Donald E. Heintschel, eds., *The Code of Canon Law: A Text and Commentary* (New York/Mahwah: Paulist Press, 1985), 71.

[84] Catherine Townsend, Darkness to Light, "Estimating a Child Sexual Abuse Prevalence Rate for Practitioners: A Review of Child Sexual Abuse Prevalence Studies" (Study Report: August 2013), 11, https://www.d2l.org/wp-content/uploads/2017/02/PREVALENCE-RATE-WHITE-PAPER-D2L.pdf. Includes an attempt at standardizing the definition to include the following:

1. Victims of child sexual abuse include both boys and girls, ages 0–17
2. Child sexual abuse includes both contact and noncontact sexual acts
3. Child sexual abuse includes any sexual act between an adult and a young child, regardless of whether force or coercion is used
4. Child sexual abuse includes any sexual act between a teen and an adult who is significantly older, regardless of whether force or coercion is used
5. Child sexual abuse includes forced or coerced sexual acts between two children when there is an age or power differential; this can include unwanted or forcible peer abuse
6. Child sexual abuse does not typically include consensual sex between peers or between an older teen and a young adult

in ten children will be sexually abused by the age of eighteen, and 20 percent of those by age eight. More specifically, by age eighteen, one in seven girls and one in twenty-five boys will be sexually abused.[85] This disparity between male and female victims is critically important to the present topic and, admittedly, there is evidence that abuse against males is less frequently reported. By what margin, we don't exactly know. But it is not likely to fully bridge the wide gap between male and female victims overall.

Two Key Characteristics of Child Sexual Abuse

To better understand the terrain and to begin to discern the victim profile of the child sexual abuse manifested in the clergy crisis, two comments act as important starting places. First, the age of a "minor" spans from zero to seventeen years of age, a long period during which there is significant physical and psychological development in the child—most notably the threshold between being prepubescent and pubescent. If the victim is a minor, it is child sexual abuse, regardless of their exact age. But the perpetrator's motives often differ and can yield a distinct clinical diagnosis depending on their age preference in victims. So, while each instance is sexual abuse against a minor, not all such instances involve characteristics of diagnosed pedophilia.

Second, in society at large, there is a greater prevalence of the abuse of minors who are female than of those who are male. These two comments, along with tables 1–4 detailing clergy sexual abuse characteristics, are important starting points in understanding the unique aspects of the clergy sexual abuse crisis. Again, it is essential to pursue an understanding of this specific phenomenon with greater accuracy to avoid stereotypes and to apply the proper corrective measures.

---

[85] Darkness to Light, "Child Sexual Abuse Statistics" (Issue Brief and Statistical Report: Darkness to Light: End Child Sex Abuse), 1, 4, https://www.d2l.org/wp-content/uploads/2017/01/all_statistics_20150619.pdf.

Four Important Qualifiers in the Field

There are four remaining qualifiers that must be expressed here in order to understand the current state of the science of sexual abuse.

Victim Age Groupings: Prepubescent and Pubescent

The delineation of victim age groupings in general literature on the subject, including literature published by the American Psychiatric Association, is not a set demarcation. Though there is some overlap of age groupings in the literature, the key distinction in age is largely intended to provide a contrast between prepubescent and pubescent children. The transition from one to the other varies slightly between boys and girls and between individuals. The age of the victim is a strong determinant in the diagnosis of the perpetrator, particularly if he or she is fixated on or generally has exclusive interest in that age grouping. Pedophilia is a specific chronophilia, a term that broadly describes an individual's sexual arousal to persons of a particular age range.

Many authorities on the subject use the age of eleven as the dividing line, with victims under this age typically associated with an offender's diagnosis of pedophilia. There are two manuals often cited in the diagnostic literature. The first is the *Diagnostic and Statistical Manual of Mental Disorders* (current version: *DSM-5*), which is a US-based manual published by the American Psychiatric Association focused solely on mental health issues. The second is the *International Statistical Classification of Diseases and Related Health Problems*, which is promulgated by the World Health Organization.

Pedophilia (*paidos* meaning "child" and *philia* meaning "love of") is recognized as a paraphilia in both the *DSM-5* and the *ICD-10*. In the *DSM-5*, a pedophilic disorder is understood to apply to those who, "over a period of at least 6 months [have] recurrent, intense sexually arousing fantasies, sexual urges, or behaviors involving a prepubescent child or children (generally age 13 or younger)."[86] The *ICD-10* describes it as "a

---

[86] American Psychiatric Association (APA), *Diagnostic and Statistical Manual of Mental Disorders,* DSM-5 (5th ed., Washington, DC: American Psychiatric Association

sexual preference for children, boys or girls or both, usually of prepubertal or early pubertal age."[87] In the *DSM-5*, the perpetrator must be at least sixteen years old and at least five years older than the victim. The mean age of victims tends to be between eight and ten. There are other terms for interest in chronologically older minors, which I will address in chapter VIII, but at this time science has not listed them in the manuals among recognized paraphilias.

The Limitations of Clinical Studies

Clinical studies over the last century have been hampered by differing definitions and terminology, methodologies and approaches, and the characteristics of the samples and sample sizes. A good majority of studies have only been able to examine incarcerated perpetrators or those who were presented for treatment. Sometimes, those civilly committed into treatment programs feel compelled to exaggerate their crimes in order to placate therapists and avoid leaving the "safe haven" and being remanded back into prison, where they rank low in the prison hierarchy and could be subject to violence.[88] Studies have nonetheless given us some insights into this dark world.

Moreover, the pool of known perpetrators is artificially small because knowledge of sexual abuse cases is complicated by low reporting. As noted earlier in chapter VI, although "false or fabricated reports by children is rare (4%-8%), only about 1/3 of sexual abuse incidents/cases are identified, and even fewer are reported. Of the reports investigated, only a portion meets the criteria for 'substantiated.'"[89] Though

---

[APA], 2013), 697 (Diagnostic Classification: 302.2), https://doi.org/10.1176/appi.books.9780890425596.

[87] World Health Organization. (2nd ed. 2010). *International statistical classification of diseases and related health problems* (10th ed.-CM), Diagnosis Code F65.4, https://icd.who.int/browse10/2010/en#/F65.4.

[88] Rachel Aviv, "The Science of Sex Abuse," *The New Yorker*, Jan. 14, 2013 issue, 9-10, pars. 49-50, https://www.newyorker.com/magazine/2013/01/14/the-science-of-sex-abuse.

[89] Darkness to Light, "Child Sexual Abuse Statistics," 7.

the Church-commissioned John Jay scope report provides some reliable abuse characteristics, low reporting is a credible basis for questioning the report's conclusion that the abuse was perpetrated by only 3–6 percent of active Catholic priests.[90] Furthermore, given the disparate number of male victims abused by clergy, this conclusion is further destabilized when considering evidence that abuse against female victims is reported more often than abuse against male victims. The lower frequency of reporting by male victims cuts both ways. If one uses this fact as a basis to suggest that the sexual abuse of males happens more frequently in society at large, then that same fact means that there could have been more unreported male victims of the clergy.

Propensity or Preference Versus Actual Abuse

It is important to distinguish between an individual who has a particular propensity or preference and one who acts on it. Not all those with a certain propensity will act those preferences out on a victim—though such persons could be disinhibited by factors like substance abuse or stress. Moreover, not every instance of sexual abuse is congruent with the perpetrator's propensity. The former point is self-explanatory. Though not stated as an excuse for their behavior, the latter point simply establishes that some who sexually abuse children outside their propensity could have other motives, could be situational offenders undergoing circumstances of personal psychological stress, or could be predators reacting to opportunities that present themselves.

To provide greater context, Darkness to Light acknowledges that "not everyone who sexually abuses children is a pedophile."[91] It is reported that the sexual abuse of minors "is perpetrated by a wide range of individuals with diverse motivations."[92] For example, "situational

---

[90]   John Jay College of Criminal Justice, "The Nature and Scope of Sexual Abuse of Minors by Catholic Priests and Deacons in the United States: 1950–2002" (Study Report, February 2004), 7, https://www.bishop-accountability.org/reports/2004_02_27_JohnJay_revised/2004_02_27_John_Jay_Main_Report_Optimized.pdf.

[91]   Darkness to Light, "Child Sexual Abuse Statistics," 2.

[92]   Darkness to Light, "Child Sexual Abuse Statistics," 2.

offenders tend to offend at times of stress and begin offending later than pedophilic offenders." They also have fewer victims and generally have a preference for adult partners. Pedophilic offenders, by contrast, tend to "start offending at an early age, and often have a large number of victims."[93] According to the DSM-5, having "multiple victims…is sufficient but not necessary for [the] diagnosis" of pedophilic disorder if it is offset by "merely acknowledging intense or preferential sexual interest in children."[94]

There is some consensus that the cure and recidivism profile of situational offenders can be more optimistic than that of diagnosed pedophilic offenders. Perpetrators are a heterogenous group and don't fall into a single clinical profile, despite the inclination to view them the same. Because the offenses vary as to type, severity, and circumstances, bishops who sent credibly accused priests to treatment were trying to ascertain a diagnosis, which would assist in assessing the offender's mindset and understanding their prognosis for successful treatment. There is reason to disagree with the practice of, and motives for, sending these priests off to treatment, particularly when doing so was coupled with a failure to notify law enforcement. This practice kept the process hidden and left the bishops with discretion that was often poorly exercised.

Exclusive Versus Nonexclusive Offenders

Finally, just as the victim age grouping is not fixed and shows some overlap, not all sexual offenders offend exclusively according to their preference. Put another way, not all pedophilic offenders exclusively victimize prepubescent children. Conversely, the abuse of postpubescent children is not necessarily pedophilic behavior in the true clinical sense.

With these essential prefatory remarks in place, I now turn to the specific profile of child sexual abuse observed in the Catholic clergy.

---

[93] Darkness to Light, "Child Sexual Abuse Statistics," 2.

[94] American Psychiatric Association (APA), *Diagnostic and Statistical Manual of Mental Disorders,* DSM-5, 698.

The John Jay Scope Report

At their June 2002 General Assembly meeting in Dallas, Texas, the United States Catholic Conference of Bishops unanimously approved a charter for the protection of children, known as the Dallas Charter. Its full title is "Promise to Protect, Pledge to Heal: Charter for the Protection of Children and Young People," and it was amended in 2011 and 2018. Article 9 of the original 2002 draft charter created a [national] Review Board, to include parents, and the bishops mandated the commissioning of a descriptive study on the nature and scope of the problem. The John Jay College of Criminal Justice of the City University of New York was engaged to conduct the research. It was the first of two reports awarded to this institution. The resulting 155-page report, hereafter referred to as the John Jay scope report, sought to amalgamate data about known priest abuse cases from 1950 to 2002. It was published in February 2004. Its preface describes the study as an "excruciating inquiry" into a "distressing sexual abuse phenomenon" with "disturbing" findings.[95]

Tables 1 through 4 detail key characteristics specific to the profile of clergy sexual abuse from 1950 to 2002 as shown in or discerned from the John Jay scope report.

Table 1: Victim Gender

Male	81%
Female	19%

Source: John Jay College of Criminal Justice, "The Nature and Scope of Sexual Abuse of Minors by Catholic Priests and Deacons in the United States: 1950–2002" (Study Report, February 2004), 9, https://www.bishop-accountability.org/reports/2004_02_27_JohnJay_revised/2004_02_27_John_Jay_Main_Report_Optimized.pdf.

---

[95] John Jay College of Criminal Justice, "The Nature and Scope of Sexual Abuse of Minors by Catholic Priests and Deacons in the United States: 1950–2002" (Study Report, February 2004), 1-2.

Table 2: Victim Age at First Instance of Abuse

Age	% of Total Victims
0–10	21.8%
11–14	50.9%
15–17	27.3%

Source: John Jay College of Criminal Justice, "The Nature and Scope of Sexual Abuse of Minors by Catholic Priests and Deacons in the United States: 1950–2002" (Study Report, February 2004), 9, https://www.bishop-accountability. org/reports/2004_02_27_JohnJay_revised/2004_02_27_John_Jay_Main_ Report_Optimized.pdf.

Table 3: Victims by Gender by Decade Examined

Decade	Period	Male Victims	Percent of total	Female victims	Percent of total	Victim Totals
1	1950–1959	488	63.62%	279	36.38%	767
2	1960–1969	1,636	75.67%	526	24.33%	2,162
3	1970–1979	2,563	85.75%	426	14.25%	2,989
4	1980–1989	1,621	86.13%	261	13.87%	1,882
5	1990–2002	402	73.49%	145	26.51%	547
Totals		6,710	80.39%	1,637	19.61%	8,347 [96]

Source: Extrapolated from John Jay College of Criminal Justice, "The Nature and Scope of Sexual Abuse of Minors by Catholic Priests and Deacons in the United States: 1950–2002" (Study Report, February 2004), 54, https://www.bishop-accountability.org/reports/2004_02_27_JohnJay_re-vised/2004_02_27_John_Jay_Main_Report_Optimized.pdf.

---

[96] Although the John Jay scope report noted that 10,667 individuals made allegations against priests, the age data on 8,347 victims was derived from victim surveys received back for the purpose of the report.

Table 4: Victim Age at First Instance of Abuse by Decade Examined

Decade	Period	Male Victims			Female Victims		
		Ages 1–10	Ages 11–14	Ages 15–17	Ages 1–10	Ages 11–14	Ages 15–17
1	1950–1959	27.70%	54.50%	17.80%	59.50%	31.90%	8.60%
2	1960–1969	22.70%	58.10%	19.20%	42.00%	39.40%	18.60%
3	1970–1979	16.90%	57.00%	26.10%	33.60%	38.50%	27.90%
4	1980–1989	13.50%	50.50%	36.10%	29.30%	41.70%	29.00%
5	1990–2002	9.70%	35.10%	55.20%	18.50%	51.70%	29.70%
Aggregate by Age		17.85%	54.19%	27.96%	38.67%	39.40%	21.93%

Source: Extrapolated from, but not depicted in this manner in John Jay College of Criminal Justice, "The Nature and Scope of Sexual Abuse of Minors by Catholic Priests and Deacons in the United States: 1950–2002" (Study Report, February 2004), 54, https://www.bishop-accountability.org/reports/2004_02_27_JohnJay_revised/2004_02_27_John_Jay_Main_Report_Optimized.pdf.

Key John Jay Scope Report Data Points

Tables 1–4 reveal three points critical to answering my first inquiry in this chapter, which seeks to answer whether *all* the clergy sexual abuse cases could be classified as clinical pedophilia.

Portion of Clergy Cases Typically Associated with Pedophilia

First, offenses against the age group typically associated with pedophilia—prepubescent children (under age eleven)—accounted for approximately 22 percent of the clergy cases. The John Jay scope report determined this age demarcation because "the literature generally refers to eleven and older as an age for pubescence or post pubescence."[97] In these cases of pedophilia, the distribution of male to female victims was

---

[97] John Jay College Research Team, "The Causes and Context of Sexual Abuse of Minors by Catholic Priests in the United States, 1950–2010" (Study Report, May 2011), 9–10, 53, http://votf.org/johnjay/John_Jay_Causes_and_Context_Report.pdf.

somewhat more balanced than that found in the overall distribution (65 percent male and 35 percent female).

Though this slightly more balanced ratio of male to female victims is more consistent with the phenomenon of pedophilia—where the perpetrator has a developmentally impaired self-concept and sexual preference—it is notable that it still skews toward male victims. The gender of victims, as a measure of propensity or preference, is a recognized category in characterizing the diagnosis of pedophilic disorder (e.g., heterosexual pedophilia, homosexual pedophilia, or bisexual pedophilia).

Portion of Postpubescent Cases with Male Victims

Second, while male victims accounted for nearly 81 percent of the total victims, if I exclude those instances generally understood to be cases of pedophilia, the distribution of male to female postpubescent victims becomes even more pronounced at a ratio of 84.6 percent to 15.4 percent.

Victim Age at First Instance of Abuse

Lastly, there was a gradual increase in the age of both male and female victims at the first instance of abuse over the five-decade period examined in the John Jay scope report. It slowly graduated to older victims over this period.

The Science and Debate Regarding Paraphilias

The data I have presented thus far appears to confirm that most of the clergy sexual abuse cases were not instances of clinical pedophilia. Before bringing final resolution to that first inquiry, I must explore the concept of, and the surrounding debate about, the umbrella clinical term "paraphilia." In an effort to de-stigmatize certain psychological conditions and focus on the source of the arousal, the *DSM-III* introduced the term *paraphilia*, replacing the old terminology of *sexual deviation*. The *DSM-IV-TR* defined a paraphilia as the "recurrent, intense sexually arousing fantasies, sexual urges or behaviors generally involving non-human objects, the suffering or humiliation of oneself or one's partner, or children or other nonconsenting persons that occur over a period of six months."[98] Pedophilia is one of eight named diagnoses in the *DSM-5*. The remaining paraphilias are exhibitionism, fetishism, frotteurism, sexual masochism, sexual sadism, voyeurism, and transvestic fetishism, as well as specified and unspecified paraphilic disorders. If clinical pedophilia does not account for approximately 78 percent of the clergy sexual abuse cases, the cause will not be found in the remaining seven named paraphilias, with the possible exception of exhibitionism in some limited cases. In the next chapter, I will explore other possible motivations.

According to the *DSM-5*, a paraphilia becomes a paraphilic disorder when a second criterion applies—namely, that it is accompanied by clinically significant stress or impairment in the subject diagnosed. This refers to the tension and the emotional or psychological stress that the paraphilia creates in the subject, which can impair healthy relationships and life functioning. As it relates narrowly to pedophilia, this second criterion can be waved in the diagnosis if "there is evidence of recurrent behaviors for 6 months" (or sustained persistence "if the 6-month duration cannot be precisely determined").[99]

Let me clarify: one doesn't have to have a paraphilia to experience "clinically significant" stress and life impairment. People experiencing such stress for conditions not identified as a paraphilia can still be treated. Therefore, for example, someone experiencing this stress due to sexual interest in postpubescent minors, even if they have not acted upon it, or someone who experiences stress with a homosexual orientation, can also present themselves for treatment.

---

[98] American Psychiatric Association (APA), *Diagnostic and Statistical Manual of Mental Disorders, DSM-IV-TR,* (Washington DC: American Psychiatric Association [APA], 2000), 566.

[99] American Psychiatric Association (APA), *Diagnostic and Statistical Manual of Mental Disorders,* DSM-5, 698.

Qualifiers for Paraphilia

What qualifies as a paraphilia is often the starting point for intense debate in the scientific community around several related questions, which can result in real societal impact. Science is not immune to social and political influence. Societal norms and beliefs, which often change and are not always anchored in objective morality, pressure the scientific community to wrestle with questions like these:

1. Where is the precise border between merely unusual sexual interests and paraphilic or disordered ones? On what basis do the eight sexual interests cited above qualify as paraphilia?
2. Is each type of paraphilia technically accurate in its description and diagnosis and supported by objective science? Various sexual interests of fallen off the list over time. Why not others?
3. Some of these paraphilic sexual interests may have victims and some may not. Does this play any role in characterizing the behavior as a paraphilia?
4. In this age of diversity, should sex-related diagnoses even be classified as mental illnesses?
5. What is the role of the perception of social stigma (taboo) in the decision to include a condition on the list, such that as behaviors become more normalized in society, they will drop off the list?
6. Is it less of a disorder if one does not exclusively prefer a particular propensity or preference?

It is beyond the scope of this book to solve these questions here, save to underscore the external pressures and issues that complicate what is still an emerging body of science. This field is not immune from political correctness and cultural relativism, and is fraught with dangerous influences that a moral society must not overlook. The societal agendas of particular subcultures are attempting to influence science, normalize certain behaviors, and thereby diminish the chances that a given behavior will induce clinically significant stress and impairment. When immoral behavior is normalized, this will have very adverse consequences on society.

Here I will provide two reflections on how science can be prone to social forces that attempt to engineer a clinical conclusion. Consider, for a moment, a 2012 article by Canadian clinical psychologist and sexologist James M. Cantor, titled "Is Homosexuality a Paraphilia? The Evidence For and Against." (Note that in 1973, homosexuality was dropped off the list of paraphilias in the *DSM*.) In his introduction, Cantor writes the following:

> Homosexuality, more than any other atypical sexual interest, has achieved great social acceptance over time, and advocates for other atypical sexual interests—BDSM, cross-dressing, diaperism, etc.—understandably seek the same recognition and rights. Thus, thinking of paraphilias as merely another sexual orientation suggests the conclusion that *everyone* with an atypical sexual interest should benefit from greater tolerance .[. .] however, I disagree that answers to scientific questions can be identified by presuming the desired outcome and then backwards-engineering one's interpretation of the research data to guarantee arrival at that outcome. Moreover, and perhaps more importantly, questions of rights fall outside the purview of science. People deserve respect and civil rights *regardless* of the scientific classification of their sexual interests.[100]

Cantor's point is that the basic human rights and dignity of a person are not the interest of science in the objective sense. Science should also not be susceptible to arriving at an outcome just because groups lobby hard for a behavior to become an accepted norm in society.

In examining homosexuality, Cantor reviewed the typical scientific data associated with a behavior, which includes prevalence, sex ratio, fraternal birth order, handedness, intelligence and cognitive profiles,

---

[100] James M. Cantor, "Is Homosexuality a Paraphilia? The Evidence for and Against," Archives of Sexual Behavior (Feb. 1, 2012) 41:237-247, 237, published online: 27, January 2012, https://www.ncbi.nlm.nih.gov/pmc/articles/PMC3310132/pdf/10508_2012_Article_9900.pdf/?tool=EBI.

physical height, and neuroanatomy. He concluded that "homosexuality is no more novel in its profile of correlates than would be any other paraphilic interest. Thus, although homosexuality is probably better said to be distinct from paraphilias, that conclusion is still quite tentative."[101]

The second example illustrates how deeply certain influencers have lobbied the scientific community to accept certain antisocial behaviors. One can only hope the following is an outlying example. On the United Kingdom news website, *The Telegraph*, Andrew Gilligan wrote an article titled "Paedophilia is natural and normal for males: How some university academics make the case for paedophilia at summer conference." Gilligan writes: "'Paedophilic interest is natural and normal for human males,' said the presentation. 'At least a sizeable minority of normal males would like to have sex with children....Normal males are aroused by children.'"[102] Gilligan notes that such reprehensible statements were not made by "anonymous commenters on some underground website....The statement that paedophilia is 'natural and normal' was made last July... as one of the central claims of an academic presentation delivered to key experts at a conference held by the University of Cambridge.'"[103] Such an alarming example underscores the attempt by some to normalize deviant behavior. Note that one of the notorious clerical sexual abuse cases involved Fr. Paul Shanley of the Archdiocese of Boston, who openly advocated for the normalcy of sex between men and boys.

Finding on Question 1: Are All the Clergy Cases Classified as Pedophilia?

Returning to my first posed question, namely, whether *all* instances of child sexual abuse by Catholic clergy align with the characteristics of

---

[101] Cantor, "Is Homosexuality a Paraphilia?" 244.

[102] Andrew Gilligan, "Paedophilia is natural and normal for males: How some university academics make the case for paedophilia at summer conference," *The Telegraph,* July 5, 2014, par. 1, retrieved /6/26/21, https://www.telegraph.co.uk/comment/10948796/Paedophilia-is-natural-and-normal-for-males.html.

[103] Andrew Gilligan, "Paedophilia is natural and normal for males," par. 3.

diagnosed pedophilia, the answer is no, based on the examination above. However, I would like to acknowledge and reconcile two points.

Pedophiles and Exclusive Preference

First, pedophiles don't all commit offenses exclusively with the characteristic prepubescent age group. Therefore, it can be conceded that some portion of older minor victims of clerical sexual abuse may have been victimized by priests who did have the classic diagnosis of pedophilia.

Reconciling the Prepubescent and Pubescent Age Ranges

Second, I would like to attempt to reconcile the age grouping (of those under eleven) used in the John Jay scope report with the definitions used by both the *DSM* and the *ICD*. The *DSM* extends its definition for pedophilia to age thirteen, and the *ICD* does roughly the same by identifying children in their early pubescence. This broader spectrum is described under the term "pedohebephilia," wherein "hebephilia" might apply to early pubescent victims in the age range of eleven to fourteen. The John Jay scope report establishes that the age of first victimization within the age grouping of zero to ten accounted for 21.94 percent of the cases of clerical sexual abuse (1,831 victims; 1,198 male and 633 female). Absent a clinical assessment of pedophilia, it is a highly speculative exercise to characterize any of the cases in the age grouping of eleven to fourteen in the John Jay scope report as distinctly pedophilia. But to prove a point, in an attempt to account for the *DSM-5* age definition that extends to age thirteen, ascribing 75 percent of the victims in the age range of eleven to fourteen as instances of distinct pedophilia would only raise the percentage from 22 percent to 60.4 percent (5,042 of the 8,347 cases). From this it is clear that not all cases involve clinical pedophilia. The overall abuse clearly includes other disordered motivations.

The evident clinical correlate for pedophilia is the strong sexual attraction to prepubescent children. There was debate in the scientific community before the *DSM-5* was released about whether to formally include early pubescent children (hebephilia) in the definition, and the notion was rejected. I don't have an explanation as to why the *DSM* scientific community rejected its inclusion as a paraphilia. By contrast, the *ICD-10* does include early pubescence, and it can be argued that it covers hebephilia. In an attempt to answer this quandary, consider the entry in the online website *Psychology Today* that characterizes an attraction to postpubescent adolescents (hebephilia at eleven to fourteen years and ephebophilia at fifteen to nineteen years):

> Most people today would believe that acting on the desire to have sex with a young adolescent, hebephilia, is abhorrent and a crime. But simply experiencing that attraction, from an evolutionary perspective, is not pathological—attraction to a teen who has undergone puberty and can reproduce is a valid reproductive behavior. Humans are wired to perceive beauty in youth, as it can be a strong indicator of fertility. But of course, that doesn't provide any justification whatsoever to predators who perpetrate abuse in today's day and age.[104]

Even if science does not classify hebephilia and ephebophilia as paraphilias, these conditions can lead to very harmful and criminal behavior.

Notwithstanding that debate in the scientific community, even though the identified phenomena of hebephilia and ephebophilia are not named as paraphilias in the *DSM-5*, it does not follow that all cases of child sexual abuse must then default to being pedophilic behavior.

The exact causes of pedophilia have not been conclusively established. Pedophiles are a heterogenous group, with some estimates reflecting a ten-to-one ratio of male to female perpetrators, and some pedophiles can be attracted to victims of either sex. They may be either married or unmarried. Offenders are usually family friends, relatives, or someone known to the victim. The prevalence of pedophiles is unknown, but the literature estimates it to be 3 to 5 percent of adult men.[105]

---

[104] Psychology Today, "Hebephilia," Psychology Today © 2021 Sussex Publishers, Inc., retrieved 6/1/21, https://www.psychologytoday.com/us/basics/hebephilia.

[105] American Psychiatric Association (APA), *Diagnostic and Statistical Manual of Mental Disorders,* DSM-5 (5th ed., Washington, DC: American Psychiatric Association [APA], 2013), 698.

The *DSM-5* notes that males with this disorder begin to feel sexual attraction toward children at about the time they enter puberty. There is arrested psychosexual development in pedophiles, leading in some cases to a confused sexual identity. The presence of, and causal relationship with, other comorbidities or pathologies is uncertain because it is unclear whether they are the source of the disorder, the disorder's result, or due to a sampling bias (for example, criminal sex offenders who display antisocial behavior).

Studies identifying notable cognitive abilities and IQ are inconclusive. Consumption of child pornography has been shown to be a strong correlate to pedophilia.[106] Evidence suggests that pedophilia cannot be cured, and it is marked by high recidivism. It is typically treated, to varying degrees of success, with psychotherapy, teaching self-management skills, and sex-drive–reducing medication.

There is evidence that the treatment centers for priests understand the incurable nature of pedophilia. In one such instance, a facilitator working on behalf of the Monastery of the Servants of the Paraclete, a religious order known to host such treatment centers, penned a September 26, 1957, letter to Bishop Matthew F. Brady of the Diocese of Manchester, New Hampshire. The letter included the following paragraph: "From our long experience with characters of this type, and without passing judgment on the individual, most of these men would be clinically classified as schizophrenic. Their repentance and amendment is superficial and, if not formally at least unconsciously, is motivated by a desire to be again in a position where they can continue their wonted activity. A new diocese means only green pastures."[107] It is credible to believe that other letters with similar conclusions were sent to various Church leaders who had priests in treatment.

---

[106] American Psychiatric Association (APA), *Diagnostic and Statistical Manual of Mental Disorders,* DSM-5 (5th ed., Washington, DC: American Psychiatric Association [APA], 2013), 698.

[107] Rev. Gerald Fitzgerald, Letter to the Most Rev. Matthew F. Brady, D.D., Bishop of Manchester, September 28, 1957, https://www.bishop-accountability.org/docs/manchester/NHAG_05926_05927.pdf.

Finally, the subsequent 2011 John Jay cause report includes a revealing statement in its executive summary: "Less than 5 percent of the priests with allegations of abuse exhibited behavior consistent with a diagnosis of pedophilia. Thus, it is inaccurate to refer to abusers as 'pedophile priests.'"[108] This finding is consistent with the prevalence of pedophilia in the broader society. Recall that many victims of pedophilia fall in the range of eight to ten years of age. Unfortunately, there are still a host of other predator types who have a preference for postpubescent minors.

Finding on Question 2: What are the Human Development Characteristics of Perpetrators in Clergy Cases?

The John Jay scope report concludes that about 22 percent of the clergy sexual abuse of minors resulted from abusers with characteristics of diagnosed pedophilia. That leaves 78 percent of the cases as having no official diagnosis. Even if most of these remaining cases were to be classified as situational offenders, it is critical to understand the causes so that prevention can be as comprehensive and effective as possible.

What have past studies shown us about the state of human development among clergy? Fr. Martin Pable, OFM Cap., in his article "Priesthood and Celibacy" written in 1981, comments on the 1971 National Catholic Conference of Bishops' Study on Priestly Life and Ministry. The timing of this referenced study fits squarely in the time frame of a vast number of clergy sexual abuse violations, which increased from the mid-1960s and reached a height in the late 1970s. (There were 2,162 reported cases between 1960 and 1969, and 2,989 cases between 1970 and 1979.) It also corresponds to the timing of a mass exodus of priests from the priesthood. Pable writes,

> It is noteworthy that in the psychological part of the NCCB [National Catholic Conference of Bishops] Study, 66% of priests were classified as 'underdeveloped,' in the sense that they have not achieved the level of psychological growth

---

[108] John Jay College Research Team, "The Causes and Context, 3.

appropriate for their chronological age. At one point the authors comment on one of the characteristics of these men: 'The chief area in which the underdeveloped priests manifest their incomplete psychological growth is in their relationships with other persons. These relationships are ordinarily distant, highly stylized, and frequently unrewarding for the priest and the other person. Underdeveloped priests report their interpersonal relationships are difficult, even though they like people and, at a deep level of their personality, would like to be closer to them. There is a certain pain involved for them in this conflict between wanting the psychological experience of being closer to people and yet finding it awkward and difficult to get themselves into close relationships with others. Underdeveloped priests are genuinely uneasy about intimacy...[which] refers to responsible closeness with other persons, one of the most important challenges of adult life.[109]

This should not come as a total surprise, given the "guardrails" around clerical continence that is the legacy of the Church's history on mandatory celibacy.

Given this description of two-thirds of the clergy in the period measured, I attempted to reconcile it with some conclusions from the 2011 John Jay cause report. Its executive summary includes the following key observations:

1. "The priests who engaged in abuse of minors were not found, on the basis of their developmental histories or their psychological characteristics, to be statistically distinguishable from other priests who did not have allegations of sexual abuse against minors."[110]

2. "Priests with allegations of sexually abusing minors are not significantly more likely than other priests to have personality or mood disorders."[111]

---

[109] Martin W. Pable, "Priesthood and Celibacy," *Chicago Studies* 20, no. 1 (Spring 1981): 59-77, 67.

[110] John Jay College Research Team, "The Causes and Context, 2.

[111] John Jay College Research Team, "The Causes and Context, 3.

3. "Priests who sexually abused minors did not differ significantly from other priests on psychological or intelligence tests."[112]

So, in summarizing the John Jay cause report on this point, the 78 percent of remaining cases not considered to be acts of pedophilia appear to be committed by priests who were not especially distinguishable by developmental histories, psychological characteristics, personality or mood disorders, or intelligence or psychological testing.

Then what were the key psychological causes, according to the John Jay cause report? The report only cites characteristics that were "more likely" to be observed in the clergy who were accused of the abuse. From what I can glean, this subset of the clergy had the following characteristics in their histories that made them more likely to abuse:

1. "Priests who were sexually abused as minors themselves were more likely to abuse minors than those without a history of abuse."[113]
2. "Priests who lacked close social bonds, and those whose family spoke negatively or not at all about sex, were more likely to sexually abuse minors than those who had a history of close social bonds and positive discussions about sexual behavior."[114]

Reflections on These Two "Likely" Characteristics

There has been increased interest in understanding the connection between sexual victimization in childhood and how it may or may not contribute to that victim's propensity to engage in deviant or criminal behavior as a juvenile or adult. It is good that science is pursuing this line of inquiry, which usually follows the framework of social learning theories, such as the "cycle of violence" or "intergenerational transmission of

---

[112] John Jay College Research Team, "The Causes and Context, 5.
[113] John Jay College Research Team, "The Causes and Context, 4.
[114] John Jay College Research Team, "The Causes and Context, 4.

family violence."[115] Having observed violence in the home or having been a victim of domestic violence as a child has been shown to influence the propensity of this behavior as an adult. But concerning the perpetration of child *sexual* abuse due to experiencing sexual abuse as a child, studies over the past two decades suffer from limitations in definitions, methodologies, and sample sizes, making the relationship inconclusive.[116] Experiencing abuse as a child can impair a healthy psychological development, but the evidence is inconclusive about the propensity of the sexually abused to perpetuate this behavior on others. So the first conclusion among the "more likely" behaviors in the John Jay Cause Report is not the strongest. I think it is important to recall that perpetrating abuse in one's past is a much more reliable determinant of perpetrating abuse in the future.

As for priests who "lacked close social bonds," this describes a fundamental problem found in two-thirds of the clergy, as reported in the 1971 United States Catholic Conference of Bishops study. It is the foundational reason why human formation has been incorporated into seminary formation since the 1990s. But it doesn't give us a clear profile for prevention.

Hence, the John Jay cause report observes that "few of the priest-abusers exhibited serious pathological, developmental, or psychological characteristics or behaviors that could have led to their identification prior to the commission of their abusive acts."[117] This conclusion, combined with an assertion that the social mores of the 1960s and 1970s may have led to a greater prevalence of deviant behavior, is all we have from this cause report. It has left many wanting a better explanation. I am among those unsatisfied with the analysis.

---

[115] Shelly A. McGrath, Ashlyn Abbott Nilsen, and Kent R. Kerley, University of Birmingham, US, "Sexual Victimization in Childhood and the Propensity for Juvenile Delinquency and Adult Criminal Behavior: A Systematic Review," *Aggression and Violent Behavior: A Review Journal,* Vol.16, Issue 6, Nov.-Dec. 2011: 485-492, 486, https://www.thestranger.com/images/blogimages/2017/05/03/14 93857245-pdf_2011_review.pdf.

[116] Shelly A. McGrath, Ashlyn Abbott Nilsen, and Kent R. Kerley, University of Birmingham, US, "Sexual Victimization in Childhood and the Propensity for Juvenile Delinquency and Adult Criminal Behavior: A Systematic Review," 489.

[117] John Jay College Research Team, "The Causes and Context, 5.

VIII

The Debate About Homosexual Behavior and the Clergy

The Balance of Cases

Left with what seem like incomplete and unsatisfactory answers from the John Jay cause report, I turn now to exploring the remaining 6,516 cases (5,512 male and 1,004 female) which are not explainable as classic pedophilia, according to the John Jay cause report. My aim is to probe possible explanations. The preponderance of male victims indicated by the data cannot be ignored. Table 5 illustrates how I arrived at these figures.

Table 5: Cases Determined Not to Be Classic Pedophilia

	Male	%	Female	%
Distribution of the 8,347 cases by gender	6,710	80.39%	1,637	19.61%
Less cases judged to be pedophilia (ages 0-10)	(1,198)	14.35%	(633)	7.58%
Balance of unclassified cases (ages 11-17)	5,512	84.59%	1,004	15.41%
Total allegations	10,667			
Victims with survey data	8,347			

Source: Extrapolated from John Jay College of Criminal Justice, "The Nature and Scope of Sexual Abuse of Minors by Catholic Priests and Deacons in the United States: 1950–2002" (Study Report, February 2004), 9, 54, https://www.bishop-accountability.org/reports/2004_02_27_JohnJay_revised/2004_02_27_John_Jay_Main_Report_Optimized.pdf. (Based on age of victim at first instance of abuse; numbers rounded to the closest whole number).

To bring these figures into sharper relief, I will repeat some important points:

1. The disparity of male to female victims may be even larger because it is generally believed that abuse against male victims is less frequently reported than abuse against female victims. In four of the five decades studied, the proportion of male victims to female victims increased.
2. The age of the victim at the first instance of clergy sexual abuse increased over the five decades studied in the John Jay scope report.

Given the profile of pedophilia, the remaining cases are more likely to have been committed by situational offenders than by serial offenders with many victims. There is also likely to be a wide variance in motivations in this group of cases.

From the clinical perspective, I can glean only three strong factors for the equation:

1. Sexual orientation
2. Likelihood of a cleric having poor social bonds
3. Likelihood of a cleric having been sexually abused as a child, particularly as it may have negatively impacted a healthy psychological development

Defining Sexual Orientation

Sexual orientation is defined by the American Psychological Association as "an enduring pattern of emotional, romantic and/or sexual attractions to men, women or both sexes."[118] In her article "Sexual Orientation: A Definition and the 13 Main Types," Isabel Rovira notes that "this implies interest in a person due to different factors: biological, psychological, economic, cultural, religious, and social (Pérez, 2014)."[119]

Terms Specifying Sexual Orientation

In exploring the first factor of sexual orientation, I will use the following definitions of the terminology as provided by James Cantor, PhD. *Heterosexuality* is "Predominant sexual interest in the opposite sex. For emphasis, the term applies both to interest in adults as well as to children of the opposite sex. Men sexually interested in adult women and men interested in prepubescent girls are both heterosexual. This usage contrasts with many contexts, in which the interest in adults is presumed."[120]

---

[118] American Psychological Association, "Sexual Orientation & Homosexuality," (2008), retrieved 6/2/2021, https://www.apa.org/topics/lgbtq/orientation.

[119] Isabel Rovira, "Sexual Orientation: A Definition and the 13 Main Types," Healthy Way Mag, March 16, 2019, https://healthywaymag.com/relationships/sexual-orientation.

[120] James M. Cantor, "Is Homosexuality a Paraphilia? The Evidence for and Against," Archives of Sexual Behavior (Feb. 1, 2012) 41:237-247, 238, published online:

Homosexuality is "Predominant sexual interest in persons of the same sex. As with heterosexuality, the term applies both to interest in adults and children of the same sex."[121]

These definitions of homosexuality and heterosexuality may appear controversial because they include a possible interest in children, including prepubescent children, and the terms often are seen to imply a presumption of interest only in adults. Pedophilic offenders aside—who may have personality disorders that impair their self-concept and sexual orientation—the definitions given by Cantor simply maintain that the orientation toward the same or opposite sex logically holds true to its nature, whether it manifests by interest in adults or minors.

If sexual interest is only in adults, there are other terms for that. The term for interest in adults is teleiophilia. Interest in male adults is androphilia and interest in female adults is gynephilia. Interest only in prepubescent or early pubescent children falls under the broad spectrum of pedohebephilia. Seen in this context, sexual interest in minors, if acted upon, is sexual abuse that can be committed by both heterosexual and homosexual persons. It cannot be presumed that either sexual orientation means an interest in adults exclusively, nor can Cantor's observation be overlooked that "although homosexuality is probably better said to be distinct from paraphilias, that conclusion is still quite tentative."[122]

Sexual Behavior Versus Sexual Orientation

The next question is whether one behaves consistently with their sexual orientation. Are heterosexual males aroused by only females and homosexual men aroused by only males? There is no definite answer. Generally, yes, but not always. And the possibility exists that not all the offending clerics fit neatly into the categories of homosexual or heterosexual orientation.

27, January 2012, https://www.ncbi.nlm.nih.gov/pmc/articles/PMC3310132/pdf/10508_2012_Article_9900.pdf/?tool=EBI.

[121] Cantor, "Is Homosexuality a Paraphilia?" 238.

[122] Cantor, "Is Homosexuality a Paraphilia?" 244.

Formation of Sexual Orientation

While the period of adolescence usually factors heavily in the formation of sexual orientation, it is not always established firmly during that time. Some evidence suggests that if it doesn't take root during one's teenage years, then it doesn't necessarily occur within any specific time frame. Therefore, some of the clerics may have had a bisexual orientation or even an undefined, or asexual, orientation.

Some who have examined this field have identified up to thirteen different sexual orientations. One that caught my attention is the so-called *demi-sexual*. With the John Jay cause report's observation about "poor social bonds" as a backdrop, this sexual orientation is defined as a sexual attraction precipitated primarily by the establishment of trust and an emotional bond with someone, presumably irrespective of the person's gender.[123] The emotional bond and trust fulfill a fundamental human longing and, once these are established, sexual attraction follows. Could this apply in some of the clergy cases involving victims who are older minors?

Case Study

Consider this story related in a 1983 article titled "Abandonment of Relationships in the Catholic Priesthood—Implications for Ministry." Agnes P. Albany provides "the story of one man's belief in his own abandonment and his struggle to find the courage to make sense out of his life."[124] I have condensed the full article, but it serves as a possible example of this *demi-sexual* orientation:

> Tom has been a priest for 20 years. He is neither content nor satisfied with his ministry. He is an able administrator who

---

[123] Isabel Rovira, "Sexual Orientation: A Definition and the 13 Main Types," Healthy Way Mag, March 16, 2019, https://healthywaymag.com/relationships/sexual-orientation.

[124] Agnes P. Albany, "Abandonment of Relationships in the Catholic Priesthood—Implications for Ministry," *The Priest*, May 1983, 39.

longs for his life to be different. He would give up his priesthood in a minute, he says, if he could find someone who
would love him unconditionally....

Tom entered the religious life at 13. He describes this as
a 'searching for the family I never had at home.' His parents
were proud of their son's decision and encouraged his departure from the family....

He recalls always wanting a big brother and he joined the
priesthood to find one. Tom is seeking that perfect relationship
which will fill the void that he believes was lost in the past....

Tom is searching for some balance in relationships, whether
male or female, which will give him what he believes he has
never gotten—the complete and unconditional acceptance he
has always longed for. He has searched in many places and in
many ways—gay bars, heterosexual relationships, prayer, and
most recently, a close relationship with a young teenage boy
in his parish. He is presently testing that relationship to see if
it will last.[125]

This case illustrates a longing for social bonds, which appears to be
the predominant predicate for his sexual attraction. There is obviously
great risk in Tom's case. Celibacy for him is neither vital nor dynamic.
His personal search could pose serious risk of creating real harm, if it
hasn't already caused some. Keeping such a priest in active ministry poses
a risk that should not be accepted.

Returning to Sexual Orientation

Although the case of Fr. Tom could well explain some additional cases,
it doesn't tell the whole story. Sexual arousal is generally consistent with
sexual orientation. The large number of postpubescent male victims
suggests the presence of a large proportion of homosexually oriented
clerics in the priesthood who could likely be suffering from poor social
bonds and possibly be the victims of sexual abuse as children. But not

---

[125] Albany, "Abandonment of Relationships," 42–44.

even the clerics who fell under this category acted with the same motivations. Some were likely situational offenders who, according to their sexual orientation, abused either male or female victims due to stress and circumstance, while others acted out their homosexual orientation in patterns of behavior like active ephebophilia and pederasty—terms I will explain shortly. This makes homosexuality in the priesthood a credible risk factor.

There are situations when one does not behave sexually according to one's orientation. Prison environments come to mind. I don't think the priestly environment is quite analogous, but I should say a word about environments composed mostly or completely of one gender.

Though I have focused on the abuse of minors as the subject of the scandal, it is not entirely implausible to also consider motivations often in play in cases involving adult male-on-male assaults. Since a preponderance of the clergy victims were older male minors, it is very possible that some of these predators blurred the line of adulthood. The Rand Corporation study for the US Air Force, cited in chapter VI, sheds light on the two categories of motives typical for male-on-male perpetration:

> Because the study of male-on-male sexual assault is still an emerging area of research, we know very little about the characteristics of male perpetrators who sexually assault other men....The existing research on the characteristics and behaviors of male perpetrators seems to indicate that they are a heterogeneous group, meaning there does not appear to be one single profile of a male perpetrator who sexually assaults male victims. Research examining known cases of male-on-male sexual assault has generally identified two different types of perpetrators based on their motivations for committing the assault (e.g., Almond, McManus and Ward, 2013; Hickson et al., 1994; Hodge and Canter, 1998). The first group consists of homosexual men who commit assault against other homosexual men primarily for intimacy or sexual gratification. The second group consists of heterosexual men who commit sexual

assault against other men as an expression of social dominance or control."[126]

These motives cannot be taken off the table in some of the clergy cases.

Research on the Link between Sexual Abuse and Homosexual Clerics

Fr. D. Paul Sullins, PhD, a married priest working for the Ruth Institute at the Catholic University of America, has challenged the claim of some that there is no link between homosexuality and the sexual abuse cases. His research has shown that there is a strong statistical link between the proportion of homosexual priests and the years of clergy sexual abuse examined in the two John Jay reports. The clear statistical link alone does not explain the precise behavior involved in each case of abuse, but neither does it discount the variant and plausible explanations I proposed above: situational offenders and active ephebophilia and pederasty. I think it's worth quoting extensively from the abstract of his forty-seven-page report titled "Is Catholic Clergy Abuse Related to Homosexual Priests?" The abstract reads,

> Sex abuse of minor children by Catholic priests has been a persistent and widespread problem in the Church in recent years. Although over 8 in 10 of victims have been boys, the idea that the abuse is related to homosexual men in the priesthood has not been widely accepted by Church leaders. The influential report of the John Jay College of Criminal Justice on the causes and context of Catholic clergy sex abuse (hereafter "JJR2," for John Jay Report 2) concluded that widespread American abuse was not related to the share of homosexual priests because the reported increase in "homosexual men

---

[126] Rand Corporation, "A Review of the Literature on Sexual Assault Perpetrator Characteristics and Behaviors," Study Report, 2015, 43–44, https://www. rand.org/content/dam/rand/pubs/research_reports/RR1000/RR1082/ RAND_RR1082.pdf.

in the seminaries in the 1980s…does not correspond to an increase in the number of boys who were abused." …To test JJR2's conclusion, I examined the available data on clergy sexual orientation to determine directly whether or not, in their words, "an increase in homosexual men in the priesthood will lead to an increase in the abuse of boys." The share of homosexual American priests over time was estimated from a 2002 survey by the Los Angeles Times newspaper that included questions about sexual orientation, age and year of ordination. Abuse was measured by reports from Catholic dioceses, the same data used in JJR2. I looked only at allegations of current abuse, and statistically adjusted the findings to eliminate differences due to the age of abuser and year of abuse. My findings showed that the increase or decrease in the percent of male victims correlated almost perfectly (.98) with the increase or decrease of homosexual men in the priesthood. Among victims under age 8, the correlation was lower but still strong (.77). This indicates that 1) the abuse of boys is very strongly related to the share of homosexual men in the priesthood, but that 2) easier access to males among older victims (ages 8-17) was also an enabling factor. The increase or decrease of overall abuse also correlated highly (.93) with the increase/decrease of homosexual priests; not surprisingly since such a high proportion of victims were male. This finding was robust; the unadjusted correlation…was still a strong .90. About half of this association was accounted for by the rise of subcultures or cliques of sexually active homosexual priests and faculty in Catholic seminaries, which was also measured by the LA Times survey. Prior to the 1950s the proportion of homosexual men in the priesthood was about the same as in the general population. By the 1980s homosexual men made up over 16% of the presbyterate, which is over 8 times that of the general population.[127]

---

[127] Paul Sullins, abstract to "Is Catholic Clergy Sex Abuse Related to Homosexual Priests?" (Study Report: The Catholic University of America; The Ruth Institute, Abstract written Feb. 16, 2019; Report posted Dec. 11, 2018 and revised May 28,

The Raging Debate

There has been robust argumentation about distancing homosexuality from having any role in the sexual abuse of minors in the clergy sexual abuse crisis. Despite a compelling link, proponents who attempt to undermine its association to the crisis appear to rely on the weaker link between homosexuality and pedophilia. But since only a relatively small portion of the cases involve clinical pedophilia, their line of argument seems just as much politically driven as scientifically driven. And yet, this postulation has been vocally and vigorously argued, as in the examples I provide below.

Why has so much effort been expended to dispel any link between homosexuality and the abuse crisis, considering the apparent mysteries and complexities of science and this scandal?

1. Is it a noble attempt to shield the homosexual community from public reaction?
2. Is it because these advocates do not want to retard the homosexual community's progress in forging normative behavior?
3. Is it because it would be too disruptive to the Church given the population of homosexually oriented priests and higher clergy that has dramatically increased over the past few decades?
4. Is it because these proponents don't want the scientific community to revisit its 1973 decision to drop homosexuality from the list of paraphilias?
5. Or is it asserted purely in the name of science?

Note in the examples provided below the concerted effort to disassociate any role of homosexuality from the clergy sexual abuse crisis.

Dr. Thomas Plante, in his 2018 article "Separating Facts about Clergy Abuse from Fiction," includes a bullet point titled "Homosexual Clerics

---

2021), https://papers.ssrn.com/sol3/papers.cfm?abstract_id=3276082, retrieved 6/21/21.

Aren't the Cause of Pedophilia in the Church."[128] This bullet point seems to imply that all instances of clergy sexual abuse are pedophilic. That was never a foregone conclusion. It appears to apply to about 22 percent of the cases and an estimated 5 percent of the abusers, consistent with prevalence in the larger society. While the cause of child sexual abuse is indeed a complex phenomenon, Plante seems to imply that homosexual clerics are not even a factor. Plante then asserts, "Homosexual men may be sexually attracted to other men, but not to children."[129] But he doesn't define *children* and so the inference is young, prepubescent children, consistent with his use of the word *pedophilia*.

In a 2009 published paper by Ryan Hall, MD and Richard Hall, MD, PA, titled "A Profile of Pedophilia: Definition, Characteristics of Offenders, Recidivism, Treatment Outcomes, and Forensic Issues," the authors explore the various categories used to describe pedophilia. They make the following entry:

> Pedophiles are usually attracted to a particular age range and/or sex of child. Research categorizes male pedophiles by whether they are attracted to only male children (homosexual pedophilia), female children (heterosexual pedophilia), or children from both sexes (bisexual pedophilia). The percentage of homosexual pedophiles ranges from 9% to 40%, which is approximately 4 to 20 times higher than the rate of adult men attracted to other adult men (using a prevalence rate of adult homosexuality of 2%–4%).[130]

Moreover, it is implausible to make the assertion, as Plante does, that homosexual men are only attracted to other adult males and never

---

128 Thomas G. Plante, "Separating Facts about Clergy Abuse from Fiction," *Psychology Today,* August 23, 2018, 2, https://www.psychologytoday.com/us/blog/do-the-right-thing/201808/separating-facts-about-clergy-abuse-fiction.

129 Thomas G. Plante, "Separating Facts about Clergy Abuse from Fiction," 2.

130 Ryan Hall, MD and Richard Hall, MD, PA, "A Profile of Pedophilia: Definition, Characteristics of Offenders, Recidivism, Treatment Outcomes, and Forensic Issues," Focus: The Journal of Lifelong Learning in Psychiatry, Vol 7, Issue 4 (Fall 2009): 522-537. https://focus.psychiatryonline.org/doi/10.1176/foc.7.4.foc522.

attracted to pubescent adolescents. I remind the reader of Dr. Cantor's definitions provided above.

Equally imprecise is a blog by Gregory M. Herek, PhD, titled "Facts about Homosexuality and Child Molestation." The term *child molestation* is generally a legal term and does not convey a psychological motive on the part of the perpetrator. In the published paper by Ryan Hall, MD and Richard Hall, MD, PA cited above, the authors note that "Child molestation is not a medical diagnosis and is not necessarily a term synonymous with pedophilia. A child molester is loosely defined as any individual who touches a child to obtain sexual gratification with the specifier that the offender is at least 4 to 5 years older than the child."[131] Herek states, "Most molesters of boys do not report sexual interest in adult men,"[132] citing the National Research Council. He does not define the term *boys* with any age demarcation.

Herek proceeds to cite a study of both homosexual and heterosexual adult men by Canadian researchers to measure their interest and sexual arousal by having them view images of "males and females of various ages (child, pubescent, and mature adult)."[133] He notes that all the participants had been prescreened "to ensure that they preferred physically mature sexual partners."[134] What does that prove, other than that a particular sample of self-professed teleiophilic (those with interest in adults only) homosexuals "responded no more to male children than heterosexual males responded to female children"?[135] How can one conclude that it represented the entire universe of homosexual interest and behavior? He then suggests that "this well known lack of a linkage

---

[131] Ryan Hall, MD and Richard Hall, MD, PA, "A Profile of Pedophilia: Definition, Characteristics of Offenders, Recidivism, Treatment Outcomes, and Forensic Issues."

[132] Gregory M. Herek, "Facts about Homosexuality and Child Molestation," Sexual Orientation: Science, Education, and Policy (blog), 3, retrieved 7/18/2020, https://psychology.ucdavis.edu/rainbow/html/facts_molestation.html.

[133] Gregory M. Herek, "Facts about Homosexuality."

[134] Gregory M. Herek, "Facts about Homosexuality."

[135] Gregory M. Herek, "Facts about Homosexuality."

between homosexuality and child molestation accounts for why relatively little research has directly addressed the issue."[136] Herek's assumptions seem flawed.

In December 2005, the *Denver Post* ran an opinion piece titled "Sex and the Church." It reads,

> In 2003, the Vatican invited experts on human sexuality to address the issue of child sexual abuse by the clergy. Among them was Martin P. Kafka, a psychiatrist at Harvard's McLean Hospital. Kafka and the others were all of one mind: Homosexuality was an irrelevant factor in the scandal. They stressed to the Vatican that it would be more effective to screen out problem priests by checking for personality traits known to be linked to sexual abuse, using already familiar methods. The experts spelled out factors that increase the risk of pedophilia, including a history of being sexually abused during childhood; a lack of adult friends and lovers; signs of antisocial behavior or trouble with impulse control; and indications that a man is conflicted and uncomfortable about his own sexuality.[137]

Again, this piece jumps to the term *pedophilia* and suggests a narrow definition of homosexuality to imply an interest in adults only. In fact, here is how Kafka is quoted according to the *National Catholic Reporter* covering this Vatican meeting of experts: "'We described it [homosexuality] as a risk factor,' Kafka said, noting that the majority of cases in the American crisis involve adolescent males between 14 and 17 victimized by adult gay priests."[138]

Finally, citing another example, the *Catholic Register* posted an article titled "Blaming Homosexuality for Sex Abuse of Minors Is 'Absolutely

---

[136] Gregory M. Herek, "Facts about Homosexuality."

[137] Keith W. Swain, "Sex and the Church," *The Denver Post*, December 5, 2005, retrieved 7/6/2020, https://www.denverpost.com/2005/12/05/sex-and-the-church/.

[138] John L. Allen Jr., "Homosexuality a Risk Factor, Vatican Told," *National Catholic Reporter*, April 18, 2003, retrieved 7/6/2020, https://www.natcath.org/NCR_Online/archives2/2003b/041803n.htm.

Immoral', Victims Say." While indeed not spoken by an authority on the subject, the headline is intended to convey a conclusion, but the article's substance shows how fast and loose people are in their descriptions. The founder of New England's Survivors Network of those Abused by Priests is quoted in the article as saying, "There has been a lot of scapegoating of homosexual men as being child predators."[139] But he goes on to say, "I will admit that if a priest is abusing a 16-, 17-, or 18-year-old boy, that part of the element that is going on there is homosexuality." But then he confidently concludes, "but that is not the root of the problem."[140] Articles like this, loose with descriptions and employing catchy headlines, do not aid in pursuing real answers. Homosexual behavior may not be at play in all the cases, but it does appear to be a noteworthy causal factor for a significant number of cases and thus demands careful investigation.

A Recent Case Demonstrating Many Questions

The Catholic News Service ran a report on July 7, 2020, titled "Cleveland priest faces multiple federal child pornography charges." The priest, now forty years old, exhibited a telltale sign of pedophilia (consumption of child pornography)—though it is unclear whether he was diagnosed as such—and through a cell phone app, he solicited a male victim who was fifteen and with whom he had sex three times.[141] The case raises interesting questions:

1. Is he a pedophile?

---

139 "Blaming homosexuality for sex abuse of minors is 'absolutely immoral', victims say," *The Catholic Register*, Feb. 20, 2019, retrieved 7/29/2020, https://www.catholicregister.org/home/international/item/29006-blaming-homosexuality-for-sex-abuse-of-minors-is-absolutely-immoral-victims-say.

140 "Blaming homosexuality for sex abuse of minors is 'absolutely immoral', victims say."

141 "Cleveland priest faces multiple federal child pornography charges," Catholic News Agency, July 7, 2020, https://www.ncronline.org/news/accountability/cleveland-priest-faces-multiple-federal-child-pornography-charges.

2. Is he a nonexclusive pedophile?
3. Was he confused about his sexual identity?
4. Why did he seek a male partner of that age? There is no evidence in the article that this victim was part of the Church community.

There are so many questions and so few answers. To acknowledge that homosexual behavior and pedophilia are distinct does not in and of itself take homosexuality off the table as one of several contenders for some answers.

The website *The Inquiry*, a site which monitors the clergy abuse crisis broadly and more specifically follows the crisis in the Diocese of Alexandria-Cornwall, Ontario, Canada, posted a 1989 article written by Fr. John Allan Loftus, SJ, PhD. Fr. Loftus, a psychologist, served as the executive director of Southdown (Emmanuel Convalescent Centre), Canada's premier facility for treating clerical sex abusers. In the article, titled "Sexual Abuse in the Church: A Quest for Understanding," Loftus speaks about the clerics credibly accused by acknowledging that "these men are not 'all the same.'"[142] Loftus's observation speaks to the complex confluence of homosexuality, clerical celibacy, and psychosexual development.

While Loftus acknowledges the "increased numbers of homosexuals in ministry,"[143] he cites a *New York Times Magazine* article (Homosexuality: who and why?"-Konner, 1989) declaring "prejudice remains rife."[144] But as shown in the articles above, that "prejudice" toward pursuing answers with candor seems to run both ways.

Unlike those in denial about the role of homosexuality or those who attempt to distance its relationship to the crisis, Loftus candidly reports that "most of the Canadian clergy/Religious in question have been

---

[142] John Allan Loftus, "Sexual Abuse in the Church: A Quest for Understanding," The Inquiry: Cornwall Ontario Sex Abuse Scandal (Emmanuel Convalescent Foundation, 1989), 14, as cited by the website: *The Inquiry*, https://theinquiry.ca/the-diocese/southdown/father-john-loftus-sj/sexual-abuse-in-the-church-a-quest-for-understanding/.
[143] Loftus, "Sexual Abuse in the Church," 19.
[144] Loftus, "Sexual Abuse in the Church," 19.

homosexually involved with postpubescent adolescents, for example, and in some cases, at least, the behaviors do appear to have been isolated acts."[145] This is a reference to situational offenders. These characteristics of the abuse described by Loftus applies in the United States as well, and there is no reason to believe the case profile and distribution differs significantly in any other country or location.

It is beyond the scope of this book to examine the etiology (that is, the causes) of homosexuality. But it is noteworthy in this regard to state that a growing body of evidence is dispelling the notion that this sexual orientation is innate or genetically caused.[146] It is also impossible, without specific clinical information in each unique case of abuse, to postulate which of the homosexual offenses against minors by clergy were committed by priests with arrested psychosexual development or confusion about sexual identity, which were committed by priests as situational offenders, or which were committed by priests who were overtly confident in their homosexual orientation.

It is beneficial here to introduce two other terms into the conversation: *ephebophilia* and *pederasty*. Though both are recognized terms in the clinical community, they are not among the eight named paraphilic disorders in the *DSM-5*. They are characterized by a sexual preference for older minors and are still forms of child sexual abuse. Table 6 delineates three categories within the spectrum of chronophilia involving minors.

---

[145] Loftus, "Sexual Abuse in the Church," 11

[146] Sara Reardon, "Massive Study Finds No Single Genetic Cause of Same-sex Sexual Behavior," Scientific American.com, August 29, 2019, https://www. scientificamerican.com/article/massive-study-finds-no-single-genetic-cause-of-same-sex-sexual-behavior/. And, Paul Sullins, "'Born That Way' No More: The New Science of Sexual Orientation," Public Discourse: The Journal of the Witherspoon Institute, September 30, 2019, https://www.thepublicdiscourse. com/2019/09/57342/.

Table 6: Spectrum of Chronophilia (Minors)

	Pedophilia	Hebephilia	Ephebophilia
Etymology	*paidos*—child; *philia*—love of	*Hebe*—Greek goddess and protector of youth, also ref. to time before manhood; *philia*—love of	*ephebos*— one arrived at puberty; *philia*—love of
Term first used	Late 19th century	1955, Hammer & Glueck	1906, Magnus Hirschfeld; 1950, Frits Bernard
Generally understood victim age	0–10 (prepubescent)	11–14 (pubescent / early pubescent)	15–19 (pubescent/ postpubescent)
DSM-5 Paraphilia	Yes	No. Was hotly debated.	No
ICD-10 Paraphilia	Yes	Arguably yes, since pedophilia def. includes prepubescent and early pubescent (F65.4)	No

Ephebophilia

The term *ephebophilia* is generally understood to mean a primary sexual preference or propensity—not mere attraction—to those in their mid-to-late adolescence (fifteen to nineteen). More narrowly, the literature has used it to mean a male's preference for pubescent, adolescent boys. *Wikipedia* notes that "The term has been described by Frenchman Felix Buffiere in 1980 and Pakistani scholar Tariq Rahman, who argued that ephebophilia should be especially used with regard to homosexuality when describing the aesthetic and erotic interest of adult men in adolescent boys in classical Persian, Turkish, or Urdu literature. The term was additionally revived by Ray Blanchard to denote adults who sexually prefer 15- to 19-year-olds."[147]

There is much speculation among clinicians about the causes of ephebophilia. The website *Healthncare.info* provides this summary:

> Some regard ephebophilia as a milder form of pedophilia in which the object of attraction is closer to the normal age of a sexual partner than with a true pedophile. Others regard ephebophilia as resulting from chronophilia, wherein the chronophile's sexual/erotic age is discordant with his or her actual chronological age but concordant with the age of the partner. Yet another theory characterizes it by a refusal to age psychologically and a desire to reconnect with one's youth. Attraction to adolescents is not generally regarded by psychologists as pathological except when it interferes with other relationships, becomes an obsession which adversely affects other areas of life, or causes distress to the subject....In men with a perverse sexual orientation under juvenile hyper sexuality, high sexual activity is manifested, in satisfaction of which the individual shows indifference how to realize the sexual desire. Many ephebophiles like the inexperience of teenage children, and they are happy to engage in 'mentoring.'[148]

Applying the category of ephebophilia to many of the clergy sexual abuse cases involving older minors may be a more congruent reflection of reality given that the data shows a gradual increase in the age of the first instance of victimization over the five-decade period examined. Changes in seminary formation were afoot over time, and there was an increase in the number of homosexual clerics. This shift could also be

---

147 Wikipedia, "Ephebophilia," last edited May 5, 2021, https://en.wikipedia.org/wiki/Ephebophilia.

148 "Ephebophilia Definition, Psychology, Symptoms, Causes, Treatment," *Healthncare.info,* 2013, retrieved 6/28/2021, http://healthncare.info/ephebophilia-definition-psychology-symptoms-causes-treatment/.

the result of an ongoing and deepening sexification in society, the earlier arrival of puberty in modern society, and active pederasty.

It is worth mentioning that the executive summary of the 2004 John Jay scope report does not mention pedophilia, nor is it among the terms defined in the terminology section of the report. But it does include a definition for ephebophilia, likely because the authors view it as a relevant cause given the preponderance of older minor victims.

Pederasty

Pederasty is generally understood to be a homosexual relationship between an adult male and a pubescent or adolescent boy. The word derives from the Greek word *paiderastia*, meaning "love of child or boy." The term has been traced back to a social custom in ancient Greece "in which an adult male would court a young Greek boy to become his model, guide, and initiator, and would become responsible for the evolution of his chosen young counterpart."[149] The relationship typically involved one active, dominant partner who acted psychologically and sexually upon a passive, submissive one.

In today's context, that construct could be acted out as straight, nonempathetic victimization, or in a role of cultivated mentorship. The perpetrator can leverage power, be in a position to offer access and enticements, and can either satisfy sexual stress or leverage this warped relationship to placate the loneliness and isolation of a celibate life. Consider the alleged behavior of former cardinal Theodore McCarrick. "Sharing a bed" with young adult seminarians—which he incredulously called merely "imprudent"—fits the model described above. A coworker of mine who was in the Army described to me how the infantry viewed a general, saying, "A general is like a god." A reasonable parallel can be drawn for how a seminarian might view his bishop.

---

[149] Mariah Cavanaugh, "Ancient Greek Pederasty: Education or Exploitation?" STMU History Media, A Student Organization of St. Mary's University, of San Antonio, Texas, featuring Historical Research, Writing and Media at St. Mary's University, December 3, 2017, 1, https://stmuhistorymedia.org/ancient-greek-pederasty-education-or-exploitation/.

Reasonable Conclusions

Even though the John Jay cause report left questions unanswered, I believe I have laid out a compelling case for the behaviors in play that are not due to classic pedophilia. These behaviors include those of situational offenders suffering from human underdevelopment and poor social bonds and also overt homosexual behaviors in conditions such as ephebophilia and pederasty. Identification of these behaviors can provide a path toward prevention and solutions.

While human formation is now more rigorous in the seminary, there could still be candidates elevated to the priesthood who may not understand celibacy and its difficulties and permanence, may not have been given the gift or embraced it, or may not be adequately psychosexually developed, because these candidates can do just enough in the formation process to be deemed suitable for ordination.

Additionally, due to the shortage of priests, it is even more common for priests to live alone, and the current atmosphere in the wake of the clergy sexual abuse crisis has made many priests even more cautious to socially engage at any real depth. It is no surprise, then, that although most clergy readily concede that the celibate life aids in their work, one of the top complaints about the priestly life is "loneliness, the feeling of abandonment and distress, which undermine all moral resistance."[150] Problems not caught in screening and formation will generally manifest themselves later at some point. Many of the clergy sexual abuse cases took place years after ordination.

Insights from Church History

The phenomenon of sexual abuse is not new in the Church's history. If any institution has roots to ancient times, where social customs like Greek pederasty were present, it is the Church.

---

[150] Pope St. Paul VI, *"Populorum Progressio* (On the Development of Peoples),"
Encyclical Letter, March 26, 1967, #67, https://www.vatican.va/content/paul-vi/
en/encyclicals/documents/hf_p-vi_enc_26031967_populorum.html.

Long before modern science, these problems were treated as moral weakness or were overlooked altogether. But some reformers decried this and other deviant behaviors. The second-century Church Father Tertullian condemned "all the other frenzies of passions—impious both toward the bodies and toward the sexes —beyond the laws of nature, we banish not only from the threshold, but from all shelter of the Church, because they are not sins, but monstrosities."151 This statement condemns all lustful behavior, but its connection to our discussion is its description of "lusts which exceed the laws of nature." The Church views homosexual behavior as a violation against nature.

In an essay titled "Catholic Clergy and the Violation of Children," Thomas Doyle, JCD, CADC, writes, "The sexual violation of minors and vulnerable adults by the Catholic clergy of all ranks has been a tragic reality in the church from its earliest days. *The Didache*, a kind of handbook for followers of Christ, which dates from the first century, states explicitly that adult men are not to engage in sex with young boys. The prohibition applied to *all* males in the community including the leaders who at that time were not known as clergy."152 Depending on the translation, *The Didache* reads, "You shall not be sexually perverse," "Thou shall not commit sodomy," or "You shall not corrupt boys."

Doyle continues, "The earliest known *law* or *canon* to condemn sex between adults and boys dates from the Synod of Elvira which took place in Spain in 309 AD. Over the centuries church leadership has been well aware of the various violations of mandatory celibacy by the secular or diocesan clergy and of similar violations of the vow of chastity by religious men. There is a body of ecclesiastical legislation that spans the centuries, all of which attempts to either eliminate or control the grave problem of the sexual violation of minors or adults by clergy and religious."153

---

[151] Tertullian, *De Pudicitia*, 4, cited from https://www.newadvent.org/fathers/0407.htm.

[152] Thomas P. Doyle, "Catholic Clergy and the Violation of Children," 1, date unknown, as cited on http://www.sjpcommunications.org/images/uploads/documents/doyle061813.pdf.

[153] Doyle, "Catholic Clergy," 1.

Later, Italian-born St. Peter Damian (born AD 1007), repulsed by what he saw at the time, wrote a book to Pope St. Leo IX titled *The Book of Gomorrah* (*Liber Gomorrhianus*, AD 1051). The document, named after the famous Old Testament story of the city with that name, rails against the scandal of sexual sin by the clergy, including those who defile men or boys, wherein they violate the soul of those entrusted to their care. According to St. Damian, such clerics, whether bishops or priests, should be condemned and removed from the clerical state and be prevented from being ordained in the first place. He was equally critical of complacent bishops and religious superiors who share in the guilt by not acting.

This long experience in the Church has led to ample insight and wisdom into human behavior and to clergy screening and formation. The 1961 Church document *Religiosorum Institutio* reflects that collective wisdom in its addressing of many aspects of candidate selection, screening, and formation. Among the admonitions is the following: "Advantage to religious vows and ordination should be barred to those who are afflicted with evil tendencies to homosexuality or pederasty, since for them the common life [living in common in religious communities] and the priestly ministry would constitute serious dangers."[154] The Church has been "on notice" for centuries that this kind of behavior was cancerous. They should have been able to spot it a mile away, long before this crisis spiraled.

This history only lends credence to homosexuality, ephebophilia, and pederasty being among the key causes in the current clergy sexual abuse crisis. It is disingenuous and dangerous in pursuing truth to deny these causes. These factors must inform a resolute and immediate path to action.

---

[154] Sacred Congregation for Religious, "*Religiosorum Institutio*: Instruction on the Careful Selection and Training of Candidates for the States of Perfection and Sacred Orders," February 2, 1961, #30, https://www.ewtn.com/catholicism/library/religiosorum-institutio-2007.

Priestly Formation

Evolution of Seminaries

A Catholic seminary is a school of theology and formation. The early Church had no seminaries. Leaders learned by oral preaching, experienced the Holy Spirit—"the Spirit of truth who will guide you to all truth"[155]—and were chosen by the twelve apostles or those in succession to them. In rarer instances, leaders were picked by the acclaim of the community in recognition of their faith and zeal. Given the cantankerous temperament of some of them, including those who were canonized saints of the Church, I think some would have struggled to endure the standards of today's formal seminary environment.

---

[155] John 16:13, *The New American Bible*, Catholic Mission Edition, St. Jerome Press (Wichita Kansas: Devore & Sons, Inc., 1987 and 1981).

By the late Middle Ages, it was clear that priests, particularly in rural communities far removed from urban universities, were not sufficiently educated. Seminaries have evolved to the demands of the age ever since. In more recent times, there were three levels of seminary appropriate to the ages of the candidates.

1. Minor seminary. This school is adapted for high school students, and general education and faith formation are the core elements. The prevalence of these schools has dramatically waned in the last thirty years due to a lack of students, the operational costs, and the belief by some that students of that age lack the maturity to understand the choice they appear to be making. Notwithstanding those real-world considerations, many in the priesthood and religious life testify to their sense of calling at a young age. Increasingly there has been a growing reemergence of career-track programs in high schools in recent decades. For these reasons, the ideals behind minor seminary formation are not completely without merit.

2. College-level seminary. As the name implies, this seminary is designed for undergraduate students. Sometimes it is a seminary that boards students while they attend local colleges and universities, and sometimes it is a self-contained school. Students receive a degree in philosophy or liberal arts, with a focus on preparing them for advanced theological studies.

3. Theologates (or major seminary). This setting represents the final four to five years of formation, typically leading to a master's degree in theology or divinity. It now includes four pillars of formation: spiritual, human, academic, and pastoral. The human formation component was added, or more strenuously emphasized, in response to both psychosexually underdeveloped clergy and the recent sexual abuse crisis. Sometimes human formation difficulties are discovered, prompting an extension of formation. But this is generally frowned upon, and sometimes these human formation difficulties disqualify the candidate.

Importance of Human Formation

While every bishop needs more priests, above all they just want normal, balanced guys. The formation in the seminary is where quality must surpass quantity. The Church document *Religiosorum Institutio* warns that "although vocations [...] are to be promoted by every means [...] still care must be taken lest an immoderate desire to increase numbers should interfere with quality and selection. Let all be convinced that, unless great zeal for an abundance of students is closely bound up with proper care for their formation, such zeal does not produce the desired effects, and even does just the contrary."[156] This is so not only because poorly formed priests give a poor example, but also because poor selection and formation can bring outright and overt harm when nonnegotiable personality flaws are missed in formation.

Under Pope Benedict XVI, the Congregation for Catholic Education summarized this facet of human formation, stating: "The candidate for ordained ministry, therefore, must reach an affective maturity. Such maturity will allow him to relate correctly to both men and women, developing in him a true sense of spiritual fatherhood towards the Church community that will be entrusted to him."[157]

Screening Candidates

When candidates present themselves as having an interest in the priesthood or religious life, the Church's ministry of discernment begins. God

---

[156] Sacred Congregation for Religious, "*Religiosorum Institutio*: Instruction on the Careful Selection and Training of Candidates for the States of Perfection and Sacred Orders," February 2, 1961, #14, https://www.ewtn.com/catholicism/library/religiosorum-institutio-2007.

[157] Congregation for Catholic Education, "Concerning the Criteria for the Discernment of Vocations with regard to Persons with Homosexual Tendencies in view of their Admission to the Seminary and to Holy Orders," #1, Given at Rome, November 4, 2005, https://www.vatican.va/roman_curia/congregations/ccatheduc/documents/rc_con_ccatheduc_doc_20051104_istruzione_en.html.

calls laborers into His harvest field[158] at different ages, in many ways, and through many mediums. An aspirant begins to understand that there is more to this life than what the world offers, that he or she has gifts to share in the service of the Church and the world. In the case of an aspirant to the priesthood, he can see himself in the role of a priest, all the while seeking the will of God. Sometimes the calling is discerned from a sudden religious experience with enduring effect, but very often it is a gentle, suasive tugging of the mind and heart. It is often fostered and nourished in the home, the "domestic church," but not always. Regrettably, sometimes parents are not open to the hand of God in their child's life, for a variety of reasons.

Because there are all kinds of factors that motivate human behavior—which is often a complex mess—the Church will codiscern with the candidate to determine whether he has the suitable spiritual and human disposition to begin priestly formation. This formation spans a period of five to twelve years, depending on the age of the candidate and other requirements. This is often a much longer time than it takes a couple to prepare for their lifelong sacramental marriage. It is generally sufficiently long enough to identify and begin to address any potential issues.

In codiscerning the motivation for interest in the priesthood, the Church must ensure that the candidate has come forth freely, has sufficient maturity, and has begun to understand the reality of a celibate life. The celibate lifestyle alone can sometimes attract the maladjusted. Consider various motivations that the Church must be on guard for: to please his parents; to solely secure his own salvation; to find a father figure or brother figure in his life or the family he never had; because his priest-friend, whom he views as a mentor, said it's one big fraternity and he'd fit right in. In seeking the well-balanced, the Church must be watchful to spot the misanthrope, the woman-hater or one with an antimarriage attitude, the recluse or loner, the self-righteous, the naive and undiscerning, and the insecure and maladjusted. This list goes on. Some of these motivations may not be overtly expressed or discovered at first.

---

[158] Matthew 9:38, *New American Bible*.

As the process gets more serious, the Church will review whether there are any obvious or significant impediments, including canonical ones, with the candidate. The Church will explore the candidate's spiritual life, look for signs of an authentic calling such as the willingness to sacrifice, and examine any experiences in ministry at his parish. The process will also include psychological testing, which became more normative since the 1970s, and background and reference checks.

Vulnerability of Priestly Formation

While human formation in the seminary has intensified in the last two decades, some character defects may never sufficiently come to light to be addressed, either because of a lack of self-awareness or because some candidates quickly understand the culture of the seminary and can navigate by avoiding the "minefields" as a survival instinct. Some simply fly under the radar, and in some cases, seminary staff and review boards will advance questionable seminarians to keep the pipeline of candidates for the priesthood moving along. Bishops accept such candidates at their own risk.

Post-ordination Support and Formation

In addition to the introduction of human formation in the seminary, post-ordination support, particularly for the first five years of priesthood, has significantly increased in the last several decades, with an emphasis on ongoing formation and development. This can be a vulnerable time for priests, with some leaving the priesthood during this period.

Having left the collegial and supportive seminary environment, a newly ordained priest must now transition into having a substantial workload while often living virtually alone. To lessen this transition's difficulty, newly ordained priests are assigned a mentor for the first five years and will join a group of newly ordained priests for support. The goal of ongoing formation—which is similar to the continuing education of other professions—is deepening their prayer life and study and developing skills for their pastoral responsibilities. There will be days of recollection, retreats, study workshops, and individual meetings with the bishop and with the whole presbyterate, including times for general instruction and addressing pastoral issues. The priest will be encouraged to maintain a relationship with a spiritual director and to remain updated and culturally enriched. His ministerial work may also be subject to evaluation at periodic intervals.

Final Thoughts on Priestly Formation

Despite a more rigorous formation process, vulnerabilities remain and must be guarded against. These include, but are not limited to, candidates subscribing to a homosexual culture within the priesthood or proceeding without the gift of celibacy, Church leaders and authorities overlooking issues in pursuit of increasing the number of priests, candidates attempting to slip through the process without transparency, and priests living alone.

Poor Shepherds and Poor Accountability

It would be better for him if a millstone were put around his neck and be thrown into the sea than for him to cause one of these little ones to sin."[159]

Beyond the sexual abuse itself, its cover-up and poor, clumsy handling by bishops (both individually and acting as a national conference) was a significant aggravating component of the crisis and a proximate cause of its prolonging. Because Vatican officials work closely with national conferences of bishops, they are implicated in this pattern of behavior as well.

Jesus frequently encountered friction from the Jewish religious leaders of his day, the Pharisees, who, in an attempt to discredit him, would accuse him of not following the Jewish Law. Often, they would present polemics around the oral tradition of practices and not the written Law itself. Jesus would then contrast their own scruples about these practices

---

[159] Luke 17:2, *The New American Bible*, Catholic Mission Edition, St. Jerome Press.

with what the Law really required of them (the interior righteousness of the Law), calling them hypocrites for missing the forest for the trees.

It is healthy for a tradition to self-reflect and hold the proper standard of conduct in high relief for its leaders to follow. The Jewish tradition has its own criticisms of the Pharisees. In Emil L. Fackenheim's book on Judaism, he recounts that the Anglo-Jewish scholar Herbert Lowe lists as follows the types of "Pharisees," false and true, that he has collated from the rabbinic sources:

1. The shoulder Pharisee (who carries his good deeds on his shoulder ostentatiously; or, according to another interpretation, tries to rid himself of the commandments);
2. The sit-a-while Pharisee (who says, "wait until I have done this good deed");
3. The bruised Pharisee (who breaks his head against the wall to avoid looking at a woman);
4. The pestle Pharisee (whose head is bent in mock humility, like a pestle in a mortar);
5. The book-keeping Pharisee (who calculates virtue against vice, or who sins deliberately, and then attempts to compensate for his sin by some good deed);
6. The God-fearing Pharisee, who is like Job;
7. The God-loving Pharisee, who is like Abraham.[160]

Similarly, the Catholic tradition is replete with examples of admonition and instruction on right conduct, for there has always been a need to call out the weeds among the wheat in the Church—even among its leaders. A prominent example is Pope St. Gregory the Great, pope from AD 590 to 604. In his *Book of Pastoral Rule*, Gregory exhorts those who aspire to rule (religious governance) by quoting the prophet in Isaiah 52:11, "Be ye clean that bear the vessels of the Lord."[161] Such a role is no light burden. Noting the examples of poor rule, he observes, "What in

---

[160] Emil L. Fackenheim, *What Is Judaism?* (New York: Collier Books, 1987) 133–134.
[161] Pope St. Gregory the Great, *Book of Pastoral Rule*, Part II, Ch. II, as cited on https://www.ewtn.com/catholicism/library/book-of-pastoral-rule-11544.

words they preach, by their manners they impugn."[162] He further points out that "certainly no one does greater harm in the Church than one who has the name and rank of sanctity while he acts perversely."[163]

Gregory reminds the pastor, the shepherd, not only that he who "speaks the highest things must exhibit the highest things,"[164] but also that he must be "unbending against the vices of evildoers through a zeal for righteousness."[165] While he must be discreet in silence at the right times, he must also be profitable in speech and not suppress what should be uttered. This means he must reprove faults, serve the office as a herald, and not be "like dumb dogs, that cannot bark (Isai. lvi. 10)"[166] (an expression used again by Pope Innocent III in the early thirteenth century). Gregory calls improvident rulers those who, "fearing to lose human favour, shrink timidly from speaking freely the things that are right, and according to the voice of the truth (Job. x. 12), serve unto the custody of the flock by no means with the zeal of shepherds, but in the way of hirelings; since they fly when the wolf cometh if they hide themselves under silence."[167] The words of St. Gregory to the bishops ring true and apply in many cases in this crisis.

The fear of losing human favor creates an emphasis on reputation. In her autobiography, St. Teresa of Avila recounts that for many years she struggled with an attachment to her reputation, to the point that it was an impediment to her spiritual progress at times. When reputation and the fear of losing human favor become focal points in Church leadership, let us be reminded of St. Teresa's words: "If they fail to remove this caterpillar, it may not hurt the whole tree, for some of the other virtues may remain, but they will all be worm-eaten. The tree will not be beautiful; it will neither prosper itself nor allow the trees near it to do so, for the fruit of good example which it bears is not at all healthy and will not last for long. I repeat this: however slight may be our concern

---

[162] Pope St. Gregory the Great, *Book of Pastoral Rule*, Part I, Ch. II.

[163] Pope St. Gregory the Great, *Book of Pastoral Rule*, Part I, Ch. II.

[164] Pope St. Gregory the Great, *Book of Pastoral Rule*, Part II, Ch. III.

[165] Pope St. Gregory the Great, *Book of Pastoral Rule*, Part II, Ch. VI.

[166] Pope St. Gregory the Great, *Book of Pastoral Rule*, Part II, Ch. IV.

[167] Pope St. Gregory the Great, *Book of Pastoral Rule*, Part II, Ch. IV.

for our reputation, the result of it will be as bad as when we play a wrong note, or make a mistake in time, in playing the organ—the whole passage will become discordant."[168] Because of a focus on reputation, Church leadership became out of tune and discordant. Unwilling to break the pattern, many bishops were prisoners of the system—a misguided mode of operation in handling these cases.

In June 1985, a confidential document was presented to the United States Catholic Conference of Bishops titled "The Problem of Sexual Molestation by Roman Catholic Clergy: Meeting the Problem in a Comprehensive and Responsible Manner." The ninety-page document, prepared by Mr. F. Ray Mouton, JD, and then-Fr. Thomas P. Doyle, OP, JCD, was initiated partly in response to the well-publicized 1984 case involving Fr. Gilbert Gauthe's repeated sexual abuse in the 1970s and 1980s. Gauthe was convicted the following year. The document adeptly and credibly raised emerging questions about civil jurisprudence, criminal law, Canon Law, insurance mitigation, clinical and medical questions, and others.

Early in the report there was a noteworthy warning. The authors wrote, "Some extremely serious issues have arisen which presently place the Church in the posture of facing extremely serious financial consequences as well as significant injury to its image. It is submitted that time is of the essence.... [The] problems with which the Project will deal are continuously arising...[and] now carry consequences never before experienced."[169]

As a society existing in the world, the Church as a living institution is entitled to competent counsel and needs to exercise human prudence in protecting and perpetuating its existence, considering its larger divine mission and constitution. But it is worth mentioning that the report

---

168 *The Life of Teresa of Jesus: The Autobiography of St. Teresa of Avila* (Garden City, New York: Image Books, 1960), 298.

169 F. Ray Mouton and Thomas P. Doyle, "The Problem of Sexual Molestation by Roman Catholic Clergy: Meeting the Problem in a Comprehensive and Responsible Manner" (final draft, June 8–9, 1985), 2-3, retrieved 6/25/2021, https://www.bishop-accountability.org/reports/1985_06_09_Doyle_Manual/DoyleManual_NCR_combined.pdf.

implicitly acknowledges that the problem is not new (as evidenced in Church history) but explicitly states that the consequences are. The stakes are high. It's a new day. It can't be business as usual. The report should have served as a wake-up call.

Over the course of this crisis, there were between 167 and 195 dioceses in the United States (new ones were created over this period). Not all bishops handled the crisis equally well. Prudent bishops dealt firmly with issues of sexual abuse, led by the compass of the Gospel. By contrast, others followed a path closer to what American psychologist Lawrence Kohlberg called the first stage in moral development, which is acting merely with an orientation of self-interest in the avoidance of punishment and consequences. Although a motive, it is among the lowest and most primitive.

The John Jay cause report, which was published in 2011, acknowledges that "By 1985, bishops knew that the sexual abuse of minors by Catholic priests was a problem, but they did not know the scope of the problem."[170] It was in their June 2002 General Assembly meeting that the US Catholic Conference of Bishops approved the charter of protection for children and called for a comprehensive scoping study—after the *Boston Globe* broke its report in January 2002. What happened in those almost twenty intervening years? By September 1993, it was clear enough for me, as a twenty-five-year-old, to address the matter in a letter to Pope St. John Paul II, and, unknown to me at the time, the pope made his first public statement on the crisis to US bishops in June of that same year.[171]

In seven or fewer years after that 1985 report, the US bishops were feverishly working with the Vatican on universal procedures in Canon Law, looking for acceptable ways to dismiss clerics from the clerical state, especially those who refused to be laicized. And in 1992, they

---

[170] John Jay College Research Team, "The Causes and Context of Sexual Abuse of Minors by Catholic Priests in the United States, 1950–2010" (Study Report, May 2011), 3, http://votf.org/johnjay/John_Jay_Causes_and_Context_Report.pdf.

[171] John Paul II, "Letter of His Holiness John Paul II to Bishops of the United States," June 11, 1993, https://www.vatican.va/content/john-paul-ii/en/letters/1993/documents/hf_jp-ii_let_19930611_vescovi-usa.html.

promulgated five principles[172] as general recommendations for dioceses to follow in handling clergy sexual abuse allegations and cases, but, as the John Jay cause report points out, the "implementation of the principles was uneven among dioceses."[173]

I am not convinced that they did not realize the magnitude of the problem. While some bishops acted resolutely and courageously, it is clear that the Conference of Bishops was slow to react as a body, and individual bishops, acting on their own autonomy, pursued different tactics and strategies to handle the crisis, with very mixed results. The John Jay cause report notes that "other bishops, often in dioceses where the Catholic Church was highly influential, were slow to recognize the importance of the problem of sexual abuse by priests or to respond to the victims."[174]

One of the authors of "The Problem of Sexual Molestation by Roman Catholic Clergy: Meeting the Problem in a Comprehensive and Responsible Manner," Fr. Thomas Doyle, OP, an active priest from 1970 to 2004, left the priesthood to work for survivors of abuse. Disillusioned by the response of the hierarchy to the report, his comments were captured in a 2019 article: "I no longer have any trust in the institutional church. None whatsoever. I naively thought that once we presented them with this information, that they would immediately get together and do something to stop it. I was totally wrong....There have been several wake-up calls....The myth is that the institution, the bishops, are

---

[172] John Jay College Research Team, "The Causes and Context of Sexual Abuse of Minors by Catholic Priests in the United States, 1950–2010," 82. Five principles: (1) respond promptly to all allegations of abuse where there is reasonable belief that abuse has occurred; (2) if such an allegation is supported by sufficient evidence, relieve the alleged offender promptly of his ministerial duties and refer him for appropriate medical evaluation and intervention; (3) comply with the obligations of civil law as regards reporting of the incident and cooperating with the investigation; (4) reach out to the victims and their families and communicate sincere commitment to their spiritual and emotional well-being; (5) within the confines of respect for privacy of the individuals involved, deal as openly as possible with the members of the community.

[173] John Jay College Research Team, "The Causes and Context," 4.

[174] John Jay College Research Team, "The Causes and Context," 4.

going to be able to fix themselves. They haven't fixed it; they've made it worse, because, in trying to fix it, they've actually gone deeper into the dishonesty, into hiding and into lying. It's systemic."[175]

Similarly, in a 2019 article by Jay Korff covering the thoughts and work of Thomas Doyle, the author writes, "The Church's historic pattern according to Doyle: Deny the abuse, minimize, shift blame, devalue the victim, intimidate, don't contact police, maintain secrecy, and move priests without telling anyone."[176]

It is worthwhile to enumerate some of the possible reasons why some Church leaders were slow, and even resistant, to respond to cases presented to them while the crisis unfolded below their noses. The following is a top-of-mind list of plausible reactions:

1. They wished to avoid public scandal (which proved shortsighted).
2. It was inconvenient (investigations and judicial proceedings under Canon Law are cumbersome and seen as a last resort).
3. They focused on the bishop–priest relationship—the problem was viewed as a moral failing and not a pathology. The bishop understood the challenges of living a celibate life and tried to counsel the priest.
4. Because of the shortage, they wanted to avoid the risk of losing a priest.
5. The priest could have been a close friend of the bishop.
6. Some leaders sent the priests off for "treatment" until the uproar subsided.
7. Some leaders mistrusted psychiatric science and preferred a pastoral approach instead.

---

[175] Jeremy Rogalski and Tina Macias, "Catholic Priest Shuns Collar to Fight for Survivors of Clergy Sexual Abuse," KHOU 11, Jan. 10, 2019, https://www.khou.com/article/news/catholic-priest-shuns-collar-to-fight-for-survivors-of-clergy-sexual-abuse/285-1d16e66d-5a17-4f14-a074-7793c8cac10d.

[176] Jay Korff, "Thomas Doyle—The Truth Seeker," WJLA News, July 15, 2019, www.wjla.com/news/the-50-year-secret/tom-doyle-the-truth-seeker.

8. Some leaders hesitated, waiting to see whether the problem was isolated or persistent. They transferred the cleric if the matter had not been publicly exposed, perhaps buying the bishop some time.

9. They prioritized confidentiality of the perpetrator over addressing the issue.

10. They wanted to avoid litigation or financial settlements, if possible.

11. The bishop didn't understand the nature of the deviant behavior or how pervasive it was.

While the list above includes shortsighted missteps by Church leaders, the list below includes more depraved motivations and deep-rooted flaws in the Church's organizational culture.

1. They did not want public exposure or notoriety due to pursuit of personal prestige or possible advancement as a career churchman.

2. They wanted to shield the priest from criminal or civil prosecution.

3. The accused priest had information that would compromise the bishop, the diocese, or other priests. They sought to avoid that risk of exposure by avoiding other issues as well.

4. The bishop himself had some history of, or sympathies for, this behavior and was internally compromised and conflicted about condemning the behavior.

So, on balance, how can the actions of Church leadership be judged? I'd say it was a very mixed bag, with plenty of both intentional and unintentional missteps, many of which had very detrimental consequences.

Some leaders argue that they did what was conventional at the time. As I laid out in chapter VII, the clinical science is still evolving. Given the priests' rights of due process, the procedures under Canon Law made it a challenge to remove priests unwilling to resign and be laicized. On the flip side, the willful shielding and transferring of priests, the failure to involve law enforcement and civil authorities, the lack of transparency, the delay tactics and intimidation, and the play on the goodwill of faithful Catholic victims to trust and be silent were absolute and abject failures of leadership. Some ignored the advice of therapists and review boards. The tidal wave was coming, and they couldn't get out of their own way. Some decided to be kings of their own castle, and sometimes absolute power corrupts absolutely.

The original draft of the document now titled "Promise to Protect, Pledge to Heal: Charter for the Protection of Children and Young People," which the US Conference of Bishops approved in their June 2002 meeting, included a provision in Article II that "Dioceses will also have a review board, the majority of whom will be lay persons not in the employ of the diocese. This board will assess allegations, regularly review diocesan policies and procedures dealing with the sexual abuse of minors, and advise the bishop on the offender's fitness for ministry."[177] That verbiage is essentially identical in the latest 2018 version of the document. As the example below illustrates, it may need further revision to strengthen this provision.

Presumably some dioceses initiated this provision even prior to its formal adoption by the Bishop's Conference. A May 2002 MSNBC article covered the story of a Roman Catholic priest in Baltimore named Maurice Blackwell. He had been shot by his alleged victim of nine years prior. The priest, who survived, "was later placed on leave after acknowledging an affair [previous and unrelated] with a teen-age boy that had taken place before his 1974 ordination."[178] It is never advisable to take matters of justice into one's own hands, but the case raises an issue for reflection. According to the news story, the diocese, then led by the late Cardinal William Keeler, sent Blackwell to a Church-run residential treatment center in Hartford, Connecticut, for psychological evaluation following the victim's initial report to police of the abuse in 1993: "He was allowed to return to the church after police dropped the investigation on grounds of insufficient evidence and after an interview

---

[177] US Conference of Catholic Bishops, "Draft: Charter for the Protection of Children and Young People," June 4, 2002, https://www.bishop-accountability. org/resources/resource-files/churchdocs/PreDallasCharter.htm, (formerly on the USCCB website before latest version was posted).

[178] Mike Brunker, Alex Johnson, Robert Hager, "Alleged Abuse Victim Shoots Baltimore Priest," NBC, MSNBC and News Services, May 14, 2002, accessed 5/14/2002, http://msnbc.com/news/732931.asp?pne=msn.

with [the Cardinal]....At that time, a panel had been appointed to review the archdiocese's handling of sex-abuse allegations against priests [and] criticized his decision. The newspaper [the Sun] said the committee noted that a team Keeler had assembled to study Blackwell's case found the accusations against him 'consistent and credible.'"[179] This case illustrates that even with a review board in place, cases can be mishandled without clear and strong rules of governance for such boards.

I must reflect on the stirring irony of comments made with a straight face by former cardinal Theodore McCarrick, even as this draft charter was being approved. McCarrick, who himself was engaged in misconduct, said at the time, "This crisis is more important than any crisis we've had in my time....Our people are waiting for the bishops to say, O.K., we've got it under control, we're on the same page, we hear you and we've listened to you and now you can be sure that this will never happen again."[180]

In Jason Berry's 1986 article titled "Anatomy of a Cover-Up," he observed, "The integrity of an institution is built on trust between those who lead and those who follow."[181] Victims and faithful Catholics have reason to be hesitant in placing any trust in the hierarchy even at this stage in the crisis, and some of those reasons are outlined below.

1. Their decisions have diminished their moral standing.
2. Many dioceses have been financially devastated.
3. The crisis has strained a great deal of "goodwill capital" between bishops and state officials and members of Congress.
4. The John Jay cause report stated that "no single 'cause' of sexual abuse of minors by Catholic priests is identified as a result of our research."[182]

---

[179] Mike Brunker, Alex Johnson, Robert Hager, "Alleged Abuse Victim Shoots Baltimore Priest."

[180] Laurie Goodstein, "Bishop Quits as Others Prepare to Meet on Abuse Scandal," *New York Times*, June 12, 2002, https://www.nytimes.com/2002/06/12/us/bishop-quits-as-others-prepare-to-meet-on-abuse-scandal.html.

[181] Jason Berry, "Anatomy of a Cover-up," *The Times of Acadiana*, Jan. 30, 1986, as posted on https://www.bishop-accountability.org/news/1986_01_30_Berry_AnatomyOf.htm.

[182] John Jay College Research Team, "The Causes and Context," 1.

I am not aware of any official "follow-up" attempts to provide clarity to this analysis. Meanwhile, Catholics are left wondering in relative silence as Church leaders try to figure it out.

Preventing future abuse and properly handling cases will be only one part of the process of restoration. Church leaders must look themselves in the mirror, dig deep into the institution, and come clean on the root causes. Even if there are multiple causes, some surely feature much more prominently than others. Church leaders should now be addressing the largest factors in this crisis: homosexual behavior in the priesthood and the screening and selection processes of candidates for episcopal orders, the priesthood, and religious life. They should continue to implement policies to minimize the prevalence of opportunities. These would be closely followed by an honest review of mandatory priestly celibacy. Anything short of this is merely addressing symptoms or side effects instead of the root problems. They should also be communicating their findings and progress with the faithful.

Zero-Tolerance Policies on Child Abuse

Former Cardinal McCarrick expressed hope "that this will never happen again." Incredulous as this comment was coming from someone who exhibited the behavior of a charlatan in leading a double life, it prompts me to say a word about zero-tolerance policies. Such policies have long been debated in business and institutional spaces. Whether regarding workplace harassment or occupational safety, the policy sounds good and tough. It shows that leadership is taking the matter seriously. But the undesirable behavior can still continue. And when the behavior continues, the scrutiny and criticism will only intensify.

Consider, for a moment, whether it is wise for an occupational safety manager to have a zero-tolerance policy for injuries. Any workplace injury would be a deviation from policy—the standard or ideal. Soon the manager realizes the discouraging truth that the target is elusive in such a program. Despite the finely tuned standard, training, and collateral support, he soon discovers that he is pursuing the wrong goal. This is the inherent danger with most zero-tolerance policies, along with possible legal liability for not meeting the self-proclaimed standard.

Instead, the occupational safety manager should take a different, more incremental approach. He may strive to eliminate the conditions and human behaviors that pose risk and that could lead to workplace injuries. For example, one is not allowed to walk past liquid spilled on the floor without cleaning it or alerting a responsible party to clean it and placing a hazard sign there until it is made safe. One is not allowed to conduct a certain type of work without the corresponding protective gear. Employees are required to immediately report observed violations of even these incremental measures to the designated authority, and failure to do so has defined consequences.

Such zero-tolerance policies are really prevention programs with best practices. They are not an assertion that a problem will never manifest itself again. Following such a program does not guarantee one is out of danger. It certainly addresses the symptoms, but it may not address the underlying causes. And, as with any such program, it is only as strong as its weakest link. It works only by implementation, trial-and-error adaptation, and dutiful follow-through.

It has also been suggested that zero-tolerance policies may discourage people from reporting if they know that a fellow worker will be dismissed with only one strike against them.

To this end, the Church has implemented background checks for clergy, staff, and designated volunteers in parishes. Mandatory training for all personnel is required, and procedures are now in place for dealing with minors and youths. These personnel are now treated as "mandatory reporters" under civil law. The Church has also implemented mandatory prompt reporting by all members of the clergy and religious orders who witness or reasonably suspect any deviant behavior of their peers, as well as consequences for not doing so. These are all important, positive steps. These efforts must be accompanied by addressing the root causes of clergy sexual abuse.

Catholics continue to pray for resolute leaders committed to solutions, transparency, and accountability.

XI

The Role of Clericalism

*It cannot be denied, and it is bitterly to be deplored, that not infrequently
one finds priests who use the thunders of their eloquence to frighten others
from sin, but seem to have no such fear for themselves and become hardened
in their faults; a priest who exhorts and arouses others to wash away without
delay the stains from their souls by due religious acts, is himself so sluggish
in doing this;...he who knows how to pour the health-giving oil and wine
into the wounds of others is himself content to lie wounded by the wayside.*
Haerent Animo, Letter to Catholic Clergy on
Priestly Sanctity, Pope Pius X, 1908[183]

There have been many news stories connecting the phenomenon known as clericalism with the clergy sexual abuse problem.
Clericalism has been defined as a disordered attitude among clergy,

---

[183] Pope Pius X, *Haerent Animo*, Apostolic Exhortation, Given in Rome, at St. Peter's,
August 4, 1908, Papal Encyclicals Online, https://www.papalencyclicals.net/
pius10/p10haer.htm.

with an excessive emphasis on moral superiority and authority. Pope Francis has made clericalism a theme of his pontificate from the beginning. Initially, he warned that a "clerical culture" can isolate clerics from truly engaging the needs of the world and the people of God. This culture can shroud or muffle the cleric's role as servant. More recently, the pope's message has also expanded to suggest that clericalism directly contributed to the clergy sexual abuse scandal and efforts at cover-up.[184]

In a Catholic News Service article by Cindy Wooden she cites Pope Francis's words in describing clericalism. Wooden writes that this "illness in the church…pretends 'the Church' means 'priests and bishops'…[and] ignores or minimizes the God-given grace and talents of the laypeople"[185]—in effect, nullifying the personality of Christians. It "emphasizes the authority of clerics over their obligation of service"…[and tries] "'to replace or silence or ignore or reduce the people of God to small elites,' generally the clerics."[186] Wooden then quotes a December 2017 report by Australia's Royal Commission into Institutional Responses to Child Sexual Abuse: "'Clericalism is linked to a sense of entitlement, superiority and exclusion, and abuse of power,' the report said."[187] This abuse can manifest itself in self-preservation, advancement and church careerism.

Clericalism can emerge when an immature, arrogant personality is combined with a distortion of, or misalignment with, a certain aspect of the Church's theology of the priesthood, and a culture or subculture that explicitly or tacitly supports it. Originating in a misguided sense of personal sanctity or some other trait, it results in the pursuit of self-interest above true service. Such a worldview can be used to justify victimization or to mistakenly minimize the suffering of sexual abuse victims.

Regrettably, clericalism is not a temptation unique to the clergy. I have witnessed what the 1994 Congregation for the Clergy's "Directory

---

[184] Cindy Wooden, "Clericalism: The Culture That Enables Abuse and Insists on Hiding It," Catholic News Service, Aug. 23, 2018, as posted on https://www.americamagazine.org/faith/2018/08/22/clericalism-culture-enables-abuse-and-insists-hiding-it.

[185] Cindy Wooden, "Clericalism."

[186] Cindy Wooden, "Clericalism."

[187] Cindy Wooden, "Clericalism."

on the Ministry and Life of Priests" document calls the "clericalization of the laity."[188] Sometimes seen in lay people serving as catechists, ministers in parishes, or officials in the chancery, there can be arrogance and an educational elitism exhibited, wholly unwarranted, which is distasteful during basic human interaction in any setting. Many genuinely have a vocation for the work, but some become "drunk" on their own form of clericalism. I say to myself, "If this is what lay formation looks like in the Church, then I want no part of it." It also raises interesting questions about whether such formation is intended to assist the laity in their mission of evangelization in the world, or whether the Church is simply creating a separate class of what Fr. James A. Fischer, CM, called "professional Church workers."[189]

Pope St. John Paul II spoke often on the nature of the laity's powerful witness and evangelization. Speaking to the US bishops on September 16, 1987, he said, "It is above all the laity, once they have themselves been inspired by the Gospel, who bring the Gospel's uplifting and purifying influence to the world of culture, to the whole realm of thought, and artistic creativity, to the various professions and places of work, to family life and to society in general."[190]

As for the clergy, I recently heard a priest say these words in a homily: "When I was just a layperson...." That is an example of either conscious or unconscious clericalism—a blind spot. This priest was not an old-timer; he was ordained in 2011. Consider the more calibrated view outlined below.

---

[188] Congregation for the Clergy, *Directory on the Ministry and Life of Priests*, Vatican City: Libreria Editrice Vaticana, January 31, 1994, #19, https://www.vatican.va/roman_curia/congregations/cclergy/documents/rc_con_cclergy_doc_31011994_directory_en.html.

[189] James Fischer, "The Non-distinctiveness of the Catholic Priest," *The Priest*, Nov. 1987.

[190] John Paul II, *Address of His Holiness John Paul II*, Meeting with Bishops of the United States of America, Wednesday, September 16, 1987, Minor Seminary of Our Lady of the Angels, #8, https://www.vatican.va/content/john-paul-ii/en/speeches/1987/september/documents/hf_jp-ii_spe_19870916_vescovi-stati-uniti.html.

In Canon Law, concerning the Loss of the Clerical State, the commentary reads, "The corresponding section of the 1917 Code was entitled, 'The Reduction of Clerics to the Lay State,' thus implying the inferiority of the laity. The insistence of the Second Vatican Council on the fundamental equality of all members of the Church necessitated more appropriate terminology (LG32)."[191]

In citing *Lumen Gentium*, the Dogmatic Constitution on the Church, it is worth reflecting on the document's direct words: "In the Church not everyone marches along the same path, yet all are called to sanctity and have obtained an equal privilege of faith through the justice of God (cf. 2 Peter 1:1). Although by Christ's will some are established as teachers, dispensers of the mysteries and pastors for the others, there remains, nevertheless, a true equality between all with regard to the dignity and to the activity which is common to all the faithful in the building up of the Body of Christ."[192]

Lumen Gentium then cites St. Augustine, who was bishop of Hippo in AD 430: "When I am frightened by what I am to you, then I am consoled by what I am with you. To you I am the bishop, with you I am a Christian. The first is an office, the second a grace; the first a danger, the second salvation."[193] When I hear a priest use the phrase, "when I was just a layperson," it suggests to me that a cultural problem still exists. He could have said, "before I was ordained a priest." I want to give him the benefit of the doubt, but I'm not convinced it was merely clumsy wording.

The New Testament's letter to the Hebrews notes that "Every high priest is taken from among men and made their representative before God, to offer gifts and sacrifices for sins. No one takes this honor upon himself but only when called by God, just as Aaron was. In the same way, it was not Christ who glorified himself in becoming high priest,

---

[191] James A. Coriden, Thomas J. Green, and Donald E. Heintschel, eds., *The Code of Canon Law: A Text and Commentary* (New York/Mahwah: Paulist Press, 1985), 929.

[192] Vatican II, "*Lumen Gentium*, Dogmatic Constitution on the Church," November 21, 1964, #32.

[193] "*Lumen Gentium*," 32, https://www.vatican.va/archive/hist_councils/ii_vatican_council/documents/vat-ii_const_19641121_lumen-gentium_en.html.

but rather the one who said, 'You are my son; this day I have begotten you.'"[194]

It has been said that when one's values are clear, decisions are made easily. When a culture gives conflicting values, it is muddled and good decisions are compromised. Both interior reform and institutional change are needed to address this muddled culture of the Church.

An editorial in *Our Sunday Visitor* describes clericalism as "a problem attached to the priesthood, not one inherent in it."[195] I would go one step further, to describe it as attempting to "serve two masters," as in the words of Jesus in the Gospel of Matthew: "No one can be the slave of two masters. He will either hate one and love the other, or be devoted to one and despise the other."[196] It is the same "double-mindedness" mentioned in James 1:5–8 and in two second-century Church writings, *The Didache* and *The Shepherd of Hermas*.

It has also been asserted by some that the laity is to blame, in part, for encouraging this culture through an overinflated, idealistic standard of seeing their clergy as impeccable and unassailable. While probably true in some cases, I certainly want to be cautious against swinging the pendulum in the other direction. The office of the priesthood, given to us by Christ, deserves respect and dignity, though it must also be effectively witnessed through the person holding that state in life.

Philosophers have been considering the ideal, the standard, since time immemorial. They ponder questions like these: What is wise? What is just? What is beauty? The goal of every priest, like every faithful Christian, is to submit his humanity to be molded by Christ's grace and to become a saint; to know, love, and serve God in this life and be happy with Him in the next. As we know, all Christians have yet to achieve this, as is also true of the clergy. Each of us is a work in progress. The

---

[194] Hebrews 5: 1, 4–5, *The New American Bible*, Catholic Mission Edition, St. Jerome Press (Wichita, Kansas: Devore & Sons, Inc., 1987 and 1981).

[195] Gretchen R. Crowe, Scott P. Richert, York Young, Our Sunday Visitor Editorial Board, "Fixing Clericalism," *Our Sunday Visitor*, Volume 108, No. 7, June 9-15, 2019, 19.

[196] Matthew 6:24, *The New American Bible*.

Catholic will apply this standard to the clergy as they do to themselves: a common call to holiness.

Holding the clergy to a standard they have yet to achieve is unrealistic. When Christ said, "Be perfect, just as your heavenly Father is perfect,"[197] He was speaking to all His followers. All Christians know how they fall short of that standard. Just as papal infallibility does not make the pope impeccable, so ordination does not make a priest perfect.

But insisting that clergy should not sexually abuse children and that Church leaders should not cover up this behavior are also proper ethical standards. Those credibly accused must step aside in the interest of justice and the good, for it is otherwise an impediment to others on the road to faith.

A concrete action taken by Pope Francis to curtail the pursuit of "clerical careerism" has been to restrict the conferral of the title "Monsignor" to diocesan priests under the age of sixty-five. The honorary title, dating back to the pontificate of Urban VIII (1623–1644) and reformed under Pope St. Paul VI, is usually requested by a bishop to recognize the service or governance role of a priest in his diocese. It has been reported that Pope Francis, when he served as archbishop of Buenos Aires from 1998 to 2013, never made such a request for this title for any priest serving in his archdiocese.

It is fitting to conclude this chapter with another quote from Pope Pius X. In his 1908 letter to the clergy, *Haerent Animo*, he writes, "We, on the other hand, though perhaps our hearts are eager for gaining honors, for increasing our wealth, or for the mere winning of renown and glory by our learning, are listless and without inclination for the supremely important and difficult task of achieving our own sanctification."[198]

---

[197] Matthew 5:48, *The New American Bible.*

[198] Pope Pius X, *Haerent Animo*, Apostolic Exhortation, Given in Rome, at St. Peter's, August 4, 1908, cited from Papal Encyclicals Online, https://www.papalencyclicals.net/pius10/p10haer.htm.

XII

The Biblical Understanding of Election

A vocation to the priesthood or religious life is rightly seen as a "calling"—an election. Clericalism emerges when the one called by God has lost sight of the biblical sense of divine election. The genuine call will be marked by a continual striving for the healthy, calibrated understanding found in Sacred Scripture. For clarity, when I use the word *election* I am not referring to John Calvin's notion of predestination, otherwise known as *unconditional election*. Despite God's foreknowledge, election is always first an initiative of God, requiring a free response by those called. As St. Augustine said, "God who created you without you, will not save you without you."[199]

Focusing on a proper biblical understanding of election will keep a priest on solid ground, centered on trust in the unfailing promises of God. It will remind the priest that his leadership follows the example of

---

[199] Libreria Editrice Vaticana, *Catechism of the Catholic Church*, 2nd ed. (Citta del Vaticana: Libreria Editrice Vaticana, 1997), 452, #1847, citing St. Augustine, *Sermo* 169, 11, 13: PL 38, 923.

Christ, who emptied Himself (Greek: *kenosis*) in obedience to the Father (see Philippians 2:7). It will reflect the antithesis of the characteristics of clericalism.

Turning to the Old Testament, Abraham is the archetype of the one who trusts in God, acts in faith and is an instrument of the embrace of God for all. In the New Testament, it is Mary, Mother of Jesus, who models this obedience to God, becoming the *Theotokos, (God-bearer)*. Below I will dissect the call of Abram, as a seminal moment in salvation history, the calling of Israel, God's Chosen People. God establishes a covenantal relationship with those He calls, and He does not abandon His part. Abram's first recorded encounter with God is found in Genesis 12:1–3, quoted below:

> The Lord said to Abram, 'Go forth from the land of your kinsfolk and from your father's house to a land that I will show you. I will make of you a great nation, and I will bless you; I will make your name great, so that you will be a blessing. I will bless those who bless you and curse those who curse you. All the communities of the earth shall find blessing in you.'[200]

In this earliest example of election, the following key elements must be noted:

1. God's free and gratuitous initiative—God addresses Abram and calls him. This is like Jesus's words in the Gospel: "It was not you who chose me, but I chose you…"[201] The personal God, who knew us before we were formed in our mother's womb,[202] makes Himself manifest.
2. God commands us to do something and solicits a response—With the words "Go forth from the land of your kinsfolk…to a land

---

[200] Genesis 12:1-3, *The New American Bible*, Catholic Mission Edition, St. Jerome Press.
[201] John 15:16, *The New American Bible*.
[202] See Jeremiah 1:5, *The New American Bible*.

I will show you"[203] and "Keep all the commandments...,"[204] God invites the one He calls into a covenant. One can't encounter God authentically and not be summoned to surrender and change—summoned to follow "the Way" (Greek: *hodos*).

3. It is part of a larger divine plan—"I will make of you a great nation."[205] The calling is an invitation to be an instrument—a partaker of God's plan. This human life is a gift and we have it on trust for a while. Its stewardship includes placing it in God's service.

4. Abram's call is a gift, not just for himself, but primarily for the community and the world—God tells Abram, "I will bless those who bless you....All the communities of the earth shall find blessing in you."[206] Similarly, St. Paul reminds the community: "Everything should be done for building up"[207] the Body of Christ.

5. The one called is free to respond—It is thus recorded, "Abram went as the Lord directed him."[208] The authentic response is also marked by praise, thanksgiving, and worship of God in recognition of His kingship over all the cosmos and one's very existence.[209]

6. God's free election is not based on merit—"It was not because you are the largest of all nations that the Lord set his heart on you and chose you, for you are really the smallest of all nations. It was because the Lord loved you and because of his fidelity to the oath he had sworn to your fathers..."[210]

7. God's call is irrevocable, and He keeps His promise—God's call and His commands stand the test of time. God loves faithfully,

---

[203] Genesis 12:1, *The New American Bible.*
[204] Deuteronomy 11:8 and 8:13–17, *The New American Bible.*
[205] Genesis 12:2, *The New American Bible.*
[206] Genesis 12:3, *The New American Bible.*
[207] 1 Corinthians 14:26, *The New American Bible.*
[208] Genesis 12:4, *The New American Bible.*
[209] Genesis 12: 8–9, *The New American Bible.*
[210] Deuteronomy 7:7–8, *The New American Bible.*

with a love that pursues us even if we falter. In the book of Romans, St. Paul affirms what has been true throughout salvation history when he writes, "For the gifts and the call of God are irrevocable."[211]

8. God maintains grace and an abiding presence—"Some time after these events, the word of the Lord came to Abram in a vision: 'Fear not, Abram, I am your shield; I will make your reward very great.'"[212] For the Christian, God is in control. St. Paul reminds us that "we know that all things work for good for those who love God, who are called according to His purpose."[213]

9. The relationship is not without its challenges and human doubts— The one called by God must continually trust: "But Abram said, 'O Lord God, what good will your gifts be, if I keep on being childless...?' Abram continued, 'See, you have given me no offspring...'"[214] Seventeenth-century philosopher Blaise Pascal pondered why God didn't just reveal everything all at once and solve the burning questions of existence. He concluded that God gave mankind just enough truth so that man might seek and find, but little enough truth to respect man's free will.[215]

10. The one called is renamed and puts on a new identity—"My covenant with you is this; you are to become the father of a host of nations. No longer shall you be called Abram; your name shall be Abraham."[216] Renaming is seen throughout Sacred Scripture, including Simon Barjona being renamed Cephas (meaning both "Peter" and "rock,"[217] and Saul of Tarsus (his Hebrew name) in-

---

211 Romans 11:29, *The New American Bible.*
212 Genesis 15:1–2, *The New American Bible.*
213 Romans 8:28, *The New American Bible.*
214 Genesis 15:2–3, *The New American Bible.*
215 Gertrude Burfurd Rawlings, trans., ed., *Pascal's Pensees or, Thoughts on Religion* (Mount Vernon, New York: The Peter Pauper Press, 1946), 33. Pascal writes: "There is enough light for those who only desire to seek Him, and enough obscurity for those contrarily disposed."
216 Genesis 17:3–6, *The New American Bible.*
217 John 1:42, *The New American Bible.*

stead using his Roman name, Paul.[218] A name is not merely what one is called. In the biblical tradition, a name is the key to the nature or essence of the given being or thing. To use or bestow a name has overtones of "knowing" the named—for the knower has a part of what is known. It is an intimacy marked by trust. A name is also a mark of one's identity; the change of the name is a change to a new identity and mission. This is why Catholics take a name at Baptism and Confirmation and why many men and women in religious orders change their name. These are all examples of having "put on Christ."[219]

When God calls, much is to be expected. Jesus tells His followers in Luke's Gospel, "When a man has had a great deal given to him, a great deal will be demanded of him; when a man has a great deal given on trust, even more will be expected of him."[220]

In discerning an authentic experience of God, I have always found to be true the threefold elements proffered by the late Fr. John Powell, SJ,[221] in *A Reason to Live! A Reason to Die!* as described below.

- The time test: An authentic experience of God is not merely a "moment of overcharged emotions" that "will soon be spent and its effects will quickly disappear."[222] For one who truly experiences God, he or she can never be the same again.
- The reality test: It will lead you into a "deeper contact with reality...more alive, more aware of others and of the world about [you]."[223]

---

[218] Acts 13:9–10, *The New American Bible.*

[219] Galatians 3:27–29, *The New American Bible.*

[220] Luke 12:48, *The New American Bible.*

[221] Despite these wise and valid observations of Fr. Powell, I must state for the record that he faced credible accusations of abuse by numerous female victims prior to his death in 2009, https://www.jesuitsmidwest.org/press-release/usa-midwest-province-jesuits-with-an-established-allegation-of-sexual-abuse-of-a-minor-2/.

[222] John Powell, *A Reason to Live! A Reason to Die!* (Allen, Texas: Argus Communications, 1972, 1975), 121.

[223] John Powell, *A Reason to Live! A Reason to Die! 122.*

- The charity test: In experiencing God, Christians realize that "our human vocation is to be loving. Experiences that produce only complacency and self-righteousness cannot be from God."[224]

As in Abraham's case, these characteristics of an experience of God are true both for one who chooses celibacy "for the sake of the kingdom" and for one who has not been given that gift. It is universally true for a relationship with God.

When the Church recommends a candidate to the priesthood, She does so based on a testimonial letter—among other things—which ideally comes with "moral certitude"[225] from those entrusted with ensuring the candidate is suitable. The letter doesn't just certify that the candidate has met the prescribed academic requirements; it also makes a good faith judgment that there is evidence of God's election, with the characteristic traits outlined above. Catholics recognize the role of a priest in their community because of the attestation of the Church. The Rite of Ordination contains this trust-filled response by the bishop having heard the testimony: "We rely on the help of the Lord God and our Savior Jesus Christ, and we choose this man, our brother, for priesthood in the presbyteral order."[226]

Though set apart to be a partner with God in fulfilling His will, a calling will always require the free, loving, and continual response of the one called to service for the community of believers and the world. The setting apart can itself be a witness, a testimonial, but such a person must be tethered to the voice of Christ and His Bride, the Church, and must always be in formation, as clay on the potter's wheel. Clericalism emerges when one or more of these characteristics goes astray—and they

---

[224] John Powell, *A Reason to Live! A Reason to Die!* 122.

[225] Pope St. Paul VI, *Summi Dei Verbum,* Apostolic Letter, given at St. Peter's, Vatican City, November 4, 1963, https://www.vatican.va/content/paul-vi/en/apost_letters/documents/hf_p-vi_apl_19631104_summi-dei-verbum.html.

[226] The International Commission on English in the Liturgy, trans., *The Rites: Volume II,* (New York: Pueblo Publishing CO, 1980), 61.

won't be the ones on God's part. God is quite capable of throwing "down rulers from their thrones"[227] if they don't keep their end of the covenant.

Quoting St. Jerome, Pius X writes in *Haerent Animo*, "'Sublime is the dignity of the priest, but great is his fall, if he is guilty of sin; let us rejoice for the high honor but let us fear for them lest they fall; great is the joy that they have scaled the heights, but it is insignificant compared with the sorrow of their fall from on high.'"[228]

---

[227] Luke 1:52, *The New American Bible.*

[228] Pope Pius X, *Haerent Animo*, Apostolic Exhortation, Given in Rome, at St. Peter's, August 4, 1908, Papal Encyclicals Online, https://www.papalencyclicals.net/pius10/p10haer.htm.

XIII

Mandatory Clerical Celibacy Examined

Setting the Stage

Although allowing priests to marry as a solution to the clergy sexual abuse problem may be a kitchen table discussion in Catholic households, I don't believe that narrowly focusing on its nexus to the crisis is, alone, a sound basis for allowing the alternative model of married priests. Admittedly on some level there is a certain logic which connects the misaligned sexual expression of clerics and the void they may experience due to loneliness or a lack of close social bonds. The impulse to make this connection is echoed in many of the classic arguments against mandatory celibacy that Pope St. Paul VI comprehensively addressed in his 1967 encyclical letter *Sacerdotalis Caelibatus* (Priestly Celibacy), including an argument that clerical celibacy is unnatural. But the unique challenge of the Gospel will often turn logic on its head. We might be inclined to believe that it is logical and natural to enact revenge against those who harm us. Yet, the radical message of the Gospel reminds Christ's followers to extend mercy and forgiveness.

I challenge those who are quick to jump to this logical fix to pause and give due consideration to several important points that cannot be easily dismissed.

1. We live in an over-sexualized culture. Society places an expectation on young people to marry, and examples of temperance and chastity are wanting. Appetites go unrestrained and people reach for anything to fill a perceived void that ultimately only God can fill. Mindful of this, the righteous ideals underpinning the discipline of clerical celibacy are too easily overlooked or dismissed. I will critically examine them in this chapter.

2. The John Jay cause report correctly observes that "an exclusively male priesthood and the commitment to celibate chastity were invariant during the increase, peak, and decrease in abuse incidents, and thus are not causes of the 'crisis.'"[229] Celibacy has been lived faithfully by many priests who have never harmed or sexually abused any person. I wish to make a qualifier here. While it is true that comparatively few exceptions to living celibacy faithfully does not, in itself, disprove the merit of the discipline, it can neither be used to support the discipline. Those who live chaste as a celibate simply demonstrate that it is possible with God's grace, and that they very likely have the gift of continence.

3. While a certain anti-Catholic, anticlerical animus often drives this messaging, comparatively rare "scandals are no more the effect of compulsory celibacy than prostitution, which is everywhere rampant in our great cities, is the effect of our marriage laws."[230]

---

[229] John Jay College Research Team, "The Causes and Context of Sexual Abuse of Minors by Catholic Priests in the United States, 1950–2010" (Study Report, May 2011), 3, http://votf.org/johnjay/John_Jay_Causes_and_Context_Report.pdf.

[230] Thurston, Herbert. "Celibacy of the Clergy." The Catholic Encyclopedia. Vol. 3. New York: Robert Appleton Company, 1908. 22 Jun. 2021 <http://www.newadvent.org/cathen/03481a.htm>.

4. Allowing priests to marry simply because continence is viewed by some as a violation of nature or as a panacea against sexual abuse overlooks the unique gift that is marriage. Sacramental marriage cannot be reduced to a measure of prevention against such ills as child abuse. It will not shield one from difficulty in living out their vocation. Even if one or two studies suggest that married men might be less likely to perpetrate sexual abuse, society wouldn't suddenly advocate for a law forcing all men to marry in order to rid us of sexual abuse in general society. Besides this solution's flawed logic, not all men would be suitable or mature enough to undertake marriage.

5. I would note that many who struggle to understand celibacy in a religious context might not give it a second thought in a secular context if someone renounced marriage to devote themselves to social work, the arts, science, or the betterment of society. It is forsaking one value for another. Such a person would be viewed as selfless and might even receive the Nobel Peace Prize.

Clerical celibacy may be a serious contextual factor in the crisis, particularly for those ill-equipped to embrace the life choice or who suffer from psychosexual pathology. But the re-imagining of the gift of continence must happen in a fuller context in the totality of its historical development. God continues to give some the gift of continence and virginity and, like all gifts, it serves as an important witness in the Christian community when done for religious reasons. The real shifts that should be considered are twofold:

1. Fostering the countercultural values of chastity and continence broadly in the Christian community and dispelling the notion that they are only something priests and those in religious community embrace

2. Asking the Church to reevaluate its regulatory role in the discipline so that clerical continence is once again embraced because it is a gift from God and not because it is mandated upon clerics. Continence was viewed as a gift in the early Church, and as it

converged with the priesthood, which is cultic in nature, it became a requirement—the ramifications of this second step will require deep reflection and study

Clerical celibacy has received much attention over the last six decades. Many had expectations that the Second Vatican Ecumenical Council (1962–1965) would reverse the disciplinary tradition of mandatory celibacy for priests in the West. This did not materialize.

In 2019, these hopes reemerged as Pope Francis and bishops contemplated provisional exceptions to help the Amazonian region of South America, where the remote location posed unique pastoral challenges. A 2019 Synod, which lasted from October 6 to October 27, released its final deliberative document on October 26. Some bishops worried that Pope Francis was opening Pandora's box by contemplating the ordination of married men of proven virtue in order to sustain Christian life in the remote Amazon region. Many voiced that it would be the end of celibacy and the end of the priesthood because the argument could be made that a shortage of priests exists elsewhere, including in many first world nations. Despite the resistance of some Church leaders, the sacramental nature of the Church, empty seminaries and scandalous behavior will keep the discipline of mandatory celibacy front and center.

Some Key Points on Clerical Celibacy

The following observations will serve to paint the landscape for a review of the discipline of mandatory celibacy.

1. The practice of perpetual sexual continence for priests, though ancient and potentially noble, was not a practice or requirement in the primitive Church (during the period when the New Testament was being written and shortly thereafter), nor is it a requirement for those priests who are married in Eastern Christianity.

2. The Church has had a persistent problem of lapse in this area, which is often the source of scandal.

3. The Church can amend its disciplinary practices and requirements in response to time, place, and circumstance for the pastoral good.

4. The Church is still ordaining candidates who lack the psychosexual maturity to understand the difficulties and permanence of celibacy, and that has real pastoral ramifications.

5. Since the mass exodus of priests in the 1970s, the shortage of priests has been at least partially masked by the Church's ordaining a larger number of homosexual candidates who are not, by definition, seeing this as a sacrificial renunciation of Christian marriage, and this has manifested a wholly different and unique set of problems.

As Church leaders periodically review this mandatory discipline, discerning the promptings of the Holy Spirit for a deepening understanding is not an openness if it is a pretext to a foregone conclusion. An overarching paradigm used in this book is that of a *wicked problem*—a problem that is both unique and has interconnected facets and codependencies. It makes solutions to the problem complex and interdependent, and every move to solve it has significance and ramifications. That does not mean leaders shouldn't try to solve the problem, but they should be mindful that there is a certain finality to some steps. Some solutions can't be initially "tested out" without setting things in motion. This truth understandably engenders hesitation and fear in some leaders.

The flip side of the coin in this crisis will be those who prefer to do little about the proximate and contextual causes. They will treat cases as they emerge, faithfully implementing best practices for prevention and little else. Taking an all-or-nothing approach, if the problem can't be solved in one step or by pulling only one lever, they won't rock the boat. They will look at a report that states that "homosexuality is not the single cause" and therefore do nothing about homosexual behavior in the priesthood. They will conclude that "celibacy is not the single cause" and they will do nothing to reexamine celibacy.

Some Reasons for the Status Quo on Celibacy

Among the reasons for insisting on the status quo, I have heard some Church leaders express with good intention the following concerns:

1. Some believe that the Evil One is at work (and he is) and relinquishing the discipline is precisely what the Evil One seeks in destroying the spotless Bride of Christ. I would just remind those holding this position that the Eastern tradition with its married priests is still part of that spotless Bride of Christ.
2. Others have frantically expressed that a change to the discipline will be the end of celibacy or the priesthood itself, as well as the doorway to women priests.
   A. This reaction is driven by two concerns. First, the Church esteems continence and virginity as a witness in the world. Second, polls have reflected that some Catholics regrettably lack a clear understanding of the Real Presence of Jesus in the Eucharist. Some therefore maintain that eliminating clerical continence will undermine its connection with the priest's role in the Eucharistic sacrifice, resulting in further harm to the coherence of the sacrament. I submit however that desacralizing the priesthood would be its demise, not the introduction of married clergy.
   B. Is the Church really saying that if She doesn't impose celibacy, it would cease to exist as a gift for the kingdom of God? Such a posture puts the notions of "gift" and "imposition or force" directly in conflict. And it shows a lack of faith about how God operates in giving His gifts.
   C. The ordination of women may seem related from a "slippery slope" standpoint of popular opinion and arguments of pragmatism, but it is a quite distinct issue. Short of an infallible statement, the subject of women in the priesthood was addressed clearly and effectively in both the 1976 Declaration *Inter Insigniores* and the 1994 apostolic letter of Pope St. John Paul II, *Ordinatio Sacerdotalis*, and was upheld by Pope Francis.

3. Still others are hesitant to work through the practical implications of a married priesthood. That indeed will require careful and diligent study and reflection, but it should be explored.

Whatever the rationale, it seems like the successors to the Apostles continue to remain on the storm-driven waters. It is worth repeating here what I said in chapter I: leaders must see this crisis with clear eyes. Clergy sexual abuse is not a rogue expression of doctrinal heresy, nor a wave of sloth. This crisis is a current-day manifestation of a persistent history of misplaced and injurious sexual expression.

In an address to the US Catholic Conference of Bishops on June 19, 2019, Pope Francis's Apostolic Nuncio to the United States said, "The process of discussing and listening leads to concrete solutions rather than simply expounding theological ideas."[231]

The Church has always celebrated both *red martyrs* and *white martyrs*. Red martyrs, which have been on the rise in the modern era, are those who shed their blood for their faith. White martyrs are those who suffer trial or persecution for their faith or who lead a life of asceticism, a self-denial or "death to self," for the sake of the kingdom. Both are held in the highest esteem. Tertullian would say of the red martyrs, "The blood of the martyrs is the seed of Christians."[232] They gave the ultimate witness that led to the conversion of many. White martyrs are also to be seeds, giving witness and nourishment to the Church. There are still exemplary models of white martyrs even today, as well as priests and those in consecrated life who live chastity faithfully and receive no media attention. But the sexual abuse scandal, and its persistence throughout Church history, has undermined this witness for many in every century. It is not enough to simply dismiss aberrations as "weeds among the wheat." It cries out for a closer examination.

---

[231] Archbishop Christophe Pierre, "Address of His Excellency Archbishop Christophe Pierre to the United States Conference of Catholic Bishops," June 11, 2019, Plenary Assembly, Baltimore, Maryland, 5, https://www.usccb.org/resources/archbishop-christophe-pierre-address-us-bishops.

[232] Tertullian, *Apologia*, 37, 39, 42, https://www.newadvent.org/fathers/0301.htm.

Gradual Change

To even the casual observer, it does appear as though the Church has been slowly and subtly decoupling celibacy and the priesthood in various steps over the last seventy years or so. This evolution has included the following:

1. The ordination of married former Protestant clergy, mostly Anglican and Lutheran, beginning with Pope Pius XII and culminating in a formalized program, called the Pastoral Provision, under Pope St. Paul VI and Pope St. John Paul II.
2. The acknowledgment by the Second Vatican Council and Pope St. Paul VI that celibacy is not demanded by the very nature of the priesthood.[233]
3. The departure from any notion of cultic or ritual purity as the primary explanation for celibacy, even though that was the Church's long-standing rationale reflected in Church canons and documents right up to 1954.
4. The reintroduction of married permanent deacons.
5. The 2014 reversal by Pope Francis of a tradition dating back to the turn of the last century that prohibited Catholic Eastern Rite married clergy from serving in the Americas and Australia.[234] Eastern Rite bishops had been lobbying for decades to get this tradition repealed and no one wanted the issue to be the grounds for schism.

---

[233] Pope St. Paul VI, "Sacerdotalis Caelibatus," Encyclical Letter, June 1967, https://www.vatican.va/content/paul-vi/en/encyclicals/documents/hf_p-vi_enc_24061967_sacerdotalis.html. "'Virginity undoubtedly,' as the Second Vatican Council declared, 'is not, of course, required by the nature of the priesthood itself.'

[234] Laura Ieraci, "Vatican Lifts Ban on Married Priests for Eastern Catholics in Diaspora," Catholic News Service, Nov. 17, 2014, https://www.ncronline.org/news/vatican/vatican-lifts-ban-married-priests-eastern-catholics-diaspora.

Most of these moves came before there was serious attention on the clergy sexual abuse crisis and were ultimately driven by pastoral concerns, including the crisis of a shortage of priests.

This notion of *crisis* has now taken on a double meaning to include the scandal caused by clergy (including bishops), some of whom have undermined any sense of the witness of celibacy "for the sake of the kingdom." One might ask whether imposing such a discipline as celibacy is really having the efficacious effect that is intended. I will explore the historical underpinnings later in this chapter. But first, let's not lose sight of the word *crisis*.

The late Archbishop Thomas J. Murphy, then-bishop of the diocese of Great Falls–Billings Montana, gave a talk at Laborers for the Vineyard—A Conference on Church Vocations, recorded in the March 1984 periodical *The Priest*. Archbishop Murphy described *crisis* this way:

> For some, the word "crisis" is charged with negative undercurrent. Yet, the definition of the word in a dictionary envisions "crisis" as a "turning point, a stage in a sequence of events at which the trend of all future events, especially for better or for worse, is determined." Another definition of "crisis" envisions it as a "condition of instability, as in social, economic, political or international affairs, leading to a decisive change." Gathered as we are to address the issue of vocations, I believe the word "crisis" is most appropriate. However, I see the word used much more in a positive sense where we are challenged to grab hold of the present moment, to recognize the issues involved, and to make the present moment a turning point. From this perspective, a "crisis" becomes a graced moment, a time of decision.[235]

One wonders if we are now at such a "graced moment." But it is in responding to this graced moment that opinions begin to diverge sharply. Some believe that there is room to pursue a path for more married priests, along the model of Eastern Christianity (discussed below). Others insist

---

[235] Archbishop Thomas J. Murphy, "Vocations to the Priesthood and to the Religious Life: A Context for Understanding Current Change," *The Priest*, Mar. 1984, 30.

that, despite the scandals, the witness of the undivided heart in apostolic life is needed now more than ever, and they are prepared to double down on the discipline of celibacy, summarized aptly in these words of Pope St. John Paul II in 1993: "This is a kind of challenge that the Church makes to the mentality, tendencies and charms of the world, with an ever-new desire for consistency with, and fidelity to, the Gospel ideal."[236] Citing the reaffirmation of celibacy by the 1971 Synod of Bishops, he stated that "even today's difficulties can be overcome, if 'suitable conditions are fostered, namely: growth of the interior life through prayer, renunciation and fervent love for God and one's neighbor and by other aids to the spiritual life; human balance through well-ordered integration into the fabric of social relationships; fraternal association and companionship with other priests and with the Bishop, through pastoral structures better suited to this purpose and with the assistance also of the community of the faithful' [*Enchiridion Vaticanum*, IV, 1216]."[237] The ongoing pastoral needs of the Church will force this debate to continue. The clergy sexual abuse scandal has placed this topic into higher resolution.

To help you fully appreciate the underpinnings and historical developments concerning the discipline of mandatory celibacy for clerics, I will now examine some key concepts, terminology, and insights from Sacred Scripture. I will be examining three angles in understanding continence: as an evangelical counsel in following Christ more perfectly, as a gift, and as a component of cultic (ritual) purity for those who are clerics (bishop, priest and deacon).

Framing the Concept of Continence

In Catholic-Christian anthropology, mankind shared perfectly in the supernatural grace of God prior to the sin of Adam. As such, man's lower

---

[236] Pope St. John Paul II, general audience, July 17, 1993, #6, Vatican City, text published in *L'Osservatore Romano* on July 21, 1993, reproduced and cited on http://www.totus2us.co.uk/teaching/jpii-catechesis-on-the-church/the-church-is-committed-to-priestly-celibacy/.

[237] Pope St. John Paul II, general audience, July 17, 1993, #6.

faculties (senses and emotions) were in complete obedience to his higher faculties (understanding and will). Through Adam's sin, moral evil entered the world because his fall was in both capacities, as an individual and as the original cell or potentiality of all humanity. This Original Sin is the state of being deprived of supernatural grace even while being destined by God for the supernatural state. Its result is concupiscence, whereby man's lower faculties are no longer in complete conformity to his understanding and will. This condition of humanity is summarized by St. Paul: "For I do not do the good I want, but I do the evil I do not want."[238] It is a disposition to sin by inheritance and by personal choice.

Its connection with the terms *celibacy, continence,* and *chastity,* which I will define, is found under the umbrella virtue of temperance. Despite misconceptions about a fixation on sexuality, temperance applies to a much broader scope of human behavior and applies to all followers of Christ, not just priests. As the *Catechism of the Catholic Church* notes, for the baptized Christian, it is about exercising one's free will, one's faculties, and one's integrated human personhood in self-mastery, "... which seeks to permeate the passions and appetites of the senses with reason"[239] so that one "...knows, loves, and accomplishes moral good."[240] In practicing this virtue, one thus respects human dignity and the moral order in God's creation, and gives witness to "...God's fidelity and loving kindness."[241] All of these attributes are founded in "the Way" of the Gospel. Grace, through Christ, builds upon weakened human nature and perfects it.

In Romans, Paul implores the followers of Jesus to "do this because you know the time; it is the hour now for you to awake from sleep. For our salvation is nearer now than when we first believed; the night is advanced, the day is at hand. Let us then throw off the works of darkness [and] put on the armor of light; let us conduct ourselves properly as in

---

[238] Romans 7:19, *The New American Bible,* Catholic Mission Edition, St. Jerome Press (Wichita Kansas: Devore & Sons, Inc., 1987 and 1981).

[239] Libreria Editrice Vaticana, *Catechism of the Catholic Church,* 2nd ed. (Citta del Vaticana: Libreria Editrice Vaticana, 1997), 562, #2341.

[240] Libreria Editrice Vaticana, *Catechism of the Catholic Church,* 2nd ed., 563, #2343.

[241] Libreria Editrice Vaticana, *Catechism of the Catholic Church,* 2nd ed., 563, #2346.

the day, not in orgies and drunkenness, not in promiscuity and licentiousness, not in rivalry and jealousy. But put on the Lord Jesus Christ and make no provision for the desires of the flesh."[242]

Catholics tend to forget the words used every year on Ash Wednesday as ashes are place on their forehead: "For you are dirt [dust] and to dirt [dust] you shall return."[243] Catholics are pilgrims on earth in this life, with a "faith [which] is the realization of what is hoped for and evidence of things not seen."[244] A pilgrim's destiny does not end here. The Christian is called to recalibrate the ways he or she defines success in this world. Jesus reminded us, "What profit would there be for one to gain the whole world and forfeit his life?"[245]

In David Bohr's book *Catholic Moral Tradition*, he notes that "the early Church's sense of the impending catastrophic end made everything in this world provisional (1 Corinthians 7:20, 31). The events of the last days are not only doctrines to be recited and professed at the end of the Creed, but truths that impose obligations. The Christian's pilgrim status serves as 'a perpetual summons to vigilance and sobriety, to responsible action in the world, to combat and struggle against the destructive powers of evil and to living hope and joyful confidence.'"[246]

St. Paul wrote, "I should like everyone to be like me, but everybody has his own particular gifts from God, one with a gift for one thing and another with a gift for the opposite. There is something I want to add for the sake of widows and those who are not married; it is a good thing for them to stay as they are, like me, but if they cannot control the sexual urges, they should get married, since it is better to be married than to be tortured."[247] This led some Church Fathers, the Gnostics, and extreme ascetics to view marriage as a mere accommodation for or remedy against concupiscence. To be fair, there were Church Fathers who

---

[242] Romans 13:11-14, *The New American Bible.*
[243] Genesis 3:19, *The New American Bible.*
[244] Hebrews 11:1, *The New American Bible.*
[245] Matthew 16:26, *The New American Bible.*
[246] David Bohr, *Catholic Moral Tradition* (Huntington, Indiana: Our Sunday Visitor Books, 1990), 37–38.
[247] 1 Cor. 7:7-9, *The New American Bible.*

praised marriage, and notable among them were Clement of Alexandria and Tertullian, who were both married.

With that biblical orientation in mind, I now turn to some key terms in the practice of living a Christian life.

Key Terminology

1. Continence. The word *continence*, in its sexual context, means refraining from all sexual acts. Before the word *celibacy* came into use in the sixteenth century, the word *continence* was predominantly used to describe the requirement for clerics. It comes from the Latin word *continentia* meaning "a holding back." It refers to refraining from sexual intimacy even at times within the context of married life.

2. Celibacy. The word *celibacy*, from the Latin word *caelibatus*, means "the state of being unmarried." Technically, anyone unmarried can be said to be celibate, but not all celibates live chastely and practice continence.

3. Chastity. The overarching moral virtue in the sexual context is *chastity*, which comes from the Latin word *castitas*, meaning "purity" or, as applied here, "sexual purity"—the virtue of being sexually pure in whatever one's state of life.

Applying These Terms to the Christian Life

1. Married Persons. Married persons practice *conjugal chastity*, which includes a healthy and ordered control of the sexual appetite, using it respectfully with one's spouse as a free and mutual gift and being faithful partners.

2. Priests and Religious. Those who profess virginity or consecrated celibacy (priests and religious persons), which enables them to give themselves to God alone with an undivided heart, practice *chastity in continence*. Those in religious institutes of men and women (the monastic tradition and institutes of consecrated

140

life like the Franciscans, Jesuits, Dominicans, etc.) also embrace poverty and obedience. These three vows are called the *evangelical counsels*, named after the word *evangelium* (from the Latin word for Gospel), voluntarily embraced to be counsels of perfection in following Christ completely.

3. Single Persons. Single persons are called to live in continence until they marry or to embrace continence in a consecrated single vocation or in the religious life.

The key takeaways are that all baptized Christians are called to practice temperance and chastity according to their state in life, with the help of God's grace, for right order and the good of society, and to be better disposed to "love our neighbor as ourselves."[248] No one said it was always easy. Failures in chastity take many forms, and abuse of children, though a form, is a multifactored and particularly tragic phenomenon in itself. Can clerical continence be a contributing contextual factor? Yes, it can, in select instances involving psychosexually underdeveloped clergy who embraced the yoke of a celibate life, or in those unprepared for its commitment and permanence, or when clergy engage in distinct sexual behavior under the guise of that life choice. Is celibacy a direct cause? Not likely. Scandals do, however, gravely undermine the intended witness to the world.

Key Scriptural Basis for Clerical Continence as an Evangelical Counsel

As mentioned in the definition above, the evangelical counsels of poverty, chastity (continence) and obedience are called counsels of perfection in following Christ. They are ways of conduct for those desiring to do more than the minimum required to follow Christ. From her earliest days, the Church has had hermits, ascetics, desert Fathers and the rich monastic tradition.

---

[248] Matthew 22:39, *The New American Bible.*

Such religious communities have been created and periodically have seen surges in membership throughout history. These religious communities were typically created and sanctioned to serve specific needs in the Church, and many people joined these communities as a reaction against societal excess and moral turpitude after the emergence of urban life in European history.

Even today, there are those who have the gift of continence and will feel called to enter a community of consecrated life. Those entering institutes of religious life join a community of prayer, ascetical practice, and self-giving for the greater benefit of the whole Church and to be wedded to Christ. Through an incremental step from temporary to perpetual vows, they practice the three evangelical counsels of poverty, chastity, and obedience in various religious communities that span the spectrum from contemplative life to apostolic work. For such communities, celibacy is a foundation and necessity of spirituality and community life, whereas having one of their members being selected for the priesthood is optional.

In the Gospel account of St. Matthew (19:1–10), Jesus was asked about marriage and divorce. He instructed His listeners that "what God has joined together, no human being must separate,"[249] contextualizing marriage in the creation story of the Book of Genesis. These words about the indissolubility of marriage would have been difficult to hear because, under the Mosaic Law, there were some narrow exceptions for divorce, viewed as a concession that Moses allowed.[250] Matthew recounts that "the disciples said to him, 'If that is the case of a man with his wife, it is better not to marry.'"[251] The disciples were not denigrating marriage. Rather, the disciples sounded much more like a nervous groom or bride having second thoughts before the wedding day.

Jesus replied, "Not all can accept [this] word, but only those to whom that is granted."[252] The Greek word used for "granted" (δέδοται)

---

[249] Matthew 19:6, *The New American Bible.*
[250] The Schools of Hillel and Shammai, interpreting Deuteronomy 24:1–4.
[251] Matthew 19:10, *The New American Bible.*
[252] Matthew 19:11, *The New American Bible.*

is understood to mean "as by the special act of God." This sentence of Jesus's is couched between the indissolubility of marriage on the one hand and the introduction of being unmarried "for the sake of the kingdom" on the other. There are some who "have renounced marriage for the sake of the kingdom of heaven. Whoever can accept this ought to accept it."[253] It raises an interesting question about to which of the two groups—the married or the unmarried—has something been granted. Likely to both, because God's help is infused in the demands He makes of us. A special grace is needed to live each of the two rewarding but difficult states of life.

Jesus said, "Let anyone accept this who can." It is a choice, but perhaps not in the typical sense that one understands choices. Jesus's invitation will always respect and acknowledge one's free will to choose. God never forces us or violates the way He created us as free beings. But there is yet another dimension to His invitation. In this chapter of Matthew, six verses later there is a story about a young rich man. The man asks, "Teacher, what good must I do to gain eternal life?"[254] He tells Jesus how he has kept all the commandments. Jesus then says, "If you wish to be perfect, go, sell what you have and give to [the] poor, and you will have treasure in heaven. Then come, follow me."[255] The passage then recounts that "when the young man heard this statement, he went away sad, for he had many possessions."[256]

Jesus is not just laying before His followers an indifferent set of equal options, like choosing between an apple and an orange. His invitation has moral and covenantal dimensions, which one can either accept or not accept. So, when the disciples questioned the merit of marriage, Jesus did not rescind His message, nor did He let the disciples off the hook so easily. He didn't send them off to pursue some "commitment-less" state of life. Instead, in offering the alternative, He assigned a purpose to such a state: "for the sake of the kingdom." And He certainly proceeded as

---

253 Matthew 19:12, *The New American Bible*.
254 Matthew 19:16, *The New American Bible*.
255 Matthew 19:21, *The New American Bible*.
256 Matthew 19:22, *The New American Bible*.

the greatest witness to that in His own life—a total giving of self, even unto death on a cross. The early Church Fathers also held His mother, Mary, as a shining example. The early Church consistently viewed virginity and continence as gifts, but they were not attached narrowly to the clergy. For these reasons, while clerical celibacy is not to be viewed as merely a capricious discipline, it is also not necessarily a gift given to all whom God calls.

Who Chooses Continence

Who are the people who discern the gift of permanent continence and would freely choose it for the sake of the kingdom of God, especially in a culture that places on them an expectation to marry?

There is no indication in the passage from Matthew that one must be unmarried in order to follow Jesus. Such an interpretation would be problematic on numerous levels, the two most obvious being the design of the Father in creation (man and woman) and the perpetuation of the human race (the commandment to "be fertile and multiply"[257]). Although the priests of the hereditary Jewish priesthood practiced temporary continence for ritual purity to offer sacrifice, few would have embraced celibacy. The New Testament prototypes of today's clergy were permitted to marry despite their expectation of Jesus's imminent return (1 Timothy 3:1–13). There is some indication that groups contemporaneous with Jesus, such as the Essenes, had members who either temporarily or permanently observed continence.

In his article "Priesthood and Celibacy," Fr. Martin Pable, OFM Cap., writes, "Thus, Donald Goergen sees celibates as 'holy radicals'— holy in the sense of striving for union with God, radical in the sense of living out a basically different lifestyle than the rest of society. 'Celibacy points toward another value system than the one society endorses.'"[258] Such "radicals" would freely choose this life of witness and sacrifice as a

---

[257] Genesis 1:28, *The New American Bible.*

[258] Martin W. Pable, "Priesthood and Celibacy," *Chicago Studies* 20, no. 1 (Spring 1981): 63.

gift from God in service of the Church, relying on the grace from God and being tethered to a strong spiritual life.

Fr. Pable reminds us that "sexuality is a complex, even mysterious phenomenon. Sexuality is a much wider reality than genital intercourse. It permeates the total being of each individual man and woman…expressed in a variety of human behaviors. […] In no way, however, does one who chooses celibacy cease to be a sexual person. If the sexual energy is not channeled, but merely repressed, there will be distortions in the personality."[259] Additionally, Fr. Pable notes that "one refrains from marriage precisely because of the deep human values (love of spouse and raising of children) it embodies. These values could not be properly actualized because of one's all-consuming commitment to his or her life task. Thus, out of respect for marriage as well as devotion to some other human value, one chooses to remain single. When that choice is made for religious reasons ('for the sake of Christ and His kingdom') celibacy is a meaningful vocation."[260] This broader definition, "for religious reasons," includes not only priests and those in religious life, but could apply to single persons who are so disposed as well. The wise counsel above states that such persons must have a self-understanding of their sexuality, and it encourages intimate relationships with people on a nongenital level.

Continence as a Gift and its Characteristics

All gifts given by God to individuals are for the edification of the Body of Christ, the Church. As I explored in chapter XII, God both calls individuals and gives them gifts, "that differ according to the grace given us,"[261] for a purpose greater than themselves. All gifts, of course, are subordinated to the call to love (see 1 Corinthians 14:1). This is a theme throughout St. Paul's letters to Christian communities.

Sexual continence is a gift. Even when freely chosen, living it faithfully requires the grace of God. It serves as a witness when it is lived as a

---

[259] Martin W. Pable, "Priesthood and Celibacy," 59-60.

[260] Martin W. Pable, "Priesthood and Celibacy," 59, 62.

[261] Romans 12:6, *The New American Bible*.

marriage to Christ, reminds Christians of their final destiny to be with God where "they neither marry nor are given in marriage,"[262] and opens their hearts to selfless love.

One who truly has the gift of continence possesses a distinct mindset. Fr. Pable cites famed psychologist Abraham Maslow: "Maslow points out that it is not sexual abstinence as such that is pathogenic, but the feelings or motivations accompanying it when sexual deprivation 'is felt by the individual to represent rejection by the opposite sex, inferiority, lack of worth, lack of respect, isolation, or other thwarting of basic needs. Sexual deprivation can be borne with relative ease by individuals for whom it has no such implication' (Motivation and Personality, Harper and Row, 1954, pp. 105–107)."[263] If it is not a gift from God, it cannot be alternatively trained into someone, nor can one fake it. It takes great maturity and virtue to honestly discern this gift. For this very reason, the Church has warned against increasing the number of vocations at the expense of the quality of those candidates.

And for those to whom the gift is given, St. Clement of Rome, in his letter to the Corinthians around AD 90, offers this admonition: "Let him that is pure in the flesh not grow proud of it, and boast, knowing that it was another who bestowed on him the gift of continence… Since, therefore, we receive all these things from Him, we ought for everything to give Him thanks; to whom be glory for ever and ever. Amen."[264] In this context, there is no specific reference to the clerical state, even though the gift was given to some for the sake of the kingdom of God and for the benefit of the whole Church. It is not a uniquely priestly gift.

Because the Church has not elevated the discernment of this gift broadly among Catholics in recent times, continence continues to be seen as something only lived by priests and the religious, some of whom have not lived it well, and oftentimes not even in joy. If this gift and value, whose "beauty may not always be immediately apparent to the

---

262 Matthew 22:30, *The New American Bible.*
263 Martin W. Pable, "Priesthood and Celibacy," 70.
264 Clement of Rome, First Epistle, Chapter 38, English translation by Roberts-Donalson, http://www.earlychristianwritings.com/text/1clement-roberts.html.

human eye,"[265] were to be more nourished in the life of the Christian community, an awareness would lead individuals to discern their gift. Such is the context and vision shared by Pope St. Paul VI when he observed that "nor can we overlook the immense ranks of religious men and women at their side, of laity and of young people too, united in the faithful observance of perfect chastity. They live in chastity, not out of disdain for the gift of life, but because of a greater love for that new life which springs from the paschal mystery."[266] A dear religious sister who taught science in my elementary school did her part in trying to advance this value. She reminded her students that the reproductive system, in contrast to various necessary (or autonomic) systems of the body like the nervous system and respiratory system, has no requirement to be exercised.

The Basis for Continence for Clerics: Regulating What Is Otherwise a Gift

Having covered the tradition of those who choose continence as a gift in following Christ more perfectly, I will now explore how the Church's regulatory role in the discipline of clerical continence handled the intersection of two key concepts: cultic purity (ritual purity, or the state of being pure in connection with the holy) and the notion of continence as a gift. The two concepts joined together at some point in history, and cultic purity became the dominant of the two rationales to the point that it was imposed even on clerics who were married. Celibacy was mandated to ensure continence. I submit that this development undermined the appreciation of continence as a gift and contributed to its own share of unintended consequences. A disciplinary tradition, no doubt well-intended, was launched even though its principal rationale, cultic purity, lost emphasis as the prevailing reason centuries later.

---

[265] Pope St. Paul VI, "*Sacerdotalis Caelibatus*," #16.
[266] Pope St. Paul VI, "*Sacerdotalis Caelibatus*," #13.

The Church's Regulatory Role Concerning Priestly Continence

The Church holds the prerogative to regulate discipline within its society. In Pope St. Paul VI's encyclical letter "Priestly Celibacy," a Church document that is among the most thorough examinations on this topic, he describes the Church's ministry of discernment: "But the priestly vocation, although inspired by God, does not become definitive or operative without having been tested and accepted by those in the Church who hold power and bear responsibility for the ministry serving the ecclesial community. It is therefore the task of those who hold authority in the Church to determine in accordance with the varying conditions of time and place, who in actual practice are to be considered suitable candidates for the religious and pastoral service of the Church and what should be required of them."[267] I have certainly pondered how well that has worked out given the recent scandals. This regulatory function of the Church, particularly as it relates to "discipline, an area in which experience can still offer more suggestions,"[268] deserves examination. A little later in this chapter, I will use a nonconventional analogy in order to examine the risks of this regulatory role.

Cultic Purity and the Priesthood

Even though the requirement of priestly celibacy now perdures under a different set of noble Christian motives, clerical continence was initially inspired in large measure by cultic purity. In his encyclical "*Sacramentum Caritatis*," Pope Benedict XVI links the discipline of celibacy to Christ's own virginity: "The fact that Christ himself, the eternal priest, lived his mission even to the sacrifice of the Cross in the state of virginity constitutes the sure point of reference for understanding the meaning of the tradition of the Latin Church. It is not sufficient to understand priestly celibacy in purely functional terms. Celibacy is really a special way of

---

[267] Pope St. Paul VI, "*Sacerdotalis Caelibatus*," #15.

[268] Pope St. Paul VI, *Ecclesiae Sanctae*, Apostolic Letter issued Motu Proprio, August 6, 1966, https://www.vatican.va/content/paul-vi/en/motu_proprio/documents/hf_p-vi_motu-proprio_19660806_ecclesiae-sanctae.html.

conforming oneself to Christ's own way of life. This choice has first and foremost a nuptial meaning; it is a profound identification with the heart of Christ the Bridegroom who gives his life for his Bride."[269]

But an article titled "The Truth About Priestly Continence and Celibacy in the Early Church" points out the following:

> Benedict's statement that Christ's own virginity must be the fundamental point of reference for understanding the tradition is true if we are looking at it from the standpoint of celibacy as an ascetical practice—a manner of living in *imitatio Christi* that signifies the priest's nuptial union to the Church. However, this is not the rationale the early Church used when discussing the discipline; in fact, Benedict's assertion—that Christ's virginity is the point of reference for clerical celibacy—does not appear a single time in any patristic source. There is simply no Church Father or synod that argues that priests should be celibate because Christ was....Not that this and other arguments do not have their place in the overall discussion; clearly they all have their own value. Yet none of them constitute the prime reason for the discipline, at least according to the Fathers....The clear and consistent teaching of the Fathers is that it is impure and impious for a man to offer the Eucharistic sacrifice to God if he is sexually active.[270]

In an article that appeared in *Chicago Studies* in 1981 titled "Celibacy and Tradition," Joseph A. Komonchak cites the following reasoning, among other considerations: "Pagan practice. (Pope) Siricius twice refers to the practice of continence by pagan priests: 'When idolaters perform their impieties and sacrifice to demons, they impose continence from women on themselves,...and do you ask me if a priest of the true God, about to offer spiritual sacrifices, must constantly be pure or if, wholly

---

[269] Pope Benedict XVI, *Sacramentum Caritatis*, Encyclical Letter, Feb. 2007, #24.

[270] "The Truth About Priestly Continence and Celibacy in the Early Church," Unamsanctamcatholicam.com, Unam Sanctam Catholicam, 2, retrieved 6/28/2019, http://www.unamsanctamcatholicam.com/history/79-history/465-celibacy-in-the-early-church.html.

given over to the flesh, he may attend to the cares of the flesh?'"[271] The Church Father Tertullian, writing in the early third century, made similar arguments. He also noted that the twelve apostles of Jesus were free to marry, but that most did not. He was the first Church Father to clearly link clerical continence to St. Paul's counsel in 1 Corinthians 7:3-5 cited below.

St. Paul, when speaking of the obligations of husband and wife, writes: "Do not deprive one another except perhaps by agreement for a set time, to devote yourselves to prayer, and then come together again, so that Satan may not tempt you because of your lack of self-control."[272] The article titled "The Truth about Priestly Continence and Celibacy in the Early Church" notes that "if St. Paul recommends periodic continence for married lay people when they seek God in prayer, how much more an ordained man who must pray without ceasing? If priests of the Old Law had to observe temporary continence when it was their turn to serve in the Temple, how much more the priest of the New Law whose ministry is unceasing? In both cases, the argument centers on the New Testament priest's role as a permanent mediator on behalf of the Church."[273]

A Deeper Dive on Cultic Purity

The Logic of Cultic Purity

On Saturday, July 17, 1993, in a General Audience, Pope St. John Paul II addressed the contrast between celibacy and marriage. He said, "Here we note the difference in vocations. Jesus did not demand this radical renunciation of family life from all his disciples, although he did require the first place in their hearts, when he said: 'Whoever loves father and mother more than me is not worthy of me, and whoever loves son or daughter more than me is not worthy of me' (Matthew 10:37). The

---

[271] Joseph A. Komonchak, "Celibacy and Tradition," *Chicago Studies* 20, no. 1 (Spring 1981):5-17, 7.

[272] 1 Corinthians 7:3-5, *The New American Bible.*

[273] "The Truth About Priestly Continence," 4.

demand for practical renunciation is proper to the apostolic life or the life of special consecration."[274] In the same General Audience, the Holy Father stated that "the Church has considered and still considers that it [celibacy] belongs to the logic of priestly consecration and to the total belonging to Christ resulting from it, in order consciously to fulfill his mandate of evangelization and the spiritual life."[275]

The pope suggests there is a reasonableness, a logic to it. What is this self-evident connection? There is a curious expression in the English language for describing a priest: he is a "man of the cloth." There is some intuitive connotation associated with this expression. Concepts like *set apart*, *close to God*, and *truth and integrity* come to mind. The very adjective *sacerdotal* (of, or relating to, the sacred), an adjective of the priesthood, includes the word *sacred*, which comes from the Latin *sacer*, meaning "purified, dedicated, set apart."

The Hebrew word is *kadosh*, meaning to be wholly "set apart;" differentiated; distinct from the common, habitual, or profane (Deuteronomy 7:6; 1 Peter 2:9). Few might realize that in Christian baptism one is set apart for God—though many baptized Christians do not act that way. This setting apart in baptism is the vocation common to all Christians.

Clerics, including the married priests in the Eastern Catholic tradition, are referred to as "sacred ministers" in Canon Law and the Catechism uses the term *consecrated*. The priest's consecration is permanent by virtue of the Sacrament of Holy Orders. He effectuates in the name and person of Christ the outward signs, instituted by Christ, to give inward grace (*sacra potestas*). Acting sacramentally in the person of Christ, a sacrament's efficacy is protected from the priest's personal moral turpitude because it is Christ who acts in the sacraments. Is his "sacredness" permanent? I would submit that "holiness" is a better substitute, for it is a state of progress and degree, always requiring an ongoing disposition that is suited for a deepening relationship to Christ. It is not a stagnant status and does not violate the free will of the priest.

---

[274] Pope St. John Paul II, general audience, July 17, 1993, #1.
[275] Pope St. John Paul II, general audience, July 17, 1993, #1.

This distinction is how you begin to avoid clericalism. Ordination is not saintly canonization.

To provide greater context, many thinkers, such as French sociologist David Emile Durkheim and Mircea Eliade, a Romanian historian of religion, have written on the distinction between the sacred and the profane in cultures across time. The word *sacred* distinguishes something from its opposite, the *profane*. In describing something as profane in this context, it's not ascribing a moral judgment of good or evil. Rather, something is profane if it is pedestrian, ordinary, routine, or mundane—in the ordinary course of life's affairs. In this worldview, the sacred, by contrast, sets something apart either because of its connection with a hierophany or theophany (a revelation or experience of the sacred or of God—like the location of the burning bush, which becomes "holy ground" in Exodus 3:2) or because it involves interaction with God (the Holy of Holies in the Jewish temple, the Last Supper). It can describe an object, a place, a time, or a person, though persons are typically viewed in terms of holiness, or moral character.

A Word about Jewish Laws on Purity

Since Christianity is intertwined with Jewish history, it may be helpful to understand ritual purity in the Jewish tradition and how it can shed light on the subject of continence and cultic purity. Ritual purity laws were not a Christian invention.

The Jewish tradition, founded on the covenants with God (Abraham and Moses), holds that 613 commandments (mitzvot) were imparted by God to His Chosen People. Of those, 365 are so-called "negative" commandments that are mandatory observances for all Jews. The other 248 are "positive" commandments, often with no particular time restrictions. Many of the mandatory commandments concerning ritual purity are found in Exodus 19:15 and Leviticus chapters 11–15.

Cecilia Wassen sums up the Jewish understanding of purity laws in her article "The Jewishness of Jesus and Ritual Purity:"

For most peoples in the ancient world, purity and impurity were part of a basic understanding of the world. This is evident in first-century Judaism which categorized people, objects and places as either pure or impure, holy or profane. The overarching function of purity regulations was to prevent impurity from coming into contact with the holy; most importantly the temple in Jerusalem, but also consecrated food (Harrington 2004: 9–12)....

The first thing to keep in mind is that impurity is an inescapable part of everyday life. Everybody was impure at times. The most obvious example is that of sexual intercourse, which rendered both the man and woman impure; a couple would have to bathe and wait until the evening to be pure again (Leviticus 15:18). Of course, this kind of impurity was not something people avoided—on the contrary, procreation was a commandment....In other words, by fulfilling certain obligations, such as the command to be fruitful and to bury one's parents, people became impure. Clearly, impurity was a part of life....We may notice as well, that biblical discourse in general conveys no negative sentiments about these carriers of impurity; instead their status as ritually impure is described in a neutral way and as a matter of fact....

Biblical laws in general do not even prescribe avoidance of ritual impurity, except in connection to the sacred. There are very few verses that warn against attracting impurity or that seek to prevent impurity from occurring. Instead, the biblical laws simply clarify how to handle impurity....

...He [referring to the scholar E. P. Sanders] rightly claims that after circumcision, purity regulations were "the most obvious and universally kept set of laws" (Sanders 1992: 214).... The importance of purity is supported by archaeological evidence. Ritual baths (*miqva'ot*) were common in first-century Palestine, including the region in Galilee.[276]

---

[276] Cecilia Wassen, "The Jewishness of Jesus and Ritual Purity," *Jewish Studies in the Nordic Countries Today* 27 (2016): 11–36, 21-22.

There were laws that governed the continence practiced by the Jewish priesthood for cultic purity, but that did not preclude them from marriage. The Church adopted a different stance on cultic purity because She did not view Her priesthood as merely a continuance of the Levitical priesthood, but a perfection of it, offering continual prayer and sacrifice, necessitating continual continence.

The Conflict Created Between the *Gift* and *Cultic Purity*

The importance of cultic purity ultimately transcended the idea that continence was a gift. In reading the Church Fathers, the canons, and regulations on continence and the priesthood, the following words routinely appear: *observing, practicing, choosing, pledged to* continence; or elsewhere, *released from the duties of marriage* or *abstaining from relations*, even if the priest was already married. Continence as a gift is not the emphasis in the canons. Consider how illogical it would be, then, to say that priests would suddenly have the "gift" of continence even if they were already married. Such married priests were *converted* to continence.

These themes continued through the Gregorian Reform (1050–1080), the Council of Trent (1545–1563), and up until the twentieth century (*Sacra Virginitas*, Pius XII, 1954). Sexual continence for cultic purity was the common tradition of the Church. Mandatory celibacy was the discipline mandated over time to achieve this purpose.

Unintended Consequences of the Conflict between the *Gift* and *Cultic Purity*

There were three critical distortions that resulted from the conflict between continence as a gift and continence as a cultic purity requirement.

1. The language of the Church emphasized a purity that led to the exact mindset that Clement of Rome warned against: namely, a boasting, because it was viewed as superior.

154

2. It led to a degradation of marriage. Even as the rationale for clerical continence changed over time, the vestiges of this history contributed to a misaligned view of sacramental marriage and created a clergy who, with their "immaculate purity" and higher education in the faith, came to be perceived as a superior caste of Christians.

3. The idea of continence as a gift was subordinated to a requirement. It became identical, in large measure, only with the priesthood and religious life.

The language of cultic purity has informed centuries of culture in the Church. It became engrained in the subconscious, in iconography, in vocabulary, and in other elements of Church life. Changing the language and emphasis since Vatican II has not turned the ship around overnight. The Church has had to push back on the dangers of clericalism and strengthen its praise of marriage.

Additionally, the discipline of clerical continence created a culture of guardrails to protect it. Those guardrails, intended to shore up human weakness, often had the impact of impeding the development of healthy relationships. As I noted in chapter VII, this has also given us a legacy of psychologically underdeveloped clergy. These factors become exacerbated in the context of a fraternity of persons in similar circumstances in a closed environment. Recall one of the hallmarks of the *wicked problem* paradigm—that one problem is a symptom of another problem.

In the writings of the Fathers and Church canons, clerical continence is associated with themes and descriptions such as ritual purity, service as mediator for the Church, being set apart, personal sanctity, worthiness, being purer than others, immaculate purity, and exceptional honor, to name a few. Many of these lofty descriptions come from the Semitic comparison to the radiance and shine of a superior gold piece that is less polluted or contaminated. But cultic purity is distinct from moral purity, though it is hoped that the one who offers the Eucharistic sacrifice possesses a radiance in both senses.

Alongside this understanding was the view that marriage and the conjugal act were seen in opposition to the requirements of the priesthood.

The failure to be sexually continent even if the priest was married was seen as moral turpitude (concupiscence), a violation of the canons, or both. This culminated in such expressions as canon 10 of the 24th Session of the Council of Trent in 1563, which reads, "If anyone says that the married state excels the state of virginity or celibacy, and that it is better and happier to be united in matrimony than to remain in virginity or celibacy, let him be anathema."[277]

Why was continence viewed as superior to marriage? It was seen as marriage to Christ, a profound renunciation in following Him, being in a pure state to welcome His return, and a mastery over the flesh.

Pope St. John Paul II is famous for his elaborate theology on the human body. In reflecting on the change in outlook following the Second Vatican Council, he tried to reconcile the role of the two states in life, marriage and perpetual virginity. In a 1990 article, Fr. Alphonse DeValk, CSB, notes, "In 1981, in a major letter on the role of the Christian family in the world, Pope John Paul reiterated that celibacy neither contradicts nature, nor maligns marriage: 'Virginity or celibacy, for the sake of the Kingdom of God, not only does not contradict the dignity of marriage but presupposes it and confirms it. Marriage and virginity or celibacy are two ways of expressing and living the one mystery of the covenant of God with his people. When marriage is not esteemed, neither can consecrated virginity or celibacy exist; when human sexuality is not regarded as a great value given by the Creator, the renunciation of it for the sake of the Kingdom of Heaven loses its meaning.'"[278]

A Shift from Cultic Purity: The Remaining Implication for the Gift?

Canon 277 of the 1983 Code of Canon Law states, "Clerics are obliged to observe perfect and perpetual continence for the sake of the kingdom

---

[277] Rev. H.J. Schroeder, O.P., ed. *The Canons and Decrees of the Council of Trent* (Rockford, Illinois: Tan Books, 1941, 1978),182.

[278] Alphonse DeValk, CSB, "Priestly Celibacy...Why? Note on Celibacy in History," (Battleford, Saskatchewan: Marian Press Ltd., 1990), 13.

of heaven and therefore are obliged to observe celibacy, which is a special gift of God, by which sacred ministers can adhere more easily to Christ with an undivided heart and can more freely dedicate themselves to the service of God and humankind."[279]

This expression in Canon Law is worthy of commentary and exploration. It couches "perfect and perpetual continence," lived out as a celibate, in very specific notions: "for the sake of the Kingdom of heaven," "to adhere more easily to Christ with an undivided heart," and to "more freely dedicate themselves to the service of God and humankind." On its face, the rationale provided in Canon Law includes the scriptural basis for celibacy, its practical spiritual fruit, and a utilitarian benefit. While Canon Law retains the inescapable term *sacred minister*, which connects continence with its true historical underpinnings, it should be noted that clerics of the Eastern Rites of the Church—even those who are married—are also referred to as sacred ministers in the Canon Law of the East. In accentuating different aspects of the same discipline, one cannot easily dismiss the discipline's legacy and its vestiges.

It is noteworthy that the official commentary on canon 277 includes the following sentence: "In this positive presentation, 'for the sake of the kingdom of heaven,' the conciliar statement [refers to Vatican II] as well as the revised law are a great improvement. 'All untenable motives for celibacy—arising from notions of cultic purity or from subliminal depreciation of the body and of sexuality—are avoided, motives still commonly mentioned until quite recently in official documents.'"[280] While this analysis of canon 277 is not the equivalent of a Church pronouncement, it does represent a shift.

In 1967 Pope St. Paul VI acknowledged that "even if the explicit reasons have differed with different mentalities and different situations, they were always inspired by specifically Christian considerations; and from

---

[279] James A. Coriden, Thomas J. Green, and Donald E. Heintschel, eds., *The Code of Canon Law: A Text and Commentary* (New York/Mahwah: Paulist Press, 1985), 209.

[280] Coriden, Green, and Heintschel, *The Code of Canon Law*, 210.

these considerations we can get an intuition of the more fundamental motives underlying them."[281]

Indeed, the fundamental motives are good. There is absolutely a role in the Church for the gifts of perpetual virginity and continence. God will continue to call members of the faithful to this lifestyle in service of the Gospel, some as monks, some as religious, some as celibate priests, and some in a consecrated single vocation. The Church should not fear losing this gift if it isn't made compulsory. Rather, She must cultivate a Christian community that is unafraid to be countercultural and that understands and values these gifts.

The Risks of a Regulatory Role

I will now consider some risks in exercising a regulatory authority. I hope that lessons from this unconventional analogy will serve to help the Church reconsider the outcomes of Her regulation on mandatory priestly celibacy.

For a period of time, I worked in the highly regulated casino industry. Regulation in this industry is intended to protect operational integrity, discourage the criminal element, and serve the public good. But regulation is not an absolute. It must still be tempered by proportionality and be in support of a probusiness environment.

More Is Not Always Better: Overregulation Often Lacks Proportionality

The casino industry had existing, sound regulations, but some regulators, even though often well intentioned, took pride in demonstrating that under their tenure they were able to exceed existing regulations. It was the mindset that "more must be better." It didn't matter to the regulator if their directive required the business to spend $100,000 to cure a $10 problem that occurred infrequently and had no consumer-facing exposure that could erode public trust, or if there was a less expensive

---

[281] Pope St. Paul VI, *Sacerdotalis Caelbatus*, #18.

work-around. Nor did it matter to the regulator's mindset that exceeding the existing standards stifled business operations such that the business was occupied—nay, consumed—almost exclusively with regulation. In some instances, overregulation threatens the very viability and existence of businesses and the industry itself. Often the regulator has no concern about the consequences of their directives until, of course, there is no business left to regulate. Clearly, more is not always better.

For this chapter's purposes, a good translation of the phrase "more is better" in Latin would be *a minori ad maius* ("from the lessor to the greater"). This was the approach of Church Fathers in insisting on clerical continence. It was largely inspired by cultic purity (as seen above in the Church's view of St. Paul's words for married persons: if you are continent for some time in prayer, how much more so should the priest who prays incessantly and serves at the altar).

I would submit, however, that the existing standard is "Whoever can accept this ought to accept it."[282] The overregulation in the West was to require all to do so. Is celibacy a gift given to some? Absolutely. Is it the call for all? Not likely.

Pope St. Paul VI noted that "celibacy is and ought to be a rare and very meaningful example of a life whose motivation is love."[283] It seems that the regulation of mandatory celibacy is forcing it to be artificially less rare and less organic, even though the desire to have this witness in the world is noble. The argument I am making here is distinct from the position that celibacy is a violence against nature. Instead, while affirming the Church's prerogative to regulate, it is an argument that the Church is overregulating what is otherwise a unique gift.

Potential for Focus to be Shifted to the Wrong Things

Going further with the regulation analogy, it is noteworthy that the Church has now spent an inordinate amount of time, money, and energy

---

[282] Matthew 19:12, *The New American Bible*.

[283] Pope St. Paul VI, *Sacerdotalis Caelibatus*, #24.

on enforcing this regulation, dealing with damage control, restoring credibility, and trying to strengthen the very prospect of future vocations.

By contrast, the Christian life, vibrantly lived with zeal in community and in a shared participation in the Eucharist, would otherwise foster the values of temperance, chastity, and a life of renunciation for the sake of the Gospel. As Pope St. Paul VI notes, "Such efforts ennoble man and are beneficial to the human community."[284] These values open the heart to charity. When these ideals are witnessed and elevated in contrast to the ways of the world, the hand of God will be at work and some will embrace this gift without forced obligation.

Lack of Imagination

Regulation tends to box one into predefined patterns of behavior and can make it difficult to be nimble and flexible. Despite being a necessity at times, it can lead to a lack of imagination and discretion. Middle management becomes very content to function within the stability and predictability that regulation creates, and then they are blamed for an inability to think outside the box. For this reason, when someone encounters a conflict with a policy, they demand to see the store owner or general manager, saying, "I want to talk to someone who can do something about this."

Regulation around doctrine is quite important. Regulation of discipline needs to be examined, according to time, place, and circumstance. Yet there are some leaders who see Pope Francis as dangerous for even raising the idea of a careful reexamination of priestly celibacy, and who would prefer to wait out his pontificate.

---

[284] Pope St. Paul VI, *Humanae Vitae*, Encyclical Letter, July 25, 1968, #20, https://www.vatican.va/content/paul-vi/en/encyclicals/documents/hf_p-vi_enc_25071968_humanae-vitae.html.

Historical Struggle

The emphasis on cultic purity—which led to a migration toward the insistence on clerical continence, even if the priest didn't have the gift and was married—naturally encountered great difficulty. In the period leading to the first millennium, when cultic purity was a key motive of the Church, there is evidence in the canons and writings of the Fathers that married clergy would be continent for a while and then return to their wives and, in some cases, have children. In some of these instances, it was prescribed that someone would accompany the cleric back home to witness that he and his wife did not live in common. The canons also required that the priest's wife was to be materially provided for.

In a 1998 *Chicago Studies* article describing the situation in the year AD 1000, Kevin Madigan writes,

> While fourth- and fifth-century canonical decrees required clerical celibacy, many (and probably most) priests of rural churches at this time lived with women. These were either wives or "heartmates." Many urban clerics (and even a few bishops) lived with wives and concubines as well. Although a few bishops and some synods in the early Middle Ages insisted on clerical continence, their words were a dead letter. Simply put, virtually no rural parishioner or priest in the year 1000 regarded clerical concubinage or marriage as practically or canonically objectionable. (In the second half of the eleventh century, and even more in the succeeding two centuries, many would. Nevertheless, old habits died hard.) It was doubtless the case that many thought celibacy as too lofty an ideal; some were probably even unaware that clerical concubinage or marriage was uncanonical."[285]

In another examination of that time, Fr. Martin W. Pable, OFM Cap., quotes Edward Schillebeeckx when he writes, "'In 1023, Pope Benedict VIII preached his outspoken sermons against the clergy who

---

[285] Kevin Madigan, "The Parish in the Year 1000," *Chicago Studies* 37, no. 3 (December 1998): 233-244, 237.

lived in concubinage or were married. The contemporary literature about this situation is alarming...a bishop of Liege complained that if he should enforce the Church's disciplinary rules, he would have to dismiss his entire clergy. Many priests justified their conduct by saying that for them marriage was a social necessity....In the long run the struggle seemed so fruitless that some bishops gave it up and advised their priests, "Si non caste, tamen caute" (If you can't live chastely, at least be discrete about it)."[286] In the wake of widespread abuse, the First Lateran Council (AD 1123) and the Second Lateran Council six years later pronounced canons that included declaring null and invalid any existing marriages of clerics. Having received Holy Orders was declared an impediment to marriage.

I've provided the entries above to illustrate one additional point beyond their face value. Some of this very activity still goes on to this day in the global Church. Views on sexuality are different in some areas of the world than in the United States—in some areas, sexuality is less hyped and more accepted. In some places in Africa, single men have no standing and are not accepted well into tribal communities. Thus, it has been suggested that the Holy See (the Vatican), looking at things from a universal perspective with two thousand years of experience in human behavior, may have been slow in reacting to clamor out of the United States in the recent crisis. Some at the Vatican, mindful of both anti-Catholic bigotry in the US and the sensationalism and obsession with sex in the media, saw this initially as a United States phenomenon.

As long as the Church continues to require mandatory celibacy for the priesthood, She will be more apt to see a mixed bag—with heroic witnesses and examples as well as disappointment and scandal. Certainly, violations against children are criminal and repugnant. The current crisis included mostly male victims. Even if the composition of the priesthood was dominated by heterosexual priests, violations against female victims would be just as grave. And scandal still exists when violations of priestly continence involve adults (of either sex). The life of the priest in such cases ceases to be an authentic witness. I've heard priests say "You're

---

[286] Martin W. Pable, "Priesthood and Celibacy," 64.

never truly celibate (chaste) until you die." This phrase is spoken not necessarily in the sense of specific actions that violate chastity, but in the sense that Jesus meant when He said, "For from the heart come evil thoughts, murder, adultery, unchastity, theft, false witness, blasphemy."[287] While there is an element of realism in that statement by some priests, given human weakness, the undiscerning ear may hear it differently—as an *a priori* excuse for such weakness. For some priests, celibacy is clearly viewed as a requirement that they must simply learn to cope with, in contrast to a gift given and freely embraced.

Traditions in Eastern Christianity Not in Communion with Rome

Some may point to the long and venerable traditions and communities of Eastern Christianity, most of which have married priests (typically married before ordination). Lest it be thought they are without issues, I will note that they must contend with issues of divorce, widowed clergy, family issues bleeding into parish life, and income sufficient to help support the priest's family.

Prior to surveying the general practices of two Eastern Christian ecclesial communities, I want to include an excerpt that shows the difficulties these communities have experienced, which in many ways mirror the issues noted in the above descriptions of the Latin Church in the year 1000. The following is an excerpt from a paper published in *The Greek Orthodox Theological Review* and revolves around the status of widowed clergy:

> Widowed clergy appear to have caused problems for their bishops throughout the later Middle Ages. The pastoral instructions of Metropolitan Peter of Moscow (1308–26) indicate that he faced the problem of widowed clergy "many times" and to prevent the scandal of concubinage, remarriage or other moral lapses he was forced to adopt measures which may seem to

---

[287] Matthew 15:19, *The New American Bible.*

us cruel and unusual: If a priest's wife dies, he must either be tonsured and enter a monastery or else leave the priesthood. In time the severity of these measures was moderated somewhat. A council in Moscow in 1503 decided that widowed priests and deacons who lead a pure life, though still prohibited from serving the Liturgy, could at least be authorized to wear the epitrachelion and orarion respectively, receive communion in the sanctuary, and serve as church singers, and that a quarter of the churches' revenues were to be set aside for their financial support. Still, married clergy were not entirely pleased with these measures. One, the priest George Skripitsa of Rostov, wrote bitterly of the 1503 council: "The Holy Apostles and the fathers of the seven ecumenical councils did not condemn priests on account of their wives' death, nor did they remove them from office....Where is there anything written that chaste priests and deacons should be deposed from office and forced to become monks? In effect, the council is unreasonably assuming that if a married priest is chaste, an unmarried one is unchaste, and yet a wifeless monk is pure." Eventually, with the Moscow Council of 1666–67, virtually all restrictions on the ministry of widowed clergy—and in particular on serving the Liturgy—were finally lifted, though vestiges of these restrictions lingered even into the twentieth century.[288]

Eastern Orthodox and Russian Orthodox Practices

The following is a brief survey of the practice in both of these ecclesial communities.

1. Marriage. To be a married cleric, one must marry prior to the ordination to the diaconate (the step in Holy Orders prior to the

---

[288] John H. Erickson, "The Council in Trullo: Monogamy and the Ordained Priesthood," *The Greek Orthodox Theological Review* (1995): 183–199, quoted on Pemptousia (blog) St. Maxim the Greek Institute, March 6, 2017, https://pemptousia.com/2017/03/the-council-in-truilo-issues-relating-to-the-marriage-of-clergy.

priesthood). Otherwise, one must declare his intent to remain celibate. He may be married only once prior to ordination and to a woman who has been married only once. Priests practice continence during their time of service at the altar.

2. Divorce. Generally, if the wife files for the divorce or the divorce is considered no-fault, the priest may be able to stay in active ministry but cannot remarry. If the priest files for the divorce, he must leave the active ministry.

3. Widowed Priest. As of 2018, the remarriage of a widowed priest is evaluated on a case-by-case basis (in Eastern Orthodoxy). Before then, a widowed priest would generally retire to monastic life.

4. Bishops. Since the sixth century, bishops have generally been chosen from the celibate monastic community (hieromonks). Widowed clergy could be eligible to become a bishop.

In exploring some of the issues facing the Church with married clergy, I would direct you to the 1995 document "Marriage and the Priesthood: A Series of Papers Prepared by the Holy Synod of Bishops of the Orthodox Church in America Concerning Contemporary Issues."[289] It explores how some of the challenges of a married priest's family can bleed over into parish life.

The Patriarch Athenagoras Orthodox Institute conducted a 2006 study of the Orthodox community in the United States called "Evolving Visions of the Orthodox Priesthood in America: A Study Report." Below are the top seven concerns "selected by more than 20%" of respondent clergy. Items one and five are particularly germane to the practical issues created by optional clerical celibacy.

1. "Providing financially for my family

---

[289] Holy Synod of Bishops of the Orthodox Church in America, "Marriage and the Priesthood: A Preliminary Study of Problems Facing the Married Priest in Contemporary Society and a Consideration of Some Possible Aids in Solving Them, Study Paper:1995, cited from https://www.holy-trinity.org/morality/synod-marriageandpriest.html.

2. Too much work
3. Uncertainty about the future of Church in America
4. Apathy among parishioners
5. Balancing time and priorities between parish life and personal family life
6. The way authority is exercised in the church
7. Inadequate administrative support: lack of secretaries, Sunday school teachers, etc."[290]

Eastern Churches in Communion with Rome

Tracing their apostolic heritage generally to one of the five main centers of early Christianity (that is, Jerusalem, Antioch, Alexandria, Constantinople, and Rome), these roughly twenty-three ecclesial communities have their jurisdictional seat principally in Eastern Europe and the Near East, generally use one of eight major Liturgical Rites of the Church, and retain their own disciplines. With some exceptions, these ecclesial communities follow the Eastern tradition described above. Their candidates for the priesthood, if they are to be married, must marry prior to ordination and have the written consent of their wife. They cannot marry after ordination. They practice temporary continence prior to their service at the altar. Their bishops are chosen from among the celibate or widowed clergy. Until recently, their married clergy served in various parts of the world, except for the Americas and Australia. If their married priests were in those locations, they were considered there "on loan." Historically, due to influence and protest from the Church hierarchy dating back to 1890 in the Americas and Australia, their married clergy have not been allowed to serve in those territories. This policy was formalized in 1929 with the decree *Cum Data Fuerit.*

---

[290] Alexei D. Krindatch, "Evolving Visions of the Orthodox Priesthood in America: A Study Report" (Berkeley, California: Patriarch Athenagoras Orthodox Institute,2006), 25, https://orthodoxreality.org/wp-content/uploads/2020/03/EvolvingVisionsFullReport.pdf.

This ban has been recently lifted under Pope Francis. The Catholic News Service ran a story on November 17, 2014, reporting, "The Vatican has lifted its ban on the ordination of married men to the priesthood in Eastern Catholic churches outside their traditional territories, including the United States, Canada and Australia. Pope Francis approved lifting the ban, also doing away with the provision that, in exceptional cases, Eastern Catholic bishops in the diaspora could receive Vatican approval to ordain married men. In recent years, however, some Eastern Catholic bishops went ahead with such ordinations discreetly without Vatican approval."[291] Signed in June 2014, and published in the *Acta Apostolicae Sedis*, the decree "concedes to Eastern Catholic bishops outside their traditional territory the faculties to 'allow pastoral service of Eastern married clergy' and 'to ordain Eastern married candidates' in their eparchies or dioceses, although they must inform the local Latin Rite bishop in writing 'in order to have his opinion and any relevant information.'"[292]

I have read authors who call the practice of married priests in the East an abuse of the tradition. One such author wrote, "It is also possible that multiple traditions can be legitimate, while one tradition is superior, on the whole, to another—put differently, that one way is better than another because it rests on a deeper foundation or coheres better with other aspects of faith. To say it is better does not mean that the Eastern rule is wrong and must be overturned, but only that it is less good."[293]

By what measure is the Eastern discipline less good? Different gifts are given variously to the servants of God, and they are living within their venerable tradition. I find such a position objectionable and remind all that "...official Catholic teaching respects the Eastern discipline. See, for example, the Code of Canons of the Eastern Churches, which was promulgated by Pope St. John Paul II. It states that 'the hallowed

---

[291] Laura Ieraci, "Vatican Lifts Ban on Married Priests for Eastern Catholics in Diaspora," Catholic News Service, Nov. 17, 2014, https://www.ncronline.org/news/vatican/vatican-lifts-ban-married-priests-eastern-catholics-diaspora.

[292] Ieraci, "Vatican Lifts Ban."

[293] Peter Kwasniewski, "When (Eastern) Catholics Argue against Priestly Celibacy," OnePeterFive (blog), Jan. 15, 2020, https://onepeterfive.com/eastern-catholics-celibacy/.

practice of married clerics in the primitive Church and in the tradition of the Eastern Churches throughout the ages is to be held in high honor.' (canon 373)"[294]

I am compelled to remark at this time that there continues to be a lack of ecumenical spirit and charity on both sides of the aisle when it comes to Eastern Christianity. I have even seen indifference in Latin Rite bishops. I find this to be a sad commentary on Christianity as a whole.

Considering Change

Given the ongoing, needed debate about a married priesthood, Catholics are currently left with some best practices to protect children, a lack of clear, officially recognized causes of the sexual abuse crisis, and some additional rigor in seminary formation, but otherwise it is business as usual. I agree with a celibate Eastern Rite Catholic priest who writes, "Any hint at change in this regard does indeed warrant the utmost prudence, honest scholarship, and wise discernment."[295]

Indeed, there are many theological and practical interdependencies that must be carefully thought through, but the Latin Church already has some married priests. To insist that this is just a difficult period that the Church must weather, a time of trial and persecution, may indeed miss the mark. Though a married clergy is not a panacea, a celibate clergy need not be the only model within the tradition.

As it relates to the clergy sexual abuse crisis, I think celibate clergy remains squarely in the contextual-factor column and not in the proximate-cause column.

---

[294] Dr. Anthony Dragani, "5 Myths about Married Priests in Eastern Catholicism," National Catholic Register (blog), Nov. 4, 2019, https://www.ncregister.com/blog/5-myths-about-married-priests-in-eastern-catholicism.

[295] Fr. Thomas Loya, "Married Priesthood, Celibacy, and the Amazon Synod: An Eastern Catholic Priest's Perspective," Catholic World Report, August 21, 2019, https://www.catholicworldreport.com/2019/08/21/married-priesthood-celibacy-and-the-amazon-synod-an-eastern-catholic-priests-perspective/.

Mandatory celibacy is a contextual problem because some, though certainly not all, candidates for the priesthood are ill-prepared to embrace lifelong clerical continence, and it can lead to or exacerbate existing psychological and behavioral problems down the road. Additionally, if celibacy is not lived in its true spirit as a charism for the benefit of the whole Church, it can contribute to clericalism, which is a proximate cause of the problem.

There are many who think the Church should double down on Her insistence of clerical celibacy. They argue that today's culture needs the countercultural witnesses to Christ and holiness now more than ever. They argue that the Church should stop apologizing for its position. I do believe the Church should cultivate and celebrate this Christian witness to the world, as it is a gift of the Lord to some. But the witness must be freely and maturely chosen by those with the gift to have any efficacious benefit.

Because continence is a gift given only to some, this means the Church should not preclude an openness to ordaining suitable mature married men (men of virtue), perhaps with grown children, as pastoral reasons suggest. This will help to slowly change the composition of the priesthood so that it is not dominated by homosexual clerics. Every effort must be exerted to resist the temptation to view such married priests, who would be sacramentally identical, as second-class priests. Given all the theological layers over the centuries, as well as practical considerations, this isn't an exercise in flipping the switch. Any change must be thoughtful and deliberate.

Two Common Arguments Against Celibacy

I will conclude this chapter with a brief overview of two other common arguments used in support of removing the requirement of celibacy.

1. It has been suggested that married men with families would be more empathetic to the real-life pastoral issues that arise in peoples' lives. Perhaps, but consider the following:

A. A priest's primary role is not as a psychiatrist. The priest's role is in the service of the salvation of souls. He directs us in Christian living, and he does so by drawing on his own spiritual life and the witness of Scripture and the entire Tradition. In confecting the sacraments, and in communion with his bishop as a coworker, he is a visible, tangible expression of Christ, acting *in persona Christi*. Additionally, he has recourse to draw upon his own experiences growing up in a family.

B. Many cultures have stories about the wise, detached, and dispassionate man in the cave whom you go to in order to find answers to life's profound questions. The guru, as it were, has time to think about these things, unfettered by allegiances and the travails of daily existence.

C. Married priests could have bad days at home and would have to temper their own biases in giving counsel on such days. You may not always be getting unbiased advice. The divorce rate among married Protestant ministers is not much better than the national average. How do you handle the scandal of divorce or other familial issues that would bleed over into parish life?

D. Catholics would need to deeply consider what a priest with divided loyalties would look like. Married priests in the Eastern tradition, as well as among Protestants, often struggle between ministerial duties and those of family and children. I spoke recently to a young man who said he left the Church, and the trigger point was the priest's unavailability to be at the deathbed of one of his grandparents, whom he described as a lifelong member of that parish.

2. It has been suggested that there would be an uptick in vocations to the priesthood if the celibacy requirement was removed. Maybe, but consider the following:

A. Issues of commitment, and attachments to this world, are still prevalent. There are fewer good examples in the domestic church (home life). Views about what constitute success in this world do not incline someone to service. If commitment to one vocation is typically hard enough, consider what would be needed to sustain two vocations.

B. Are Catholics in the pew prepared to support the added cost? (In the Eastern Orthodox tradition in the US, the parish must support the priest and his family. If the parish is too small and cannot afford it, the priest may be only part time as he secures a livelihood elsewhere.)

C. Dispensing all the existing celibate clergy from their obligation so they could marry would be highly problematic on multiple levels.

D. Would laicized priests, now married, return? Some, of course, do not wish to return even if given the option. The Church recognizes that many priests in leaving to marry consciously reversed a commitment they had previously made.

These complexities simply underscore the interdependent dimensions of a *wicked problem* and require thoughtful discernment and study.

XIV

Homosexual Behavior and the Priesthood

It is an intentional mischaracterization to claim that those individuals who have raised the concern that homosexuality (among other issues) is linked to some of the clergy sexual abuse cases are doing so because it is an easy scapegoat. In an earlier chapter, I differentiated the characteristics of diagnosed pedophilia from other motivations for abusive behavior. Though there have been female victims in this scandal, and though causes of sexual abuse are manifold—including developmental pathologies, childhood experiences, past behaviors, and contextual circumstances that trigger situational offenders—two points are incontrovertible and demand honest attention:

1. The Church's long-held position on homosexuality, from Sacred Scripture, Tradition, and natural law that is inscribed in God's created universe
2. The preponderance of male victims, especially postpubescent boys

Clarity on the Church's Position on Homosexuality

The Church's position on homosexuality, which distinguishes between homosexual orientation and acting on that orientation, states that homosexual persons must not be the subject of ill will or ill treatment or be subject to any behavior that demeans the dignity of their person. Homosexually oriented persons, like all persons, are God's children and are entitled to the protections of their natural rights derived from having "received an incomparable and inalienable dignity from God himself."[296]

Society has been conditioned to believe that a moral judgment, given in charity, cannot be made about behavior. It is God who has original jurisdiction of over one's moral life, but His eternal law is knowable to man by reason and revelation. It would be a contradiction in God for Him to will man's final end and simultaneously make it unattainable by keeping the means to that end hidden. The Church, as custodian of this divine law, simply proclaims it for the salvation of souls- man's last end. Moral judgment about a behavior is not the same as a judgment about the person or the culpability of the person who is doing the act. Doing the latter is what is referred to in Jesus's admonition, "Do not judge, and you will not be judged."[297]

Yet, it is in a commitment to another, in the demand of charity, that the Christian loves the sinner but hates the sin. The Christian is called to exercise a compassionate and loving fraternal correction concerning behavior that violates God's law (1 Corinthians 12:24; James 5:19; Galatians 6:1). This is the more loving response when compared with an indifferent tolerance.

In reality, society routinely makes judgments about behavior to determine what is beneficial for its citizens and to maintain social order. Do we believe that murder (the direct killing of innocent life) is bad only because it is forbidden by society? Murder gets its evil quality not

---

[296] Pontifical Council for Justice and Peace, *Compendium of the Social Doctrine of the Church*, #105, 2004, https://www.vatican.va/roman_curia/pontifical_councils/justpeace/documents/rc_pc_justpeace_doc_20060526_compendio-dott-soc_en.html.

[297] Matthew 7:1, *The New American Bible*, Catholic Mission Edition, St. Jerome Press (Wichita, Kansas: Devore & Sons, Inc., 1987 and 1981).

because of a custom or convention of man subject to arbitrariness, but because it is intrinsically bad (of its own nature). This reality is knowable by reason and necessitates society to forbid it. If the intrinsic character of a human act is used in the moral evaluation of those named behaviors, why would other behaviors be exempt from having this criterion applied? For example, society uses criteria to make moral judgments about rape, racist behavior, and other bad behaviors.

Because of its position on homosexuality, the Church is accused of bigotry and homophobia. *Bigotry* is stubbornly holding an unreasonable belief or opinion, often hateful and based on emotion, against a person or group of people. *Homophobia*, quite literally, is a fear of homosexuals. Neither term holds water here. The Church's position weighs in on the behavior and orientation to the behavior, and not without reason. Critics will call the Church an ancient dinosaur, not in tune with the times. They will discredit Scripture as myth, long cemented in a bygone age. But without even appealing to Sacred Scripture, the Church understands one's sexual faculty as a gift from God and as a creative power to be used responsibly in the natural complementariness and reciprocity between a man and a woman in marriage. This is knowable by reason alone in natural law, which is unchanging, immutable.

But opponents now attack natural law as well. This attack leads to social policies like unisex public restrooms, used simultaneously by men and women, and transgender men competing in women's sports.

Celibacy is a sacrificial renunciation of what is otherwise good and ordered in God's design—the sacramental marriage of man and woman and conjugal acts that are both unitive and procreative. That same union, which forms a family as the basic unit of society, mirrors the Trinitarian love of the three persons of the Godhead and Christ's love for His Spouse, the Church (see Ephesians 5:32). The homosexual inclination or orientation is not ordered to that purpose; hence, the Catechism describes the "acts" as "intrinsically disordered" and the inclination or orientation, though not sinful in itself, as "objectively disordered."[298]

---

[298] Libreria Editrice Vaticana, *Catechism of the Catholic Church*, 2nd ed (Citta del Vaticana: Libreria Editrice Vaticana, 1997), 566, #2357.

In accord with the Church's consistent teaching, all of us need pastoral care as God's children. Some may accuse the Church of having the "Christian life become essentially a matter of avoiding sin rather than following Christ and living the Good News, with [an] emphasis upon the nature of the individual moral act."[299] While human acts do have an intrinsic moral character, the Church embraces all persons, including those with a homosexual orientation, but reminds us that the full Christian life includes a call to the human vocation of love in response to God within the design of the gift of the human person, which includes human sexuality. Using the beautiful metaphor of the stone that closed the tomb of Christ after His crucifixion and death, Pope Francis highlighted at the 2019 Easter Vigil Mass that the Church reminds each Christian to consider which stones in their lives must be rolled away so they too may encounter the Risen Lord.

When sin and scandal become disruptive to the life of the Church, She must be resolute in calling it out and correcting it in both fraternal charity and justice, reminding all persons of their human vocation of love in God's design. If it becomes a cultural cancer within the Church, marked by publicly and obstinately propagating, by word or example, behaviors and positions that are contrary to the Divine Law, She cannot merely feign Christian fraternity. She must prudently and firmly root it out for the common good. The Church engages society with the powerful, countercultural witness of the Gospel. She adds nothing of value if She succumbs to society's norms. Following in the footsteps of Christ, She understands that "no prophet is accepted in his own native place."[300]

Seminary Sympathies toward Homosexuality

In the early 1990s, while visiting a friend who was a student at St. Patrick's Seminary in Menlo Park, California (run by the Sulpician Fathers for over a hundred years by that time) I noticed several seminarians walking

---

[299] David Bohr, *Catholic Moral Tradition* (Huntington, Indiana: Our Sunday Visitor Books, 1990), 52.

[300] Luke 4:24, *The New American Bible.*

down the hallway wearing the same distinctly colored armbands. I inquired about what they represented. I listened in disappointed incredulity as I was told, in essence, that they were supporting homosexuality. I asked myself how Catholic seminarians could willfully make this a cause of activism! In the span of some four decades, some seminaries went from rules to dissuade particular friendships, to telling seminarians not to shy away from intimacy, to this bold and overt expression—all under the watchful eye and apparent cognitive dissonance of many bishops. Years later, several former students of St. Patrick's seminary described the environment at the time they were there as a "moral and doctrinal sewer."

From my experience, breakdowns in complex organizations are often not the result of losing sight of its big macro goals, but rather in the key daily operating processes and oversight informed by cultural or ideological differences on the micro-level.

In his 1963 Apostolic Letter *Summi Dei Verbum*, an Address on Seminaries and Vocations, Pope St. Paul VI cites a prophetic statement when he writes, "We therefore readily endorse, after the example of Pius XII, the wise sentence pronounced by Leo XIII, of unforgettable memory, about seminaries: 'With their estate the fortune of the Church is inextricably linked.'"[301] It seems some Church leaders did not exercise the required oversight to follow this counsel.

Not surprisingly, Fr. Gerald Coleman, who served for sixteen years as president and rector of St. Patrick's Seminary, contributed a chapter to Santa Clara University psychology professor Thomas Plante's book *Sin Against the Innocents: Sexual Abuse by Priests and the Role of the Catholic Church,* published in 2004. The chapter seeks to dispel the notion that clergy sexual abuse is always linked to homosexuality and states that gay men should be allowed to be considered for the priesthood. In his 2018 article "Separating Facts about Clergy Abuse from Fiction," Dr. Plante states, "Sexual orientation is not a risk factor for pedophilia."[302]

---

[301] Pope St. Paul VI, *Summi Dei Verbum,* Apostolic Letter, given at St. Peter's, Vatican City, November 4, 1963, https://www.vatican.va/content/paul-vi/en/apost_letters/documents/hf_p-vi_apl_19631104_summi-dei-verbum.html.

[302] Thomas G. Plante, "Separating Facts about Clergy Abuse from Fiction," *Psychology Today,* August 23, 2018, 2, https://www.psychologytoday.com/us/

Yet, we know empirically that most of the victims were postpubescent boys. Plante's conclusion re-directs the conversation to only a relatively small portion of the cases. The facts should give Church leaders pause and an incentive to evaluate the candidate screening, selection, and formation process.

Some who try to discount the role of homosexuality in some cases of child sexual abuse put forward faulty lines of logic as their argument. Activists say homosexuality is not always linked to sexual abuse,[303] or they claim it cannot be blamed as the single factor because there is a complex confluence of factors. I can concede both of their points without destroying a link. They are not mutually exclusive realities. Even if one argues that clergy sexual abuse is acted out only amid such conditions as easy access to victims, stress, and human weakness, the predominance of male victims means that one who has a homosexual orientation would have one less obstacle to overcome with a male victim.

The 1983 "Educational Guidance in Human Love: Outlines for Sex Education" promulgated by the Sacred Congregation for Catholic Education reads, "Homosexuality, which impedes the person's acquisition of sexual maturity, whether from the individual point of view, or the inter-personal, is a problem which must be faced in all objectivity by the pupil and the educator when the case presents itself."[304] The document does not specify "homosexuality only when it is acted out." It goes on to call the condition a "social maladaptation."

So, though heterosexual candidates for the priesthood could also be maladapted (and this must be discerned in screening and formation),

---

blog/do-the-right-thing/201808/separating-facts-about-clergy-abuse-fiction.

[303] Tom Gjelten, "As Catholic Sex Abuse Crisis Deepens, Conservative Circles Blame Gay Priests," NPR, Sept. 19, 2018, 3, https://www.npr.org/2018/09/19/647919741/sex-abuse-scandal-deepens-divide-over-gay-priests. "'Clearly, the vast majority of [clergy abuse] cases are men preying on boys and adolescents. We have to be clear about that,' says James Martin, S.J., a Jesuit priest and editor-at-large of *America*, a Jesuit magazine. 'But that does not mean that every gay priest is an abuser.'"

[304] Sacred Congregation for Catholic Education, *Educational Guidance in Human Love: Outlines for Sex Education,* November 1, 1983, (Boston, MA: Daughters of St. Paul) #101, 36.

homosexuality is prima facie a maladaptation on the grounds of natural law. Yet the Church has invited these candidates to Holy Orders so long as they are bound to chastity. With an ever-evolving science, and the Church's long-held teaching, Church leaders are not being consistent. Then there are activists who might say, "The Church is rife with it anyway, so why not recognize it?"[305]

Those who call this link a distraction are under enormous pressure to be politically correct and do not want to add fire to the claim that the Church is being homophobic due to its position on homosexuality in general. The pastoral push to be a welcoming Church community has, in practice, very well trumped the concerns about dealing frankly with some of the cases in the clergy sexual abuse crisis.

Acknowledging a Long-Held Exhortation

In April 2002, Pope St. John Paul II called the US cardinals to Rome, as well as the president and vice president of the United States Catholic Conference of Bishops. The pope asserted that "there is no place in the priesthood or religious life for those who would harm the young."[306] In covering this event, a news agency reported as follows:

> Bishop Wilton D. Gregory, president of the U.S. Conference of Catholic Bishops, said Tuesday's morning session with the pope had been "very cordial."
>
> "Obviously, the question of the credibility of bishops is a real concern," he said. "Those bishops who have made judgments that have proven to be in error, in fact tragic, are looking for ways to make sure they handle all future cases appropriately and in whatever ways they can to rectify the

[305] Russell Shaw, "The Priest's Confused Identity," *Crisis Magazine* (Dec. 1, 2000), https//www.crisismagazine.com/2000/the-priests-confused-identity.

[306] Stephen Weeke, Kelley O'Donnell, Mary Ann Ahern, Alex Johnson, "Pope Blunt Before U.S. Cardinals," MSNBC, April 23, 2002, retrieved 4/23/2002, http://www.msnbc.com/news/732931.asp?pne=msn&cp1=1.

mistakes and the errors in judgment from the past that they may have been guilty of."

Gregory blamed part of the problem on gay priests and a perceived proliferation of gay men in seminaries.

"It is an ongoing struggle," he said. "It is most importantly a struggle to make sure that the Catholic priesthood is not dominated by homosexual men. [...] Not only is it not dominated by homosexual men, but to make sure that candidates that we receive are healthy in every possible way—psychologically, emotionally, spiritually."[307]

In regard to the question of homosexuality, the *Catechism of the Catholic Church*, #2357–2359, combines the subjects of chastity and homosexuality. The Church distinguishes between having a homosexual orientation or tendency and acting on that orientation. Thus, an equivalency of sorts is drawn between both homosexual and heterosexual orientation, for both types of individuals are called to live a chaste life. The homosexual is chaste when refraining from sexual activity, and the heterosexual is chaste within the context of marriage or when refraining from sexual activity if unmarried.

Living a sexually continent life is an abstinence and has parallels to the discipline of fasting. Many of us remember the parish priest explaining fasting right before the season of Lent. It is giving up what is otherwise good (that is, food) so that one might focus undistractedly on the Lord and hunger for Him. The operative parallel here is *giving up what is otherwise good*. Clerical continence is the free choice of giving up marriage between a man and a woman and physical procreation. The heterosexual will understand this as the sacrificial choice it is. Despite civil laws permitting homosexual partners to marry, marriage is not lawful in the Church between two of the same sex. The homosexual, then, is not giving up the good of marriage designed by God because their orientation is not inclined to that good, by definition.

---

[307] CNN, "Pope Says Bishops' Decisions 'Wrong,'" CNN, April 23, 2002, retrieved 8/9/2020, https://www.cnn.com/2002/WORLD/europe/04/23/pope.scandal/index.html.

Both the heterosexual and homosexual, in theory, could be celibate "for the sake of the kingdom of God." Both could also embrace celibacy in the utilitarian sense of freedom to serve the whole. But the sacrifice of marriage, as between a man and a woman, which gives it its true meaning, is characteristically different between the two.

To that point, in the 2002 meeting with Pope St. John Paul II covered in the April 23, 2002 MSNBC story cited above, Cardinal Francis George, then-archbishop of Chicago, said, "'The important thing in seminary formation is to ask whether or not a candidate is capable of marriage and family...because an ordained priest is a married man. He's a committed man, the bride of Christ. The difficulty in formation...is whether a man can see himself as married and bringing forth new life, which is what a priest is supposed to be.'"[308]

It is worth repeating a 1981 quote from Pope St. John Paul II that was also noted in the previous chapter:

> Virginity or celibacy for the sake of the Kingdom of God not only does not contradict the dignity of marriage but presupposes it and confirms it. Marriage and virginity or celibacy are two ways of expressing and living the one mystery of the covenant of God with His people. When marriage is not esteemed, neither can consecrated virginity or celibacy exist; when human sexuality is not regarded as a great value given by the Creator, the renunciation of it for the sake of the Kingdom of Heaven loses its meaning.[309]

In the 2002 meeting with the pope, the bishops, now with a mess on their hands, seemed to be echoing what was already the wise counsel of the Church. Perhaps they lost sight of it in the pursuit of more vocations.

---

[308] Stephen Weeke, Kelley O'Donnell, Mary Ann Ahern, Alex Johnson, "Pope Blunt Before U.S. Cardinals."

[309] Pope St. John Paul II, *Familiaris Consortio* (Apostolic Exhortation on the Role of the Christian Family in the Modern World, November 22, 1981), #16, as cited on https://www.vatican.va/content/john-paul-ii/en/apost_exhortations/documents/hf_jp-ii_exh_19811122_familiaris-consortio.html.

This prescription was stated twenty years prior to Pope St. John Paul II's 1981 words, in *Religiosorum Institutio*: "Therefore, let them [candidates for the priesthood] be so instructed that, with a clear understanding of the advantages of Christian matrimony, they may deliberately and freely embrace the greater good of priestly and religious chastity."[310]

Homosexuality: Prevalence and Culture

I am not claiming that it is impossible for a homosexual priest to live a celibate life. A priest will be judged by his actions. Some of the abuses involving homosexual behavior were committed by homosexual clerics who lacked strong social bonds and healthy development or who were acting as situational offenders. Yet, the phenomenon that Fr. D. Paul Sullins has described as "the lurid homosexual cultures and homosexual activity in Catholic seminaries"[311] cannot be ignored.

Diving deeper into this homosexual culture, consider the reflections in an April 2001 article titled "The Gay Priest Problem" that appeared in the periodical *Dossier* and that predates the *Boston Globe* stories and both of the reports commissioned by the US Catholic Bishops. I will quote liberally from its author, Fr. Paul Shaughnessy, SJ.

Fr. Shaughnessy begins by reflecting on the coverage by the media addressing the emergence of Catholic priests dying from HIV/AIDS. He opens with a news clip from the Associated Press by Judy L. Thomas that appeared in January 2000 that cites reportage from the *Kansas City Star* newspaper: "The newspaper said its examination of death certificates and interviews with experts indicates several hundred priests have died of AIDS-related illnesses since the mid-1980s. The death rate of

---

[310] Sacred Congregation for Religious, "*Religiosorum Institutio*: Instruction on the Careful Selection and Training of Candidates for the States of Perfection and Sacred Orders," February 2, 1961, #29c, https://www.ewtn.com/catholicism/library/religiosorum-institutio-2007.

[311] Matthew Bunson, "Is Catholic Clergy Sex Abuse Related to Homosexual Priests?"-an interview with sociologist Fr. Paul Sullins, National Catholic Register, November 2, 2018, https://www.ncregister.com/news/is-catholic-clergy-sex-abuse-related-to-homosexual-priests.

priests from AIDS is at least four times that of the general population, the newspaper said."[312] Yet, the reporter notes a Church leader's incredible response: "Kansas City Bishop Raymond Boland says the AIDS deaths show that priests are human."[313] Explaining his shock and exasperation with the whole matter, Fr. Shaughnessy writes,

> From almost all sides one heard the complaint "Why doesn't somebody do something?" Why not indeed. A large part of the answer is implicit in the remarkable response to the situation tendered by Bishop Boland. To aver that a priest shows he is human by dying of AIDS is to say either that yielding to this sort of temptation is something that might happen to any normal person or that it is somehow natural to our human state to engage in acts of passive consensual sodomy, from which the resultant infection takes its predictable course. In reality, the fact that priests die of AIDS proves that they commit sin, by which they show not that they are more genuinely human but that they act in a sub-human manner; sub-human not in any special sense, but in the ordinary sense in which each of us falls short of his true human dignity by sinning, whatever our sin may be.
>
> But Bishop Boland, like many of his brethren, is unwilling to concede any moral component to the phenomenon. "I would never ask a priest how he got [AIDS]," he told Thomas, "just like nobody asked me two years ago how I got cancer of the colon. But I would provide for him. I would not write him off and say, "Because you've got AIDS and because there are doubts about how one can acquire it, therefore you're not a good priest." Well, let's take the case of a three-year-old girl brought into the emergency room with a broken jaw and cigarette burns on her rib cage. Suppose the hospital personnel said, "Look, there's more than one way to pick up these

---

[312] Paul Shaughnessy, "The Gay Priest Problem," Dossier (March/April 2001), initially retrieved on 4/22/2002 at http://catholic.net/rcc/Periodicals/Dossier/2001-04/article4.html. Now available at https://www.catholicculture.org/culture/library/view.cfm?recnum=12047.

[313] Paul Shaughnessy, "The Gay Priest Problem," Dossier (March/April 2001).

injuries, and the girl's medical treatment will be the same whatever the cause, so there's no point in asking how she got them."[314]

In 2019, while I was engaged as a catechist in my parish, I completed the mandatory background process and training that is now in place through the Virtus.org platform, which is intended to help church organizations prevent wrongdoing, manage risk, and improve service to their communities through education, training, and best practices. As part of the training and in light of the clergy sexual abuse scandal, the parish showed a video on the protection of children. I was very surprised to see Bishop Raymond Boland, now bishop emeritus of Kansas City, with a prominent speaking role in the video. Given the narrative above, he would not have been my choice to speak credibly on this issue.

In the same article, Fr. Shaughnessy also quotes a story reported ten years earlier in the *National Catholic Reporter*, saying the liberal National Catholic Reporter cited this example as typical:

> "'Father Smith (not his real name) is a Jesuit priest working in a Philadelphia parish in one of the older parts of the city. He is a closeted gay priest and does not want his name used. "In my worst moments," he said, "I fear I will have been a collaborator in supporting an institution that oppresses gay people...." He said he became a Jesuit after falling in love with an older, 40-year-old Jesuit priest. Smith was 20 then and studying at St. Joseph's College in Philadelphia. "As a Catholic priest, I know there would be no church without gay people....I assume priests are gay until proven otherwise.'"

In the same vein, such priests routinely gloat about the fact that gay bars in big cities have special "clergy nights," that gay resorts have set-asides for priests, and that in certain places the diocesan apparatus is controlled entirely by gays. What is significant is that these are not claims made by their opponents, not accusations fired off by right-wing

---

[314] Paul Shaughnessy, "The Gay Priest Problem," Dossier (March/April 2001).

Catholics in a fit of paranoia; rather they are gays' words about gays themselves. Their boasts include having blackmailed the Connecticut Catholic Conference into reversing its opposition to a gay rights law by threatening to "out" gay bishops—a reversal that is difficult to understand without resort to the blackmail explanation....Hence, their influence must be gauged not only by their numbers, but by the focus and force of their hostility. To this end, it is instructive to ponder the following message (below) to his fellow gay clergy by South Africa's Bishop Reginald Cawcutt, penned in response to a rumor that Cardinal Joseph Ratzinger's Congregation for the Doctrine of the Faith was about to issue a letter prohibiting the acceptance of gay seminarians.

> "'Kill [Ratzinger]? Pray for him? Why not just f—him??? Any volunteers—ugh!!!...I do not see how he can possibly do this—but...if he does, lemme repeat my statement earlier— that I will cause lotsa s—for him and the Vatican. And that is a promise. My intention would be simply to ask the question what he intends doing with those priests, bishops (possibly "like me") and cardinals...who are gay. That should cause s— enough. Be assured dear reverend gentlemen, I shall let you know the day any such outrageous letter reaches the desks of the ordinaries of the world.'"

Bishop Cawcutt's actual communication, be it noted, contained no prudish dashes.[315]

Cawcutt resigned in July 2002.

This prevalence of homosexual behavior among some clergy and Church leaders is a serious issue and will undoubtably make this matter very contentious and difficult to solve.

Impact on Screening Candidates for the Priesthood

This prevalence of homosexual sympathies within some quarters of the Church has in turn impacted the screening process of aspirants to the

---

[315] Paul Shaughnessy, "The Gay Priest Problem," Dossier (March/April 2001).

priesthood as well as the selection of episcopal candidates. It transforms the problem into a cyclic and multigenerational issue when those with such sympathies perpetuate the problem by selecting candidates with a similar persuasion. In the same article referenced above, Fr. Shaughnessy writes, "One religious order that doesn't require the test [to determine sexual orientation] is the Society of the Precious Blood. The Rev. Mark Miller, provincial director of the Kansas City province, said the testing raises issues that he does not wish to address. 'When you ask a question, you need to know why you are asking it,' Miller said. 'The answers that would come up put it in a category where we don't want to go.'"[316]

As an active homosexual subculture perpetuates itself multi-generationally, some have protected their own and leveraged their positions once inside the power structure. Sub-groups have always existed in one form or another. When I was in the seminary, I heard the expression "Foreign Born Irish (FBI)," referring to the Irish-born priests in America who formed a tightly-knit clique. Today, some priests speak of the "gay mafia."

Why Bishops Won't Act

In the same article, under the heading of "Why Bishops Won't Act," Fr. Shaughnessy writes,

> I define as corrupt, in a sociological sense, any institution that has lost the capacity to mend itself of its own initiative and by its own resources, an institution that is unable to uncover and expel its own miscreants. It is in this sense that the principal reason why the action necessary to solve the gay problem won't be taken is that the episcopacy in the United States is corrupt, and the same is true of the majority of religious orders. It is important to stress that this is a sociological claim, not a moral one.
>
> By the same token, in claiming the US episcopacy is corrupt, I am not claiming that the number of scoundrel bishops

[316] Paul Shaughnessy, "The Gay Priest Problem," Dossier (March/April 2001).

is necessarily any higher than it was when the episcopacy was healthy. I am simply pointing to the fact that, as an agency, the episcopacy has lost the capacity to do its own housecleaning, especially, but not exclusively, in the arena of sexual turpitude. Can you name a single instance in which the district attorney or the media did not get there first?[317]

A 2019 article by Stephen Wayne documents an interview with Fr. D. Paul Sullins by the news service *Church Militant*. Discussing his new report cited in chapter VIII, Sullins was asked what role the bishops have had in propagating the abuse. Fr. Sullins replied, "In the past, bishops enabled the crisis by ordaining homosexual men to the priesthood, despite the clear guidance of the popes that this was not to be done. Bishops also allowed priests to continue to prey on child victims, sometimes shielding them from exposure and using nondisclosure payments to keep victims silent. Today, the bishops are collectively compounding the problem by a lack of transparency about their role in enabling the abuse and avoiding declaring politically uncomfortable teachings of the Church about the sinfulness of homosexual behavior or the ideals of the gay lifestyle."[318]

What Has Attracted So Many Homosexuals to the Priesthood

On several occasions, George Weigel, biographer of Pope St. John Paul II, has commented on the state of the clergy at the beginning of the pontificate of John Paul II. Weigel has described it as being in the worst condition since the sixteenth century. Thousands of priests had left active ministry: "Between 1966 and 1972, there were nearly 10,000 such priests [seeking dispensation from their obligations] in the U.S. alone."[319]

---

[317] Paul Shaughnessy, "The Gay Priest Problem," Dossier (March/April 2001).

[318] Stephen Wynne, "Researcher Links Abuse Crisis to Influx of Gay Clergy," Church Militant, June 18, 2019, https://www.churchmilitant.com/news/article/fr-paul-sullins.

[319] Martin W. Pable, "Priesthood and Celibacy," Chicago Studies 20, no. 1 (Spring 1981): 70.

In a 2017 article titled "How the Catholic Priesthood Became an Unlikely Haven for Many Gay Men," author Ross Benes, who wrote a book called *The Sex Effect*, said he

> came across many scholars who suggested that preventing priests from marrying altered the makeup of the priesthood over time, unintentionally providing shelter for some devout gay men to hide their sexual orientation....Because the church denounces all gay sex, some devout gay men pursue the celibate priesthood as a self-incentive to avoid sex with men, which can help them circumvent perceived damnation....
>
> In the last half century there's also been an increased "gaying of the priesthood" in the West. Throughout the 1970s, several hundred men left the priesthood each year, many of them for marriage. As straight priests left for domestic bliss, the proportion of remaining priests who were gay grew....
>
> Sexual sublimation is by far the most common theory in the literature as to why there are so many gay priests. There has also been speculation that as a discriminated-against minority group, gay men may be more sensitive to empathize with people—a strong desire to help others leads some of these men to the altruistic priesthood....
>
> The U.S. Conference of Catholic Bishops' National Review Board reported that "certain homosexual men appear to have been attracted to the priesthood because they mistakenly viewed the requirement of celibacy as a means of avoiding struggles with their sexual identities." As gay former-priest Christopher Schiavone put it, "I thought I would never need to tell another person my secret, because celibacy would make it irrelevant."[320]

Perhaps for others, the fraternity of other gay men was an attraction. There can be no pregnancies in homosexual activity, no trace or evidence to give scandal.

---

[320] Ross Benes, "How the Catholic Priesthood Became an Unlikely Haven for Many Gay Men," Slate, April 20, 2017, https://slate.com/human-interest/2017/04/how-the-catholic-priesthood-became-a-haven-for-many-gay-men.html.

The Church is dealing with this issue of homosexuality on two fronts: those already ordained and those being considered as candidates for formation. As to the latter, in 2002 the Congregation for Catholic Education "proposed guidelines on psychological testing for seminary candidates. Church officials view homosexuality as a potential problem that could be disclosed by testing. Church officials, who asked not to be named, said the Vatican was not trying to impose an arbitrary norm against homosexuals but was trying to make 'prudential decisions' based on individual cases at the seminary level. They noted that the Vatican views the issue as mainly dealing with future priests, not those already ordained."[321]

As for those already ordained, I will cite a December 2, 2018, article referencing a new book by Pope Francis, in which the reporter opens with the following sentence: "Men with deep-rooted homosexual tendencies should not be admitted to the Catholic clergy, and it would be better for priests who are actively gay to leave than lead a double life, Pope Francis says in a new book."[322] I resoundingly agree.

Bishops certainly appear conflicted on this issue. Some leaders are still in denial about any link between homosexual behavior and clergy sexual abuse. Some, pressured by societal forces and wanting to appear welcoming and pastoral, must still be consistent with, and accountable to, the Church's teaching on homosexuality in true charity. As the final report of the 1985 Synod of Bishops recounted, "doctrinal and pastoral responsibilities" cannot create a "false opposition."[323] Sound doctrine is the basis of a sound moral life. Some have incorrectly interpreted this axiom to mean that doctrinal positions can be overlooked in the effort to be pastoral. But a better interpretation of the axiom means that pastors must not water down doctrinal positions in order to be compassionately

---

[321] John Thavis, "Screening out Homosexual Candidates," Catholic News Service, 2002, retrieved 4/2/2002.

[322] Philip Pullella, "Be Celibate or Leave the Priesthood, Pope Tells Gay Priests," Reuters, Dec. 2, 2018, https://www.reuters.com/article/us-pope-homosexuals-book/be-celibate-or-leave-the-priesthood-pope-tells-gay-priests-idUSKB-N1O10K7.

[323] *The Extraordinary Synod—1985*, (Boston, MA: St. Paul Editions,1985), 49.

pastoral. Most bishops continue to feel the pressure for more priests. Finally, still others may be acting in self-interest due to their own orientation. These pressures must be peeled away so we can see the solution with clarity. While this matter is likely to be a tumultuous part of change in the Church, the bishops must not act like "prisoners in the system."

XV

The Shortage of Priests and Priesthood Today

Among the contextual factors in the clergy sexual abuse crisis is the ongoing shortage of priests and, among practical considerations, the investment required to bring a candidate to ordination. The Church is a sacramental Church. The sacraments are outward signs instituted by Christ to support the Catholic faithful in their journey to their heavenly inheritance; they are the primary and ordinary means of grace. Christ empowered His twelve apostles and their successors, the bishops, to go out into the world, sanctifying and healing in these signs that remind us that Christ is with us until the end of time.

The bishop, who governs his locality, jurisdiction, or diocese, cannot do so alone. From the earliest days, he had coworkers—deacons and priests—who shared in varying degrees in the ministerial priesthood of Christ, who is Priest, Prophet, and King. With a dwindling number of new vocations, a diocesan priestly median age of sixty-plus, and a sense of stewardship for the sunk costs of over $250,000 in seminary training for each priest,[324] many bishops were inclined to go the extra mile for their priests, especially as they consulted with their episcopal brethren for shared strategies and common methods of dealing with aberrant behavior. (If a candidate for priesthood was accepted during his undergraduate years, the cost was even higher.) For reference, and for contrast, the average cost to onboard a new employee in most organizations in 2015 was about $4,000, according to Deloitte.

Some bishops retained misaligned clergy, treated their behavior as a moral weakness, and sought to rehabilitate and reform them, and were sometimes unaware of the gravity and scope of the disorder. Sadly, in other instances they *were* aware and handled matters egregiously. It is reasonable to estimate the cost of rehabilitative and clinical treatment for credibly accused clergy as being between $12,000 and $25,000, though it is perhaps a small price to pay to preserve the existing sunk costs. In hindsight, this approach proved to be penny-wise and pound-foolish. These factors and circumstances are relatively self-evident and, therefore, I will shift to reviewing the state of vocations today and the impact of this crisis on the faithful clergy.

Priestly Shortage after the Second Vatican Council

As to the first topic—the shortage of vocations—I have previously noted the mass exodus of clergy in the 1970s. Perhaps some left after they realized that the Second Vatican Council was not going to relax the obligation of celibacy or bring about other anticipated changes. Perhaps some were uncomfortable with the pivots in doctrinal emphasis resulting from the council, the liturgical experimentation it seemed to unleash, or the inpouring of pop psychology and the social sciences. Whatever the reasons, the mass exodus left a void.

When history is written, I think Catholics will look with sorrow on the deleterious effects of years of experimentation on some aspects of the liturgy over recent decades following Vatican II. The history

---

[324] Jerry J. Pokorsky, "What Price Truth?" The Catholic Thing, November 20, 2014, https://www.thecatholicthing.org/2014/11/20/what-price-truth-2/.

in England under Henry VIII and the subsequent Edwardian reforms of his son also proved to be a sad chapter. The liturgy was the most prized possession of the Catholic faithful, and villagers went to their death in attempting to ward off changes in the liturgy. Even then, the changes were intentionally subtle and intended to escape the notice of the people, until eventually later generations could no longer differentiate the changes. In recent times, this sense of free experimentation bled into other areas of Church life, including the expression of dogma and moral teaching.

To digest the magnitude of this exodus of priests, consider a snapshot of the crisis as provided by a December 2000 article by Russell Shaw in the periodical *Crisis* titled "The Priest's Confused Identity." The data he provides is from the time immediately prior to the sexual abuse crisis getting national attention in the series of *Boston Globe* articles in early 2002. Shaw writes,

> The number of priests in the United States has been falling for the past three decades, from more than 59,000 in 1970 to 46,000 now [the year 2000]. About 30,500 of these are diocesan priests, and some 15,000 are religious. During these years, according to the Center for Applied Research in the Apostolate (CARA), the percentage of active diocesan priests between the ages of 25 and 34 has declined by half (it is now about 5 percent), while the percentage over 55 has increased 50 percent (priests older than 55 now are about 59 percent of the total, including a substantial number over 75). The average age of diocesan priests in active ministry in the United States is 59. For religious priests, it is 63.
>
> Seminary enrollments have declined sharply, from slightly over 8,000 in theologates in 1967 to 1968 (5,000 diocesan; 3,000 religious) to fewer than 4,000 now (just over 3,000 diocesans, well under 1,000 religious). There has been a parallel drop in ordinations. As a result, CARA researchers report, "Dioceses now face the problem of too few active priests

available to administer parishes." In 1960, about 500 parishes lacked a resident pastor. Today, about 13 percent, nearly
2,500, do.[325]

Statistics Since the *Boston Globe* Stories

Have the trends changed since the *Boston Globe* news stories on the clergy
sexual abuse scandal in 2002 that heightened national attention? To illustrate its continued downward trajectory, I have gathered the following
data, presented as a bulleted list and chart 7.

1. According to the Center for Applied Research in the Apostolate
   (CARA), the following US figures from CARA provide a comparison of key data from 2000 to 2019:
   - diocesan clergy: 24,857, down from 30,607
   - religious: 11,072, down from 15,092
   - priestly ordinations: 468, up from 442
   - seminarians in theologates: 3,293, down from 3,474
   - religious sisters: 44,441, down from 79,814
   - religious brothers: 3,931, down from 5,662
   - parishes without a resident priest pastor: 3,572, up from 2,843[326]

2. The mean age of priests, both diocesan and religious, in the
   United States has steadily risen.

---

[325] Russell Shaw, "The Priest's Confused Identity," *Crisis Magazine* (Dec. 1, 2000),
https://www.crisismagazine.com/2000/the-priests-confused-identity.

[326] Center for Applied Research in the Apostolate, Frequently Requested Church
Statistics, Georgetown, https://cara.georgetown.edu/frequently-requested-
church-statistics/.

Chart 7:

	Year				
	1970	1985	1993	2001	2009
All Priests	35	52	57	61	63
Diocesan	34	51	55	59	62
Religious	37	55	60	64	66

Note: The mean age of priests, both religious and diocesan, has therefore ticked upward in each successive decade, as reflected in available surveys through 2009. Mary L. Gautier, Paul M. Perl, Stephen J. Fichter, *Same Call, Different Men: The Evolution of the Priesthood Since Vatican II* (Collegeville, MN: Liturgical Press, 2012).

Note that from 1970 to about 2000, there was a decline of 13,493 priests in the United States, or 449.77 per year. By contrast, from 2000 to 2018, the net decline was 9,770, or 514.21 per year, but only over a nineteen-year period instead of thirty. From 1970 to 2019, diocesan priests are down by one third, and religious order priests are down by nearly 50 percent. The annual decline is now at an even faster clip.

Why the Problem Persists

By looking at macro themes, it can be discerned that many young people struggle with commitment, particularly those who come from homes where it has been violated. Many parents, confused and disillusioned themselves, are not passing on any religious traditions in the home. They leave their children rudderless. Many young people might view celibacy as too lofty an ideal in today's sexualized culture. Many hear about the clergy sexual abuse crisis and have no desire to be part of any organization with that mess on their hands. Many, frankly, may not see enough holy priests or happy and joyful priests. All of these could be contributing factors as to why vocations are dwindling and have been skewing toward an older age. Young people have plenty to reckon with as they develop their own identities in a society all too happy to form them on their behalf. These conditions have led to what Russell Shaw called a "shortage...of vocational discernment."[327] Arguably, it is also a serious crisis of faith.

Challenges for Today's Priests

There is no single greater witness for vocations than the lives of those who live them. The joy and satisfaction they derive from their calling must be evident in order to be contagious. The clergy today bear many challenges and a confluence of circumstances. For many, these challenges have likely been something they didn't anticipate when first responding to the call. Today's environment is anything but stereotypical of a priest's life. Consider what they might be navigating:

- disappointment in, and betrayal by, the arrogance, behavior, and decisions of Church leaders and some of their brother priests
- the tensions that arise as their homosexual clergy–brethren may feel they are now under the microscope
- a struggle with the notions of healthy relationships and appropriate boundaries in today's environment
- some of the Catholic faithful who might view them with skepticism
- worry, as public figures, about whether they may someday be falsely accused and what due process will look like in a zero-tolerance environment
- the pressures of navigating a clerical culture without being accused of clericalism
- working alongside priests in an environment of generational gaps, as methods of formation have changed
- multicultural gaps, as clergy from various countries converge into one diocese

---

[327] Russell Shaw, "What Vocation Shortage?", America (The Jesuit Review), March 29, 2004 Issue, 1, https://www.americamagazine.org/issue/479/article/what-vocation-shortage.

- piety and conservative leanings being criticized and mocked; they might be called too "rigid," so, some conform to the program but maintain an "inner space"
- divisions on doctrine and spirituality that could be creating disunity

A Closer Examination of Today's Environment in the Church

Preaching

Some, even if they privately struggle, still preach in fidelity to the Church's teachings. Others preach something entirely different, claiming their views should be protected under the broad umbrella of "Catholic thought." And there are those who avoid topics altogether to avoid dividing a fractured congregation.

In this respect, homiletics (or preaching) has changed. Some "experts" tell us that the homily is not the place for catechesis, as those who attend Mass are already baptized and "in the fold," sharing at the banquet table. It is good and fitting to focus on the Scripture of the day, for "an effective homily takes its cue from the very nature of the Scriptures."[328] Those same Scriptures call Christians to deepen their interior life and respond to issues of social justice. But there is very little instruction or catechesis anymore for a captive audience you will see once a week if you're lucky—that is, before they wander off to a Protestant church, or no church, because they never had deep enough roots to understand their own tradition and the wind of scandal blew them away. Man's highest faculty is reason (*ratio*), and his "faith seeks understanding" (*fides quaerens intellectum*).[329] As Benedict XVI reminded the Church, "the catechetical aim of the homily must not be forgotten."[330] Benedict XVI's good

---

[328] United States Conference of Catholic Bishops (USCCB), *Preaching the Mystery of Faith: The Sunday Homily* (Washington DC, 2012), 27, https://www.usccb.org/resources/usccb-preaching-document_0.pdf

[329] St. Anselm of Canterbury (AD. 1033-1109), *The Proslogion*, AD. 1078.

[330] USCCB, *Preaching the Mystery of Faith*, 2.

counsel means that an arbitrary "wedge should not be driven between the proper content and style of the Sunday homily and the teaching of the Church's doctrine."[331]

In recent years, I've sensed an anti-intellectual trend in the Church; things seem to be dumbed down, while Catholics are searching for credible and substantive answers to counter the culture. Knowledge of the Church's teachings alone is no guarantee of sanctity, but, in the words of Catholic writer and theologian F.J. Sheed such "knowledge does serve love. It serves love in one way by removing misunderstandings which are in the way of love, which at the best blunt love's edge a little...each new thing learned and meditated about God is a new reason for loving him."[332] By encountering the inexhaustible mysteries of the Word of God, preaching must be unafraid to correct the spirit of the age, transforming the Christian by the renewal of their mind.[333]

Push to Desacralize the Priesthood

Let us not forget the forces within the Church that have long wanted to redefine the priesthood and are trying to maximize this sexual abuse crisis, and the shortage of priests, to that effect. Russell Shaw writes, "But the desacralizers have had an impact. Many Catholic intellectuals in western Europe and America now 'either reject the concept of ministerial priesthood or redefine it in ways that make it scarcely distinguishable from the concept of ministry in Protestant Congregationalism,' Avery Dulles, S.J., reports in his book, *The Priestly Office*."[334]

One hears an echo of this kind of thinking in the increasingly frequent use of the word "presider," not *priest*, for the ordained celebrant of the Eucharist. And I would add to this the relatively new title of "priest-minister," to designate a priest serving in a parish led by a non-priest pastoral leader, which is becoming increasingly frequent. All of

---

[331] USCCB, *Preaching the Mystery of Faith*, 24.

[332] F. J. Sheed, *Theology for Beginners* (Ann Arbor Michigan: Servant Books, 1981), 5.

[333] See Romans 12:12, *The New American Bible*, Catholic Mission Edition, St. Jerome Press (Wichita, Kansas: Devore & Sons, Inc., 1987 and 1981).

[334] Shaw, "The Priest's Confused Identity."

this terminology seems to be used in order to combat clericalism, without much thought for its ambiguity and long-term implications. This is similar to the intentional strategy used in England during the shift to Protestantism. Make enough subtle changes over time, and after a generation or two, no one will know the difference. Exceptions soon become the norm, sometimes by necessity and sometimes by design.

Real Renewal

Today does not seem to be an encouraging time for priests or prospective vocations, but it still can be for those who are committed to Christ, love His Church, and wish to generously manifest the catalyst for meaningful reform in their generous self-giving.

I will close this section on a positive and prophetic note. Both are taken from Pope St. John Paul II's "Letter to All Priests" on the occasion of Holy Thursday, 1979, and directly speak to the issues raised above.

Noting both the hierarchical and ministerial nature of the priesthood and confirming the Second Vatican Council's language that this priesthood differs "essentially and not only in degree" from "the common priesthood of the faithful,"[335] he writes, "It constitutes a special ministerium, that is to say 'service,' in relation to the community of believers. It does not, however, take its origin from that community, as though it were the community that 'called' or 'delegated.' The sacramental priesthood is truly a gift for this community and comes from Christ himself, from the fullness of His priesthood."[336]

In speaking of the indelible character imprinted on the soul through the sacrament of orders, he wrote something very prophetic:

> The people from among whom we have been chosen and for whom we have been appointed want above all to see in us such a sign and indication, and to this they have a right. It may

---

[335] Pope St. John Paul II, *Letter to All Priests, Holy Thursday 1979* (Washington, DC: United States Catholic Conference, 1979), 8.
[336] Pope St. John Paul II, *Letter to All Priests, Holy Thursday 1979*, 11.

sometimes seem to us that they do not want this, or that they wish us to be in every way "like them"; at times it even seems that they demand this of us. And here one very much needs a profound "sense of faith" and "the gift of discernment." In fact, it is very easy to let oneself be guided by appearances and fall victim to a fundamental illusion in what is essential. Those who call for the secularization of priestly life and applaud its various manifestations will undoubtedly abandon us when we succumb to temptation. We shall then cease to be necessary and popular. Our time is characterized by different forms of "manipulation" and "exploitation" of man, but we cannot give in to any of these. In practical terms, the only priest who will prove necessary to people is the priest who is conscious of the full meaning of his priesthood: the priest who believes profoundly, who professes his faith with courage, who prays fervently, who teaches with deep conviction, who serves, who puts into practice in his own life the programme of the Beatitudes, who knows how to love disinterestedly, who is close to everyone, and especially to those who are most in need."[337]

How does a priest come to appreciate the guidance of Pope St. John Paul II above, and yet intermingle with all so the sanctuary meets the streets, as Pope Francis calls for? It seems this is a training that is most needed. While not a favored theologian by orthodox Catholics for several reasons, the late Hans Küng makes a salient point when he writes, "When love is merely a decision of the will and not also a venture of the heart, it lacks genuine humanity. It lacks depth, warmth, intimacy, tenderness, cordiality. Christian charity often made little impression just because it had so little humanity."[338] Put another way, as theologian Karl Rahner, SJ, writes, "If a man can find in us another man, a real Christian, with a heart, who cares about him and is really delivering the message of

---

[337] Pope St. John Paul II, *Letter to All Priests, Holy Thursday 1979*, 17-18.
[338] Hans Küng, *On Being a Christian* (Garden City, New York: Fount Paperbacks, 1978), 262.

God's mercy towards us sinners, then more is happening than if we can hear the impressive and unmistakable hum of bureaucratic machinery."[339]

In his autobiography, St. Anthony Mary Claret notes, "Well, what does it profit a priest to have completed the ecclesiastical career and to have graduated in Sacred Theology and in Canon and Civil Law, if he has not the fire of charity? It will be unprofitable for him. Such a one will be of no use to others, because he will be as the engine without fire, and it may be that instead of being a help to others, as he should be, he will be a hindrance."[340]

My Message to Priests

Rejoice, beloved, in your calling! Rejoice in the bountiful gifts and mercy of the Lord! Rejoice in the opportunity to serve in the vineyard and share Christ by your preaching and example! Rejoice when you act *in persona Christi* in the sacraments! In the unique call of service to the Church and the world, you have generously responded with trust in the Word of God that does not return to Him empty. Your cup overflows when you drink from the well of Living Water. Because you have "put on a new man,"[341] as St. Paul says in Ephesians, you continually configure yourself to Christ, the Healer and Good Shepherd. This is priesthood!

Closing

In the talks I have given over the years, which are intended to stimulate self-reflection, I frequently use two very telling indictments against Christianity made by thinkers of note. The first is a quote universally attributed to German philosopher Friedrich Nietzsche: "I might believe in the Redeemer if his followers looked more redeemed." And Mahatma

---

[339] Karl Rahner, SJ, *The Christian Commitment* (New York: Sheed and Ward, 1963), 32–33.

[340] *The Autobiography of St. Anthony Mary Claret*, (Rockford, Illinois: TAN Books and Publishers, 1945, 1985), 120.

[341] Ephesians 4:24, *The New American Bible*.

Gandhi, when questioned if he would become a Christian, replied, "If it weren't for Christians, I'd be a Christian."[342]

What, then, appears to be lacking in the Christian witness? Two strong candidates are indispensable: love and joy. Christ's mandate of love is recorded in John's Gospel with these words: "This is how all will know that you are my disciples, if you have love for one another."[343] Love is the greatest of the theological virtues; it is a sharing in the unconditional love of God. Together with faith and hope, it is the source of Christian joy. The Christian's trust in the ever-faithful God is a source of confident joy. If Church leaders struggle to reflect these virtues, then what does that say to the world? Christians give witness to the Lord's invitation to the world not in words or theology alone, but in how their lives have been impacted by God's presence. This resulting joy is among the greatest fruits of Christianity and makes it both attractive and countercultural. The joy and happiness of the redemption in Christ will bear a witness noted by the believer and unbeliever alike.

In a quote attributed to Gandhi, he noted that "happiness is when what you think, what you say, and what you do are in harmony." The aspiration expressed in this quote from Gandhi is expressed symbolically every time Catholics stand at Mass to hear the Gospel proclaimed. They etch a sign of the cross on their forehead, lips and heart. It signifies that the Gospel is permeating our whole being, bringing about an internal cohesion and a tranquility of order, which is Christian peace—a fruit of the Holy Spirit.

[342] Lama Chuck Stanford, Arvind Khetia, "Voices of Faith: Why did Ghandi say, 'If it weren't for Christians, I'd be a Christian?'" Kansas City Star, April 17, 2015, https://www.kansascity.com/living/religion/article18756585.htm

[343] John 13:35, *New American Bible*.

XVI

The Bishop–Priest Relationship

As an essential element of organizational and pastoral culture in the Church, the relationship of a bishop to his priest is a unique contextual factor in the clergy sexual abuse crisis. The bishop is responsible for the care of all souls in his territory, including the souls of his coworkers, the priests, with whom he shares a particular sacramental closeness in Sacred Orders. A healthy friendship should develop, which Pope St. John Paul II characterized as a "fraternal and understanding affection."[344] This relationship has often led some bishops to view the sexual abuse by priests, particularly that of situational offenders, as a moral weakness in need of reform rather than focusing on the criminal character of the act and its ramifications. With the science of sexual abuse still in relative infancy, and with a disposition to love the sinner but hate the sin, the emphasis was

---

[344] Pope St. John Paul II, Homily of the Holy Father, addressed to priests, deacons and seminarians, Nov. 17, 1980, Fulda Cathedral, Fulda, Germany, https://www.vatican.va/content/john-paul-ii/es/homilies/1980/documents/hf_jp-ii_hom_19801117_fulda-germany.html.

to heal and reform the offender, in view of the compelling image of the Good Shepherd who rejoices with the return of the lost sheep (Matthew 18:12–14; the Prodigal Son, Luke 15:11–32).

The Three Orders of Ministerial Service

The three orders of ministerial service in the Church are bishop, priest, and deacon. The word *bishop* comes from the Greek word *episkopos*, meaning "overseer" or "guardian." The bishop possesses the fullness of Holy Orders, a gift to the Church "so that the truth of the gospel might remain intact for you."[345] The word *priest* comes from the Greek word *presbyteros*, which means "elder" or "senior." The word *deacon* comes from the Greek word *diakonia*, meaning "to serve" or "to support those in need." Though all baptized Christians share in Christ's role as priest, prophet, and king, from the beginning the twelve apostles chose their successors in the commission of ministerial service, given to them by Christ, through prayer and the laying on of hands (Acts 1:23–26, 13:1–3; 1 Timothy 4:14, 5:22; 2 Timothy 1:6; Titus 1:4).

With roots described in the New Testament, these roles were alive in the primitive Church. In the Latin or Western Church, through an unbroken chain of succession, any given bishop traces that succession back to the apostles, who after Christ's death went to various parts of the known world and established Christian communities, typically beginning in towns of significant size and import. So central was their role in the Christian community that St. Ignatius (AD 50–108) declared in his Letter to the Smyrnaeans, written circa AD 107, "You should regard the Eucharist as valid which is celebrated by the bishop or by someone he authorizes. Where the bishop is present, there let the congregation gather, just as where Jesus Christ is, there is the Catholic Church. It is a

---

[345] Galatians 2:5, *The New American Bible*, Catholic Mission Edition, St. Jerome Press (Wichita, Kansas: Devore & Sons, Inc., 1987 and 1981).

fine thing to acknowledge God and the bishop. He who pays the bishop honor has been honored by God."[346]

A bishop exercises religious governance in a territorial jurisdiction known as a diocese, named after the smaller, regional jurisdictions created by the Roman Emperor Diocletian (born AD 245). In overseeing this local Church, a bishop exercises pastoral care, including preaching the Gospel, upholding the faith that comes to us from the Apostles, overseeing the integrity of the liturgy and sacraments, helping the community to grow, and overseeing those in the clerical state.

As to this last duty, the relationship between a bishop and his priests is a special one, as they are coworkers in the harvest of the Lord. Various Church documents characterize the relationship as "Father–son," "filial," but also "fraternal," as brothers who share a common ministerial priesthood through Holy Orders. Bound by the priest's promise of obedience to his bishop, it is often marked by guidance, care, and mentorship, and based on openness, dialogue, and availability to each other. It is an essential element of organizational culture in the Church.

Key Church Documents Speaking of This Relationship

The documents of the Church that touch on the relationship between a bishop and his priests are quite numerous. The three cited below are particularly expressive and detailed on the topic.

1. *Pontificalis Romani*, June 18, 1968 (Liturgy and Rites of the Church): In the Rite of Consecration of a Bishop, the "sample" homily is rich with these themes, quoted here in part.

   In the person of the bishop, with his priests around him, Jesus Christ, who became High Priest forever, is present among you. Through the ministry of the bishop, Christ himself continues to proclaim the Gospel and to confer the mysteries of

---

[346] Cyril C. Richardson, ed., *Early Christian Fathers* (New York: Collier Books, 1970), 115.

faith on those who believe. Through the fatherly action of the bishop, Christ adds new members to his body….

The title of bishop is not one of honor but of function, and therefore a bishop should strive to serve rather than to rule. Such is the counsel of the Master: the greater should behave as if he were the least, and the leader as if he were the one who serves….

Since you are chosen by the Father to rule over his family, always be mindful of the Good Shepherd, who knows his sheep and is known by them and who did not hesitate to lay down his life for them.

As a father and a brother, love all those whom God places in your care. Love the priests and deacons who share with you the ministry of Christ.[347]

2. *Christus Dominus*, Decree on the Pastoral Office of Bishops in the Church, October 28, 1965: In section II-C, *Christus Dominus* addresses the bishop's relationship to the diocesan clergy. Number 28 reads, "All presbyters, both diocesan and religious, participate in and exercise with the bishop the one priesthood of Christ and are thereby constituted prudent cooperators of the episcopal order. In the care of souls, however, the first place is held by diocesan priests who are incardinated or attached to a particular church, for they have fully dedicated themselves in the service of caring for a single portion of the Lord's flock. In consequence, they form one presbytery and one family whose father is the bishop."[348]

Expounding on this familial theme, number 16 reads,

---

[347] The International Commission on English in the Liturgy, trans., *The Rites: Volume II,* (New York: Pueblo Publishing CO, 1980), 90-91.

[348] Pope St. Paul VI, Second Vatican Ecumenical Council Decree *Christus Dominus*, #28, October 28, 1965, https://www.vatican.va/archive/hist_councils/ii_vatican_council/documents/vat-ii_decree_19651028_christus-dominus_en.html.

In exercising their office of father and pastor, bishops should stand in the midst of their people as those who serve. Let them be good shepherds who know their sheep and whose sheep know them. Let them be true fathers who excel in the spirit of love and solicitude for all....

In order effectively to accomplish these things, bishops, "ready for every good work" (2 Tim. 2:21) and "enduring all things for the sake of the chosen ones" (2 Tim. 2:10), should arrange their life in such a way as to accommodate it to the needs of our times.

Bishops should always embrace priests with a special love since the latter to the best of their ability assume the bishops' anxieties and carry them on day by day so zealously. They should regard the priests as sons and friends and be ready to listen to them. Through their trusting familiarity with their priests they should strive to promote the whole pastoral work of the entire diocese.

They should be solicitous for the spiritual, intellectual and material welfare of the priests so that the latter can live holy and pious lives and fulfill their ministry faithfully and fruitfully....

With active mercy bishops should pursue priests who are involved in any danger or who have failed in certain respects.[349]

3. *Sacerdotalis Caelibatus*, (On Priestly Celibacy), Pope St. Paul VI, June 24, 1967: In this 1967 Encyclical Letter, Pope St. Paul VI more fully explores this relationship between bishops and priests.

It was you who called them and destined them to be priests; it was you who placed your hands on their heads; with you they are one in sharing the honor of priesthood by virtue of the sacrament of Orders; with you they are united in a spirit of trust and magnanimity....

It is your fraternal and kindly presence and deeds that must fill up in advance the human loneliness of the priest, which is

---

[349] Pope St. Paul VI, Second Vatican Ecumenical Council Decree *Christus Dominus*, #16.

so often the cause of his discouragement and temptations.... be their master, fathers, friends, their good and kind brothers, always ready to understand, to sympathize and to help. In every possible way encourage your priests to be your personal friends and to be very open with you. If they are your devoted friends and if they have a filial trust in you, your priests will be able... to open up their souls and to confide in you their difficulties in the certainty that they can rely on your kindness to be protected from eventual defeat, without a servile fear of punishment, but in the filial expectation of correction, pardon and help....

There will be times when you must exercise your authority by showing a just severity towards those few who, after having resisted your kindness, by their conduct cause scandal to the People of God; but you will take the necessary precautions to ensure their seeing the error of their ways.[350]

Calibrating the Relationship

While this relationship between bishop and priest is rightly close, it must still be grounded in truth and accountability. The impulse for fraternal correction and spiritual restoration cannot interfere with doing what is right for the circumstances.

In an April 2002 speech to US cardinals addressing the clergy sexual abuse crisis, Pope St. John Paul II included this statement reflecting a commitment to God's power to heal those in sin: "At the same time, even while recognizing how indispensable these criteria are [reliable criteria to ensure that such mistakes are not repeated], we cannot forget the power of Christian conversion, that radical decision to turn away from sin and back to God, which reaches to the depths of a person's soul and can work extraordinary change."[351] But clearly, accountability demands that

---

[350] Pope St. Paul VI, "*Sacerdotalis Caelibatus,*" Encyclical Letter, June 1967, #91, 93, 94, https://www.vatican.va/content/paul-vi/en/encyclicals/documents/hf_p-vi_enc_24061967_sacerdotalis.html.

[351] Pope St. John Paul II, *Address of John Paul II to the Cardinals of the United States,* Tuesday, April 23, 2002, Vatican City, https://www.vatican.va/content/john-paul-ii/en/

credibly accused offenders forfeit de facto any credibility to continue to serve in community leadership, as this poses danger and harm.

Further, credibly accused offenders must be reported to civil authorities. In David Cito's article in *Ave Maria International Law Journal* titled "The New Delicta Graviora Laws," Cito notes the responses of Msgr. Charles Scicluna, then Promoter of Justice for the Congregation for the Doctrine of the Faith, in a 2010 interview: "Msgr. Scicluna...stresses that 'the laws on sexual abuse have never been meant to prohibit the reporting of these crimes to the civil authorities.... It is an onerous duty, a Bishop reporting his Priest is comparable to a parent reporting his child.'"[352]

In summary, the disposition for forgiveness and reform of the offender that was founded in the special relationship between bishop and priest, combined with other factors, sometimes clouded the need for justice to be served. These other factors included scandal avoidance, a poor understanding of the disorder, reluctance to offer fraternal correction when early signs were manifest, and, in some cases, compromised bishops. On May 11, 2010, during a visit to Portugal, Pope Benedict addressed this topic, saying, among other things, that "forgiveness cannot be a substitute to justice."[353]

The reexamination of the relationship between bishop and priest in today's environment will create its own challenges. This is a time when priests need the support of their bishops more than ever, and when priests are viewed with an arms-length, independent-contractor status, and bishops become more guarded and cautious, priests may now feel a loss in this critical dimension of their priesthood.

---

speeches/2002/april/documents/hf_jp-ii_spe_20020423_usa-cardinals.html.

[352] Davide Cito, "The New Delicta Graviora Laws," *Ave Maria International Law Journal*, Vol. 1, Issue 1, ISSN no. 2375-2173 (Fall 2011): 90-116, 94, https://ave-marialaw-international-law-journal.avemarialaw.edu/Content/iljarticles/2011. Cito.DelictaGraviora.final.pdf.

[353] Cito, "The New Delicta Graviora Laws," 97.

XVII

Shortcomings in Canon Law

Lack of clarity and ineffective provisions in Canon Law that provide remedies for violations of social order in the Church were impactful as a contextual factor in the clergy sexual abuse scandal. These shortcomings in Canon Law complicated or exacerbated the often poorly exercised discretion of bishops in handling these cases. In tracing the incremental, concrete steps taken by popes John Paul II, Benedict XVI, and Francis, I will underscore six key areas in this chapter:

1. the failure to proceed with the concurrent jurisdiction of civil authorities
2. the Church Law's definition of a "minor" for violations of this nature
3. Canon Law's treatment of this behavior in proportion to its true severity
4. the statute of limitations for this offense

5. procedural steps that were needed to balance prompt action with the due process of law for the accused
6. accountability of Church leaders

I will also review the concerns of legal due process for the clergy and transparency as well as offer a reflection on Pope Francis's revision to the penal laws of the Code of Canon Law, promulgated just prior to the publication of this book.

Defining Canon Law

The word *canon* comes from the Greek and means a measuring rod, ruler, or normative measure or standard. This word was adopted to describe the body of books understood by the early Church to be the normative measure of divinely inspired writings, consistent with the teaching of the Apostles, and thus to be included in the New Testament.

In its relation to Church Law, the word *canon* dates back to the Council of Nicaea in AD 325 and describes that body of laws and legal principles that help govern the life of the Church. That law has continued to develop and evolve ever since. In this chapter, I am examining the Canon Law of the Latin or Western Church. But the development of Christianity witnessed various geographical differences in customs, traditions, and disciplines, such that other Eastern ecclesial communities in communion with Rome have their own traditions and laws, though many are shared with the West.

The two most recent codified bodies of Church Law followed ecumenical councils. As the council fathers (pope and bishops) of each gathered to address the Church's self-understanding (or ecclesiology), its role and posture in the world, and various theological and pastoral issues, the adaptation of its juridical–legislative norms followed. But the Church does not move fast. The 1917 Code, which was among the most comprehensive attempts in history to systematize the canons of the Church, came forty-seven years after the close of Vatican I (1869–1870), and the 1983 Code came along eighteen years after the close of Vatican II (1962–1965).

In promulgating the current version of Canon Law in 1983, Pope St. John Paul II reminded the Church in *Sacrae Disciplinae Leges* that "its purpose is…to create such an order in the ecclesial society that, while assigning the primacy to love, grace and charisms, it at the same time renders their organic development easier in the life of both the ecclesial society and the individual persons who belong to it. As the Church's principal legislative document founded on the juridical–legislative heritage of revelation and tradition, the Code is to be regarded as an indispensable instrument to ensure order both in individual and social life, and also in the Church's own activity."[354]

Providing some historical context to Canon Law, the online Encyclopedia Britannica includes the following entry: "Many scholars assert that a church cannot exist without authority—i.e., binding rules and organizational structures—and that religion and law are mutually inclusive.… International law owes its very origin to canonists and theologians, and the modern idea of the state goes back to the ideas developed by medieval canonists regarding the constitution of the church. The history of the legal principles of the relation of *sacerdotium* to *imperium*—i.e., of ecclesiastical to secular authority or of church to state—is a central factor in European history."[355]

Justice and Penalties

Because Canon Law regulates the discipline and order of the ecclesial community, it also reflects the beliefs and culture consistent with the Church's self-understanding, mission, structure, and organization.

---

[354] John Paul II, *Sacrae Disciplinae Leges*, Apostolic Constitution for the Promulgation of the New Code of Canon Law, January 25, 1983, https://www.vatican.va/content/john-paul-ii/en/apost_constitutions/documents/hf_jp-ii_apc_25011983_sacrae-disciplinae-leges.html.

[355] Ladislas M. Örsy, "Canon Law," *Encyclopedia Britannica*, Feb. 12, 2020, https://www.britannica.com/topic/canon-law.

Canon Law addresses a wide spectrum of topics, including but not limited to the sacraments, the handling of the goods of the Church, administrative processes, and penalties. With some exceptions, penalties may be applied to persons for acts or omissions in the external forum (visible or known to the public or the community) which cause harm. At various times in history, the Church had recourse to the state to enforce discipline as rulers had a mutual interest in seeking order and stability in society. Today, ecclesiastical law and civil law (laws of the state) are decidedly more distinct.

Why must a community of believers, called to love, have a law encompassing penalties? According to *The Code of Canon Law: A Text and Commentary*, the "disciplinary action taken by church authorities is not done precisely on their own initiative; it is rather the consequence of an action(s) of an individual who breaks or seriously disturbs his or her unity with the community."[356] Canonical penalties exist for the following reasons:

1. The faith community cannot be silent and idle when there are "significant breaches of its faith and order." [357]
2. After the breach, peace and order must be restored.
3. The response to the breach helps to restore reliance for those within and without the community, including the effect of deterrence.
4. The response is intended to reflect the Church's "redeeming, healing character...through faith and charity."[358]
5. The response is marked by a gentle, patient and pastoral charity (love is kind, gentle—1 Corinthians 13:4–7) and by fraternal correction (Galatians 2:11–14).[359]

---

[356] James A. Coriden, Thomas J. Green, and Donald E. Heintschel, eds., *The Code of Canon Law: A Text and Commentary* (New York/Mahwah: Paulist Press, 1985), 894. Commissioned by the Canon Law Society of America.

[357] Coriden, Green, and Heintschel, *The Code*, 894.

[358] Coriden, Green, and Heintschel, *The Code*, 894.

[359] Coriden, Green, and Heintschel, *The Code*, 894.

To What and Whom Penal Law Applies

The objects of ecclesiastical penal law are generally public offenses (acts or omissions) against the Church's faith or order that damage the Church's spiritual–moral integrity. Current Church Law (changed somewhat from the 1917 Code) more generally applies to persons of the Roman or Latin Rite who have either been baptized Catholic or were received into the Church and who have attained a sufficient age of reason, generally understood to be age seven and up (canons 1 and 11). Penal laws do not apply to those who have not reached age sixteen,[360] and even then they are applied with diminished imputability—or moral responsibility—until adulthood.[361]

I will only mention the 1917 Code as needed, because most of the recent clergy sexual abuse cases were handled using the superseding 1983 Code. The 1917 Code would have provided remedies to the Church for clergy sexual abuse up until 1983. For the purpose of illustration, the penal law of the Church serves as a means to "repair the scandal, restore justice, reform the offender."[362] Canon 1341 of the 1983 Code continues in the spirit of canon 2214.2 of the 1917 Code. Penal law uses a legal-pastoral framework to resolve offenses or violations and resulting harm in the external forum.

Reforming the Offender

It is opportune here to say a word about one of the pillars of penal law: reforming the offender. Just like in civil law, Church penal law envisions multiple purposes for its prescriptions such as the rehabilitation of the offender and restoring the offender to normalized relationship with the community whenever possible, justice which can include punishment, and deterrence. Put succinctly, the goal is the healing and recovery of

---

[360] Coriden, Green, and Heintschel, *The Code*, canon 1323, 902.

[361] Coriden, Green, and Heintschel, *The Code*, canon 1324, 903.

[362] Coriden, Green, and Heintschel, *The Code*, 911, and http://www.jgray.org/codes/1917CIC.txt.

a lost sheep (Luke 15:4-7) and the avoidance of an offender's hopeless despair like that of Judas (Matthew 27:5). Because the approach is characterized as a "gentle, patient, and pastoral charity" cited above, this has led some thinkers to question "whether at times a non-penal pastoral approach would be more appropriate than inflicting a penalty in leading an individual to a fuller life in Christ."[363] It is on this very note, however, that the balance between healing and justice was distorted in this crisis. In instances involving grave severity and the persistence of the behavior, the offense could trigger a separation from the community in recognition of irreparable scandal or harm.

Nature of the Priesthood and Canon Law

It is important to understand both the nature of ministerial priesthood in Catholic theology and the rights afforded to such persons under Canon Law. People often, understandably, speak in frustration about abusive priests, saying in effect, "Just remove him from the priesthood if he has committed these acts."

A priest receives the Sacrament of Holy Orders. The sacraments, instituted by Christ, are outward signs that effect inner grace. Three of the seven sacraments of the Church, including Holy Orders, are nonrepeatable and change one's ontological character, placing a permanent, indelible, and irremovable seal. The other two are Baptism and Confirmation. Therefore, one cannot remove or dismiss a priest from his ontological priesthood once he is validly ordained. He can, however, be removed from the clerical state.

Catholic priesthood differs from hereditary Jewish Levitical priesthood. As the Book of Hebrews says, Melchizedek is an archetype of Christ: "His name first means righteous king, and he was also 'king of Salem,' that is, king of peace. Without father, mother, or ancestry, without beginning of days or end of life, thus made to resemble the Son

---

[363] Coriden, Green, and Heintschel, *The Code*, 894.

of God, he remains a priest forever."[364] A Catholic priest shares in the priesthood of Christ, the eternal High Priest, so much so that even if he were to be excommunicated, he could absolve a penitent in danger of death.[365]

There are two elements necessary to exercise the priestly office: a valid ordination and the legal authority to exercise this ministry in the visible Church. Theologically, an ordination, in order to be valid, must have a minister with episcopal orders who has the intention to ordain, a recipient who is a baptized male with the free intention to receive the sacrament, and the laying on of hands along with the prescribed prayer of ordination. Once ordained, the priest must have the authorization of the bishop to licitly exercise his ministry publicly. Through administrative decree or penalty, a priest may be temporarily suspended from exercising that ministry.

But penalties involving a more perpetual or irrevocable consequence—for example, removing a priest from the clerical state (laicization)—tend to involve more thorough and cumbersome processes under Church Law. A judicial process would be invoked, and a priest, attempting to exercise due process, might resist and appeal such penalties. This resistance is where some of the challenges lie.

Key Themes and Characteristics of the 1983 Code: Subsidiarity and Discretion

Just as nations and societies have laws and structures that come from their respective constitutions, Canon Law bears the mark of its own structure and self-understanding. The 1983 Code emanates from the Church's self-understanding from the Second Vatican Council. Among the Code's hallmarks is that, though the Church is hierarchical, it is the people of God, sharing in a common priesthood through baptism, called to share in Christ's work as King, Prophet, and Priest in the world, each

---

[364] Hebrews 7:2–3, *The New American Bible*, Catholic Mission Edition, St. Jerome Press (Wichita, Kansas: Devore & Sons, Inc., 1987 and 1981).

[365] Coriden, Green, and Heintschel, *The Code*, canon 976, 688.

according to the degree of his or her own state. Certain understandings flow from this view.

The principles of subsidiarity and discretion counter a false view that the Church is monarchical and that rights and duties are somehow merely delegated from upper levels of the hierarchy. The notion manifests itself, among other places, in the governing role of bishops in their diocese. They are not seen as delegated envoys or territorial representatives of the pope. Rather, they have an authority inherent in their own pastoral office. Therefore, the complementary concepts of collegiality and subsidiarity are reflected in the Vatican II documents.

The term *collegiality* refers to the manner of governing the Church in which the pope, the bishop of Rome, works in collaboration with his fellow bishops, respecting the autonomy that comes inherently from each bishop's pastoral office. The term *subsidiarity* refers to the approach in which certain decisions are pushed down to the lowest possible level, the diocesan level, and rest with the bishop—except for those items expressly reserved by the Holy See.[366] For example, canon 87 of the 1983 Code reads, "As often as he judges that a dispensation will contribute to the spiritual good of the faithful, the diocesan bishop can dispense from both universal and particular disciplinary laws established for his territory or for his subjects by the supreme authority of the Church."[367] In the application of penalties, subsidiarity "should facilitate the adaptation of penal discipline to the concrete circumstances of different persons and places."[368] Thus, decisions to address an abusive priest were typically handled locally.

Discretion and Guiding Principles in the Recourse to Penalties

The elements of discretion and due process are guiding principles seen throughout the application of penal laws. Canon 221 prescribes that one

---

[366] Coriden, Green, and Heintschel, 8–13.
[367] Coriden, Green, and Heintschel, 65.
[368] Coriden, Green, and Heintschel, 896.

has "a right not to be punished with canonical penalties except in accordance with the norm of law."[369] This suggests there should not be an arbitrariness to the infliction of penalties. Penalties are to be just, suggesting proportionality. Canon 1317 states that "penalties should be established to the extent to which they are truly necessary to provide more suitably for ecclesiastical discipline. Dismissal from the clerical state, however, cannot be established by particular law."[370] In other words, the infliction of any penalty must be truly necessary, and the dismissal of a priest from the clerical state cannot be initiated through a local precept, only through the universal law of the Church.

Canon 1341 provides the following guidance: "Only after he has ascertained that scandal cannot sufficiently be repaired, that justice cannot sufficiently be restored and that the accused cannot sufficiently be reformed by fraternal correction, rebuke, and other ways of pastoral care, is the ordinary [the bishop] then to provide for a judicial or administrative procedure to impose or to declare penalties."[371] In other words, every nonpenal pastoral step or alternative must be considered whenever possible: "No sanction can be imposed unless a person has externally violated a law or precept, has done so gravely, and is personally imputable for the act."[372]

In addition to discretion and the use of penalties as a last resort, there is one other characteristic or guiding principle of Church Law worth noting. Canon 1316 calls for penal laws to be enacted uniformly in a city or region. I believe this is why clergy sexual abuse cases were handled so similarly in dioceses across the country, as bishops conferred with one another both privately and in their formal conferences.

---

[369] Coriden, Green, and Heintschel, 899.
[370] Coriden, Green, and Heintschel, canon 1317, 899.
[371] Coriden, Green, and Heintschel, canon 1341, 911.
[372] Coriden, Green, and Heintschel, canon 1321.1, 155.

The Weight of Discretion

While discretion may appear liberating, any executive officer of an organization knows that processing critical pieces of information can be overwhelming. Sometimes it can stifle decisions or lead to poor decisions. But when an organization's values are clear, including the ranking of competing values into a hierarchy of importance, decisions should become clearer and more resolute. Below I list some of these deliberative considerations that may have been in play before the Church enacted recent reforms that crystalized its value system and process for handling cases of clergy sexual abuse. For each individual case, such deliberations and proposed solutions are meant to be the result of a calculation of the three pillars of penal law described above: repairing the scandal, restoring justice, and reforming the offender.

1. After an administrative investigation, can it be ascertained that an offense has occurred, or is there a serious suspicion that one has committed an offense?
2. If the above is as yet undetermined, how will the good name of both the priest and the accuser be preserved in the community?
3. If an offense has been determined, how grave were the consequences? How visible and damaging were they to the external forum? Did the offense cause physical harm, injury, danger, scandal, and/or harm to souls?
4. Has the priest admitted to the offense? Is the priest willing to be laicized?
5. What is known about the cause of the offense and its severity, and what (if any) factors are affecting or impeding imputability (moral responsibility), such as mental illness or alcohol or substance abuse?
6. How will the due process for the accused be preserved?
7. How can justice and healing come to the victim?
8. Who knows about the offense? Who has a right to know? How has the parish community been affected, so that this can be factored in crafting a remedy?

9. What are the options for remedy in Canon Law? Should the bishop prescribe a discretionary penalty or a preceptive penalty (prescribed in the law or precept)? This could include postponing, suspending, or refraining from applying the penalty; waiving the penalty; or weighing penalties in cases of multiple offenses. Is the offense serious enough to invoke the elaborate judicial process under Canon Law to remove the priest from the clerical state? (This is viewed as a cumbersome last resort.)

Other Factors Considered

In addition to details about the specific offense, a bishop may also weigh or be affected by the factors below.

1. Is reform or rehabilitation of the offending priest an option here for his true spiritual well-being? Perhaps this is a first-time offense by a priest who otherwise seemed to lead an exemplary life.
2. What has been the uniform practice among bishops across the country in cases such as this?
3. Are there any issues concerning the priest's material well-being that would cause him to struggle if he lost his clerical state?
4. If the offense is not too severe, will assigning a public penalty to the priest worsen the scandal?
5. Has due weight been given to any counsel from diocesan attorneys on potential liability?
6. Has the bishop been compromised by his own present or past behavior?

Problem One: Failure to Involve Civil Authorities with Concurrent Jurisdiction

With this essential background information regarding the guiding principles of Church Law, one can see that many bishops used their discretion intentionally to not refer sexual abuse cases to civil authorities with concurrent jurisdiction.[373] While each case involved a unique set of circumstances and there was a spectrum of severity in the behavior of the priests, in some cases the bishops made decisions to avoid invoking the most severe penalties. They went to great lengths to avoid or repair scandal by meeting with the accuser in isolated cases, perhaps offering confidential settlements in the name of justice, and then sought other pastoral ways of handling the credibly accused priest, such as temporary suspension, penance, and therapy. This pattern took place across the United States.

Solution to Problem One: Involving Civil Authorities

In the United States Catholic Conference of US Bishops' Charter for the Protection of Children and Young People—from its 2002 draft through its current revision—article IV requires a diocese to report an allegation of the sexual abuse of a minor (even if the victim is no longer a minor) to the public authorities. The diocese is to comply with all applicable civil laws and cooperate in their investigation. Diocesan officials are also expected to advise the victim of his or her right to make a report to civil authorities, if this has yet to be done, and to support this right. The diocese will also conduct a concurrent investigation on the priest's conduct and, if the evidence is credible, "removal from ministry is required whether or not the cleric is diagnosed by qualified experts as a pedophile or as suffering from a related sexual disorder that requires professional treatment."[374]

---

[373] Failure to contact police (Cardinal Edward Eagan, while bishop of Bridgeport, Conn) as chronicled in MSNBC Staff and Wire Writers, "Egan said to have concealed priest's love affair with teen," April 12, 2002, retrieved April 12, 2002, http://www.msnbc.com/news/732931.asp?pne=msn&cp1=1. And Staff writers, "Egan: I was unaware of sex abuse by priests," CT Post, February 11, 2012, https://www.ctpost.com/news/article/Egan-I-was-unaware-of-sex-abuse-by-priests-3295841.php. transferring of clergy (Cardinal Bernard Law, who transferred Fr. Paul Shanley); among many other examples.

[374] US Conference of Catholic Bishops, "Promise to Protect, Pledge to Heal: Charter for the Protection of Children and Young People," 27, USCCB (website), last

It is not clear what standard will be used to readmit an accused priest into active ministry. If, for example, the civil authorities conclude that there is insufficient evidence, due to the high bar used for successful prosecution, will that be the applicable standard for permitting a priest to return to active ministry? What role, if any, does the diocesan review board, made up mostly of laypersons, play in this decision? What are the rules of governance for such boards? Can their recommendations still be overridden? At the time of this writing, I am not aware of the answers to these serious questions. I think that both Catholics in the pew and priests serving in parishes will want to know the answers.

A Word about Canonical Penalties

Before I probe the remaining deficiencies in Canon Law that require remedy, I must describe two key types of canonical penalties. Most penalties are inflicted or imposed by a competent authority, like a bishop (*ferendae sententiae*). Only a few penalties relating to the gravest offenses are automatically incurred by virtue of the offender's act itself (*latae sententiae*), similar to a "strict liability" in secular law parlance.

Most laws in secular society do not carry strict liability, wherein the violator automatically incurs the penalty by virtue of doing the act itself. Most crimes in secular law require consideration not only of the act (*mala in se*) but also an examination of the intention (*mens rea*, or the mental element) of the actor as well as the elements surrounding the action and attendant circumstances. Consider, for example, the elements the Church defines as conditions for mortal sin: namely, grave subject matter, full knowledge, and the deliberate consent of the will. Some circumstances, like substance abuse, passion, and pathology, can impair knowledge and the free exercise of the will and thereby can mitigate imputability, even if the act itself is a grave subject matter. Secular laws also acknowledge some offenses as being "crimes of passion," which can partially mitigate culpability or a violator's sentencing.

revision: June 2018, https://www.usccb.org/test/upload/Charter-for-the-Protection-of-Children-and-Young-People-2018-final(1).pdf.

Problem Two: The Age of a Minor

The specific violation or offense addressed in Canon Law that most commonly applies to the sexual abuse crisis is canon 1395.2: a violation against the sixth commandment of the Decalogue. Catholics understand the sixth commandment, "You shall not commit adultery,"[375] to broadly encompass the totality of human sexual expression in dignity and in accordance with God's law. The canon states, "If a cleric has otherwise committed an offense against the sixth commandment of the Decalogue with force or threats or publicly or with a minor below the age of sixteen, the cleric is to be punished with just penalties, including dismissal from the clerical state if the case warrants it."[376] Because this canon is found in the Code, the Church already anticipates the possibility of this occurrence, due to its history with these problems. A prominent example from history includes a letter from St. Peter Damian to Pope Leo IX in 1049 complaining about clerics committing these crimes and yet remaining in office.

Thus, problem two lies in the definition of a minor. Canon 97 defines a minor with the following words: "a person who has completed the eighteenth year, below this age, a person is a minor."[377] Canon 1395 draws a line for the offense "below the age of sixteen."[378] It is unclear why this age was chosen, but, perhaps because it is the Church's universal law, it reflects the age of consent in many countries across the globe. A 2021 case in France involving three firefighters accused of sexually assaulting a teenage girl has exposed similar problems in French law. In the United States, one does not reach the age of consent until they are eighteen; also, in cases involving minors in their late teens, the age differential between perpetrator and victim is a considered factor. As for specific sexual crimes, one would have to conduct a state-by-state survey to determine the age demarcation in the law at the time of the offense.

---

[375] Exodus 20:14, *New American Bible.*

[376] Coriden, Green, and Heintschel, canon 1395.2, 929.

[377] Coriden, Green, and Heintschel, canon 97, 71.

[378] Coriden, Green, and Heintschel, canon 1395.2, 929.

Solution to Problem Two: Clarifying the Age of a Minor

Realizing that the age in canon 1395 did not capture the full age spectrum of victims nor square with comparable laws in other jurisdictions, the Holy See in 1994 "granted an indult to the Bishops of the United States (and eventually to other jurisdictions): the age for the canonical crime of sexual abuse of a minor was raised to 18."[379] An *indult* is a permission by a competent authority, in this case Pope St. John Paul II, to proceed with something not otherwise sanctioned by the common or universal law of the Church.

In chapter VII, I characterized other situations and vulnerable members that could fall under the category of sexual abuse. Since abuse against minors is only one such situation, Pope Benedict XVI and Pope Francis added additional categories of offenses and expanded abuse to include the use of child pornography:

1. Benedict XVI. In revising the norms in 2001, the following was added:
   A. Anyone over eighteen who is developmentally disabled is equated to a minor for purposes of applying these laws.
   B. The list of delicts was expanded to include the "acquisition, possession, or distribution of pornographic images of minors under the age of 14...in any way and by any means."[380] This was further amended on May 3, 2011, to apply the federal legal age for defining this delict, which is eighteen in the United States of America.

---

[379] Congregation for the Doctrine of the Faith, "The Norms of the Motu Proprio '*Sacramentorum Sanctitatis Tutela*': Historical Introduction," 2001, https://www.vatican.va/resources/resources_introd-storica_en.html.

[380] William Cardinal Levada, Prefect, "Letter to Bishops and Ordinaries and Hierarchs Regarding the Modifications Introduced in the *Normae de Gravioribus delictis*," Congregation for the Doctrine of the Faith, May 21, 2010, and the accompanying document: "A brief Introduction to the modifications made in the Normae gravioribus delictis, reserved to the Congregation for the Doctrine of the Faith," B15.

2. Pope Francis. In his motu proprio on May 6, 2019, titled *Vos Estis Lux Mundi* ("You are the Light of the World"—a reference to Matthew 5:14), the following was added:

A. "Forcing someone, by violence, or threat, or through abuse of power, to perform or submit to sexual acts."[381] (This differs from canon 1395 because it appears to apply the aggravating circumstances of sexual abuse even to those who are not minors.)

B. "Performing sexual acts with a minor or a vulnerable person."[382] (This is generally consistent with past directives but goes beyond those developmentally disabled or incapacitated and uses the broad term "vulnerable.")

C. "The production, exhibition, possession or distribution, including by electronic means, of child pornography, as well as by the recruitment of or inducement of a minor or a vulnerable person to participate in pornographic exhibitions."[383] (The first part of this delict was already added by Pope Benedict XVI. The latter portion is new.)

Problem Three: The Relatively Light Severity of the Offense in Canon Law

Problem three lies in the comparative severity of sexual abuse as judged by the penalties inflicted for other violations of clerical chastity. While this canon provides for "just penalties," going as far as dismissal from the clerical state, it does not carry an automatic penalty (*latae sententiae*). Instead, it is the type of penalty that the Church inflicts by means of the

---

[381] Pope Francis, *Vos Estis Lux Mundi* ("You are the Light of the World), Apostolic Letter issued Motu Proprio, May 7, 2019, Art. 1, 1(a)i, https://www.vatican.va/content/francesco/en/motu_proprio/documents/papa-francesco-motu-proprio-20190507_vos-estis-lux-mundi.html.

[382] Pope Francis, *Vos Estis Lux Mundi*, Art. 1, 1(a)ii.

[383] Pope Francis, *Vos Estis Lux Mundi*, Art. 1, 1(a)iii.

competent authority—usually done administratively by a bishop, or by a judge through a judicial or tribunal process.

To illustrate the comparative severity, I will contrast the violation in canon 1395 (above) with that in canon 194 of the 1917 Code and canon 1394 of the 1983 Code, which states that "a cleric who attempts even a civil marriage incurs an automatic suspension."[384] This act is one of strict liability—a violation that results in a *latae sententiae* penalty. One can argue that marriage is, by definition, incompatible with clerical continence and a canonical impediment to the priesthood, thus triggering the automatic penalty. But on the grounds of severity, damage, and scandal, the abuse of children is far worse.

Consider the commentary provided for canon 1395:

> Paragraph two deals with certain *non-habitual* clerical sexual offenses, which are especially serious if they are perpetuated publicly, or with force or threats, or with a person of either sex under sixteen years of age. Initially such an offense is not viewed as seriously as the preceding ones [attempted marriage] since only 'just penalties' are imposed. Yet, if remedial measures are unsuccessful, even such a cleric may ultimately be dismissed from the clerical state.
>
> Great care should be exercised by church authorities in this delicate area. Frequently the most beneficial approach is a therapeutic rather than a penal one, especially if there is diminished imputability on the part of the cleric. However, while the well-being and future ministry of the offending cleric are key considerations, due cognizance also has to be taken of the damage done to the community and individuals within it.[385]

That seems to be a pretty tepid analysis to me. I have already covered the difference between strict liability laws and laws that require the examination of intent (*mens rea*). Child sexual abuse offenses under Canon Law fall into the latter category. Because many of the sexual abuse

---

[384] Coriden, Green, and Heintschel, canon 1394.1, 928-29.
[385] Coriden, Green, and Heintschel, *The Code*, 929.

cases involved elements that diminished imputability (like alcohol use or pathology), they were often met with rehabilitation, albeit perhaps with penance and temporary suspension of faculties and, sadly, transfer and cover-up. Any inflicted penalties, either by rebuke, admonition and warning, individual decree from the bishop, or tribunal decision, would then be placed in the diocesan secret archive.[386] Typically, only the bishop or a trusted designee has the physical key. Even if the offender has died, or if ten years have passed, "a brief summary of the case with the text of the definitive sentence is to be retained."[387] The archives are secret for reasons of confidentiality, but they can give evidence to constructive notice about a priest's behavior and reveal a pattern of case management.

Solution to Problem Three: Addressing the Relatively Light Severity of the Offense

In 1988, Pope St. John Paul II issued the Apostolic Constitution *Pastor Bonus,* which addressed the operation of the Apostolic See and the Roman Curia (Vatican operations). The previous reorganization was under Pope St. Paul VI in 1967. *Pastor Bonus* addresses how the structures within the Vatican assist the Holy Father in governing the Church. It lays out the role of various dicasteries—the name coming from the Greek *dikasterion,* which means "law-court." One such dicastery is the Congregation for the Doctrine of the Faith (CDF), led at the time by Cardinal Joseph Ratzinger, who later became Pope Benedict XVI. Article 52 of *Pastor Bonus* reads: "The Congregation examines offences against the faith and more serious ones both in behaviour or in the celebration of the sacraments which have been reported to it and, if need be, proceeds to the declaration or imposition of canonical sanctions in accordance with the norms of common or proper law."[388]

---

[386] Coriden, Green, and Heintschel, *The Code,* canon 1339.3, 910.

[387] Coriden, Green, and Heintschel, *The Code,* canon 489.2, 396.

[388] Pope St. John Paul II, *Pastor Bonus,* Apostolic Constitution (June 28, 1988) #52, https://www.vatican.va/content/john-paul-ii/en/apost_constitutions/documents/hf_jp-ii_apc_19880628_pastor-bonus.html.

In response to the sexual abuse scandal, Pope St. John Paul II issued an Apostolic Letter, known as a *motu proprio*, titled *Sacramentorum Sanctitatis Tutela*, on April 30, 2001. A motu proprio, which means "of his own impulse" in Latin, is a decree and instruction, with or without petition by another, to bring clarity to the precepts of Canon Law to promote its fulfillment. Typically, these decrees are not doctrinal but pertain to discipline and presuppose existing law.

The purpose of *Sacramentorum Sanctitatis Tutela* was to identify specific delicts (or offenses) that are considered graver and therefore not to be treated with a mere pastoral attitude by bishops but are to be reserved for review by the CDF. Delicts are primarily offenses in the external forum (visible to others or the public), since one's conscience and one's relationship with the Lord are in the internal forum and thus inaccessible for ready discernment by others. The document listed offenses against the Eucharist, the sanctity of the Sacrament of Penance (including solicitation of crimes against the sixth commandment in the confessional), and the sexual abuse of minors. Elevating sexual abuse to the CDF tribunal served three purposes:

1. These offenses were not just moral failings; they were a violation against the faith.
2. The matter received heightened attention and seriousness.
3. It was intended to streamline the dismissal of credibly accused clergy (including bishops) from the clerical state.

Problem Four: The Statute of Limitations for These Cases in Canon Law

The statute of limitations for the offense in canon 1395 (abuse of a minor) was a period of five years as prescribed in canon 1362.2 and measured in continuous time from the date of the offense or after the cessation of a continuing habitual offense. Considering how these cases tend not to be reported immediately, this duration needed to be lengthened, just as statutes of limitation in many civil jurisdictions have been extended in recent times.

Solution to Problem Four: Extending the Statute of Limitations for These Cases

The extension of this prescription of time has evolved in several stages. In 1994, at the same time that the indult on the victim's age was promulgated, the prescription of time "was extended to a period of ten (10) years from the 18th birthday of the victim."[389] Msgr. Charles Scicluna, Promoter of Justice (lead prosecutor for these cases at the Vatican), would later note that "experience has shown that a term of ten years is inadequate for these types of cases and that it would be desirable to return to the former system in which these delicts were not subject to a (time) prescription at all. On 7 November 2002, the Holy Father granted to the CDF (Congregation for the Doctrine of the Faith, to whom these cases were directed) the faculty to derogate from prescription on a case-by-case basis upon the request of an individual bishop."[390] In 2005, under Benedict XVI, the time frame was extended to twenty years beyond the victim reaching their eighteenth birthday, applied retroactively.[391] The CDF's faculty to derogate beyond twenty years remains intact, with or without the local bishop's request.

---

[389] Congregation for the Doctrine of the Faith, "The Norms of the Motu Proprio 'Sacramentorum Sanctitatis Tutela': Historical Introduction," 2001, https://www.vatican.va/resources/resources_introd-storica_en.html.

[390] Charles Scicluna, "The Procedure and Praxis of the Congregation for the Doctrine of the Faith regarding Graviora Delicta," https://www.vatican.va/resources/resources_mons-scicluna-graviora-delicta_en.html.

[391] Davide Cito, "The New Delicta Graviora Laws," *Ave Maria International Law Journal*, Vol. 1, Issue 1, ISSN no. 2375-2173 (Fall 2011): 90-116, 110. https://avemarialaw-international-law-journal.avemarialaw.edu/Content/iljarticles/2011.Cito.DelictaGraviora.final.pdf.

Problem Five: Removal from the Clerical State; Administrative Process v. Judicial Process

Assuming the bishop had determined the credibility and severity of a given case and recommended that the offending priest be dismissed from the clerical state, two questions came into play in navigating the appropriate process:

1. Because the priest has rights of due process and, as a public figure, could be the subject of false allegations, is he willing to voluntarily leave and seek a petition of laicization from the Holy See, or might he demand an ability to defend himself?
2. If the latter, what process must be invoked to inflict this perpetual and irrevocable penalty?[392] Such a proceeding would typically trigger a very formal and cumbersome judicial process under Canon Law.

In describing the situation at the time, canon lawyer Msgr. John A. Alesandro writes,

> The bishops of the United States have been struggling to resolve such a matter in a canonically acceptable manner. Most bishops have been loath to invoke the process in the Code of Canon Law for punitive dismissal of the priest from the clerical state. In some cases, however, use of the process has become a necessity....
>
> ...some bishops seemed to indicate that what was needed in lieu of the judicial penal process was an administrative process....The goal was to streamline the cumbersome judicial process required by the Code whenever a priest faced the severe and permanent penalty of dismissal for a canonical delict by placing it in the hands of the diocesan bishop....
>
> ...The vision by canon lawyers, however, of an administrative process, was the imposition of the penalty of dismissal

---

[392] Coriden, Green, and Heintschel, *The Code*, canon 1342.3, 911. "Perpetual penalties cannot be imposed or declared by decree."

from the clerical state by a diocesan bishop in a non-judicial manner, but with due process protections for the priest. In other words,...many bishops were looking for a 'non-penal' procedure....

It soon became apparent that while a judicial procedure may be cumbersome and, more importantly, may remove the ultimate decision from the diocesan bishop to a collegiate tribunal of three qualified priest-judges, simply converting the judicial penal process into an administrative penal process would not provide diocesan bishops with what they were seeking.[393]

In the early 1990s, bishops from around the country worked with the United States Catholic Conference of Bishops (USCCB) to share notes and strategies. The Conference was engaged in discussions with the Vatican on how to streamline the process to remove a credibly accused priest from the clerical state.

While this exchange with Vatican officials was taking place, the USCCB recommended the following process:

Accordingly, the [National Conference of Catholic Bishops] proposed not "dismissal," but administrative "removal" from the clerical state. The pastoral facts and circumstances, past, present and future (e.g., likelihood of recidivism), would determine whether grounds for removal existed. Thus, in 1992, the NCCB's Canonical Affairs Committee developed for discussion purposes a process modeled on the administrative removal from the pastorate.

Although the proposed process could not be initiated unless there was proof that the priest had committed a canonically proscribed offense, it was not a penal process. There was no statute of limitations, and the reasons for or against removal balanced both the gravity of the harm and need for correction, reparation and restoration of justice with practical

---

[393] John A. Alesandro, "A Study of Canon Law: Dismissal from the Clerical State in Cases of Sexual Misconduct," *The Catholic Lawyer*, 36, no. 3 (1996): 257–300, 257–259, 261.

judgments about the feasibility of the priest's continued ministry in any form as well as his potential danger to others. The central basis for removing the cleric is analogous to the reason for administrative removal of a pastor. Removal would result if the cleric's ministry had become permanently harmful (*noxium*) to the Church or completely ineffective (*inefficax*) in any reasonable ecclesial situation because of his past acts and if, all things considered, his continued ministry in any form whatsoever would represent a grave danger to the Church."[394]

This administrative work-around of Canon Law still retained much room for the bishop's discretion and avoided a formal judicial process. This discretion could still be abused while a better solution was being sought.

Solution to Problem Five: Providing a Clear Process for Removal from the Clerical State

To provide clarity on the process of handling offending priests, including their dismissal from the clerical state, the CDF made "special procedural norms 'to declare or impose canonical sanctions'"[395] to comply with Pope St. John Paul II's motu proprio *Sacramentorum Sanctitatis Tutela*.

The CDF's procedural norms stipulate that "as often as an ordinary [a bishop]...has at least probable knowledge of a reserved delict, after he has carried out the preliminary investigation, he is to indicate it to the Congregation for the Doctrine of the Faith, which unless it calls the case to itself because of special circumstances of things, after transmitting appropriate norms, orders the ordinary...to proceed ahead through his own tribunal."[396] This instruction confirms that such cases must be handled

---

[394] Alesandro, "A Study of Canon Law," 262.

[395] Cardinal Joseph Ratzinger, "Letter from the CDF to Bishops and Religious Superiors on More Grave Delicts," Congregation for the Doctrine of the Faith, May 18, 2001, https://www.vatican.va/roman_curia/congregations/cfaith/documents/rc_con_cfaith_doc_20010518_epistula-graviora-delicta_en.html.

[396] Cardinal Joseph Ratzinger, "Letter from the CDF."

through the judicial process, even at the local diocesan level, not merely administratively. It also means that someone other than the local bishop is required to be notified of the case, thus raising its profile and seriousness.

Prior to these changes by the CDF, a priest could appeal decisions in such cases as follows: (1) an individual, administrative decree by his bishop would be appealed to the Congregation for the Clergy (a dicastery) and (2) a judicial decision appealed to the Roman Rota (Latin, meaning "wheel"), a tribunal at the Vatican that hears appellate cases of the second instance. These cases are now reserved for the CDF and its tribunal function. In keeping with the seriousness of the matter, and each case's connection to a violation of the faith, this provision assures consolidation with the CDF.

On May 21, 2010, Pope Benedict XVI, focusing on the exceptionally serious nature of these offenses, approved a revision to the 2001 norms. This revision granted the ability to revisit cases where only procedural laws have been violated by an inferior tribunal, with deference to the right of a proper defense for the accused. In cases of extreme gravity, where there is no question of the delict and a proper defense has been exercised, the CDF could present a case directly to the Holy Father, resulting in a dismissal from the clerical state, the deposition of a Church leader, and the dispensation from the obligation of celibacy.[397]

Problem Six: Accountability for Church Leaders

There was another significant problem pervasive throughout this scandal that was not fully addressed by the earlier norms and procedures: the accountability of Church leaders. Various Church leaders have been implicated in clumsy mismanagement of cases, in overt cover-ups that impeded justice, and even as sexual perpetrators themselves, either prior

---

[397] William Cardinal Levada, "Letter to Bishops and Ordinaries Regarding the Modifications Introduced in the *Normae de Gravioribus delictis*," Congregation for the Doctrine of the Faith, May 21, 2010, and the accompanying document: "A brief Introduction to the modifications made in the Normae gravioribus delictis, reserved to the Congregation for the Doctrine of the Faith," A4, A6.

to being consecrated as bishop or in the role of shepherd. The list is long enough and is still growing.

If there are scoundrel bishops in the hierarchy, what can be done about it? What role can other bishops play? This was a touchy issue because each local ordinary (bishop of a diocese) is the sacramental head of the local church entrusted to him. He is the "legislator, administrator, and judge."[398] And while one might hope that bishops are open to each other in providing fraternal support and correction, this is certainly not always the case. During the June 2019 US Catholic Conference of Bishops meeting to discuss bishop accountability, a very well-intended bishop from Texas was asked by the EWTN news anchor about the idea of bishops "policing" other bishops. He gave a theologically sound but "churchy" reply. In essence, his response was that all the bishops are equals and so, theologically, this policing is not possible.[399] To the casual listener who knew that part of this problem laid squarely on the shoulders of the Church's leaders, this will likely sound like an excuse or avoidance of the question instead of an openness to a plausible solution. This is an example of the recent observation delivered to US bishops by the Papal Nuncio to the United States when he spoke about "simply expounding theological ideas."[400] Ineffective communication with the Catholic in the pew continues to erode confidence about whether Church leaders are serious about finding solutions.

This posture of simply expounding on theological ideas can be just as much a part of the cover-up as the abuse itself if it is used as a pretext for a lack of transparency. It illustrates the difficulties and interdependent facets of a *wicked problem*. The light has been shone on one of the underlying problems—the decisions of bishops—and many bishops have egg on their face for choices they have made. The conciliar concepts of collegiality

---

[398]   Coriden, Green, and Heintschel, *The Code*, 12.

[399]   EWTN News Nightly with Lauren Ashburn - 2019-06-12, interview with Bishop Joseph Strickland, https://www.youtube.com/watch?v=S2DTKZzTHI0.

[400]   Archbishop Christophe Pierre, "Address of His Excellency Archbishop Christophe Pierre to the United States Conference of Catholic Bishops," June 11, 2019, Plenary Assembly, Baltimore, Maryland, 5, https://www.usccb.org/resources/archbishop-christophe-pierre-address-us-bishops.

and subsidiarity work well for bishops when they work in their favor. But these concepts are not esteemed by the discerning faithful when they result in morally intolerable decisions, as we have seen in this crisis.

Solution to Problem Six: Providing for Church Leader Accountability

In May 2010 the Congregation for the Doctrine of the Faith issued a letter to bishops that codified revisions Pope Benedict XVI had made in 2005. The letter stated that all norms and reforms relating to the clergy sexual abuse issue under Pope John Paul II are expressly applicable to cardinals, patriarchs, legates of the Apostolic See, bishops, and others, for all of them are clerics under Canon Law.[401] This addressed their own personal behavior as it relates to sexual abuse and related behaviors.

But what about an account of their role in mishandling cases? In Pope Francis's 2019 motu proprio titled *Vos Estis Lux Mundi*, which was approved *ad experimentum* for a period of three years, he named the following offense of intending to cover up abuse or ward off any interference: "Conduct carried out by the subjects referred to in article 6 [Cardinals, Patriarchs, Bishops and Legates of the Roman Pontiff] consisting of actions or omissions intended to interfere with or avoid civil investigations or canonical investigations, whether administrative or penal, against a cleric or a religious regarding the delicts referred to [above]."[402]

To further comply with Pope Francis's motu proprio, the US bishops, during their 2019 General Assembly meeting, established a third-party reporting system to hold bishops responsible for any culpable action in this crisis. The system includes a national reporting number (800-276-1562) and a website (ReportBishopsAbuse.org).

---

[401] William Cardinal Levada, "Letter to Bishops and Ordinaries Regarding the Modifications Introduced in the *Normae de Gravioribus delictis*," Congregation for the Doctrine of the Faith, May 21, 2010, and the accompanying document: "A brief Introduction to the modifications made in the Normae gravioribus delictis, reserved to the Congregation for the Doctrine of the Faith," A1.

[402] Pope Francis, *Vos Estis Lux Mundi*, Art. 1, 1(b).

One might wonder why Pope Francis's motu proprio was approved as an experiment for only three years. The answer lies in the truth that reform is ongoing. Returning to the *wicked problem* paradigm in chapter II, the following principles are clearly at play here: "there's no way to know whether your solution is final; solutions are not true or false, they can only be good or bad; every solution is not a 'one-shot' operation."[403] As the Church (and the Holy See) discovered more cases, they increasingly learned more about the variation of offenses, the circumstances involved, and the need to modify their approach accordingly in order to achieve justice. The ongoing learning process requires continual reflection in order to keep on track.

Pope Emeritus Benedict XVI later reflected on the effectiveness of these procedures in an essay:

> This arrangement also made it possible to impose the maximum penalty, i.e., expulsion from the clergy, which could not have been imposed under other legal provisions. This was not a trick to be able to impose the maximum penalty but is a consequence of the importance of the Faith for the Church. In fact, it is important to see that such misconduct by clerics ultimately damages the Faith....
>
> The severity of the punishment, however, also presupposes a clear proof of the offense—this aspect of guarantorism remains in force.
>
> In other words, in order to impose the maximum penalty lawfully, a genuine criminal process is required. But both the dioceses and the Holy See were overwhelmed by such a requirement. We therefore formulated a minimum level of criminal proceedings and left open the possibility that the Holy See itself would take over the trial where the diocese or the metropolitan administration is unable to do so. In each case, the trial would have to be reviewed by the Congregation

---

[403] Euphemia Wong, "What is a Wicked Problem and How Can You Solve It?", Interaction Design Foundation, retrieved 8/15/20, https://www.interaction-design.org/literature/article/wicked-problems-5-steps-to-help-you-tackle-wicked-problems-by-combining-systems-thinking-with-agile-methodology.

for the Doctrine of the Faith in order to guarantee the rights of the accused. Finally, in the Feria IV (i.e., the assembly of the members of the Congregation), we established an appeal instance in order to provide for the possibility of an appeal.

Because all of this actually went beyond the capacities of the Congregation for the Doctrine of the Faith, and because delays arose which had to be prevented owing to the nature of the matter, Pope Francis has undertaken further reforms.[404]

Remaining Issues

Having noted the progress to date on the critical shortcomings in Canon Law, I now turn to a few remaining aspects of the crisis that require further reflection by the Church.

Handling Accused Clerics and Legal Due Process

In adjudicating cases in courtrooms and tribunals, Fr. Michael Orsi, Research Fellow in Law and Religion at Ave Maria Law School, reminds us that "justice demands that the guilty pay, but it also demands that the innocent not suffer."[405] Such is the basis of fair law—affording due process to every person. Because a cleric is a public figure, this protection, long held in both civil and canonical law, must have integrity.

The toxicity of and rightful attention to these sexual abuse cases still requires that the investigations are objective and are not a rush to judgment. The same vanity of reputation protection that enticed bishops

---

[404] Anian Christoph Wimmer, trans., "Full text of Benedict XVI essay: 'The Church and the scandal of abuse,'" Vatican City, Catholic News Agency, April 10, 2019, Section II of essay, https://www.catholicnewsagency.com/news/41013/full-text-of-benedict-xvi-essay-the-church-and-the-scandal-of-sexual-abuse https://www.catholicnewsagency.com/news/41013/full-text-of-benedict-xvi-essay-the-church-and-the-scandal-of-sexual-abuse.

[405] Michael P. Orsi, "Reconsidering the Dallas Charter," Catholic League for Religious and Civil Rights, June Issue 2011, https://www.catholicleague.org/reconsidering-the-dallas-charter/.

to cover up scandals cannot now come in the form of railroading the due process rights of priests who might be falsely accused, nor should it be a pretense for weeding out unfavored priests by not giving them the benefit of the doubt.

The documents on the national level that provide policy guidance for the handling of these cases is the Charter for the Protection of Children and Young People, along with the 2006 Essential Norms for dealing with allegations. This *particular* law of the Church in the United States cannot usurp *universal* Church Law on due process for clerics.

Essential phrases such as *credible allegation* and *sexual abuse of a minor* are not well defined in the Church's documents. The interplay of concurrent jurisdiction between civil and canonical processes is also not well defined. These points require clarification.

Credible Allegation

Recognizing the concurrent jurisdiction of civil authorities, article IV of the charter provides that "dioceses/eparchies are to report an allegation of sexual abuse of a person who is a minor to the public authorities."[406] The qualifying word *credible* is not even used. This is likely because the Church does not want to appear as though it is acting as a gatekeeper in determining credibility from a civil jurisprudence perspective. Reporting an allegation that has not been determined credible has the potential to indicate guilt and jeopardize reputation. Though likely rare, the cleric could be the subject of frivolous or malicious allegations made by those angry with him.

The charter states that the accused cleric "is to be afforded the presumption of innocence during the investigation of the allegation and all

---

[406] United States Conference of Catholic Bishops, *Promise to Protect, Pledge to Heal: Charter for the Protection of Children and Young People*, 2018, Art. 4, pg. 10, https://www.usccb.org/test/upload/Charter-for-the-Protection-of-Children-and-Young-People-2018-final(1).pdf.

appropriate steps are to be taken to protect his reputation. He is to be encouraged to retain the assistance of civil and canonical counsel."[407]

A cleric is to be removed from ministry if he admits to the offense or if it has been established "after an appropriate process in accord with canon law."[408] But it is not stated clearly whether he will be removed from ministry based solely on unproven accusations or whether this decision will be made on a case-by-case basis. If the cleric is removed from ministry only on an unproven allegation, this could be interpreted as guilt, and restoring a priest's good name if the allegations later prove to be unfounded will seem like an afterthought and a clean-up operation at the end.

Defining the Sexual Abuse of a Minor

In chapter VII on the clinical science of abuse, I pointed out the complications caused by inconsistent definitions of sexual abuse in studies that have been conducted. The charter also does not have a clear clinical definition of the sexual abuse of minors.

Instead, the charter relies on the definition in canon 1395, the various delicts defined in the motu proprios of Pope St. John Paul II and Pope Francis, and the guidance provided by Pope Benedict XVI in determining whether the offense was "an external, objectively grave violation."[409] The charter advises dioceses that, if in doubt, they can consult "the writings of recognized moral theologians," and "the opinions of recognized experts."[410]

Substantiated Allegations

Since substantiated cases will involve concurrent jurisdiction between civil and canonical processes, it is unclear how the findings of civil

---

[407] USCCB, *Promise to Protect, Pledge to Heal*, Art. 5, pg. 11.

[408] USCCB, *Promise to Protect, Pledge to Heal*, Art. 5, pg. 11.

[409] USCCB, *Promise to Protect, Pledge to Heal*, Note 1, pg. 18.

[410] USCCB, *Promise to Protect, Pledge to Heal*, Note 1, pg. 18.

authorities will bear on the canonical process for the cleric. Because district attorneys use a high bar to ensure successful prosecution, what happens if a case is not sufficiently substantiated for the civil jurisdiction to proceed with prosecution? How should the Church take this into consideration, if at all? Is the cleric then returned to ministry? Is he removed from ministry but not removed from the clerical state, instructed to live a life of prayer and penance?

Continued Vulnerabilities in Transparency

In this ongoing evolution of remedies, the process is still open to vulnerabilities. Because humans are involved, justice is not always fair or perfect. Humans interject bias, judgment, and discretion.

In the case of priests, the diocesan-level tribunals handling these cases are required to be composed of other priests (serving in the roles of judge, promoter of justice/prosecutor, notary, and legal representative or advocate). When the Supreme Tribunal of the CDF hears a case, only the CDF can dispense with the requirements of priesthood and a doctorate in Canon Law for these participants. Similarly, in cases involving bishops or other Church leaders, every decision-maker is a bishop or higher. In some sense, it is a "jury of one's peers" and can also be a very sympathetic jury. There is a provision to recuse oneself if one has a bias, but it is ultimately an honor system. The trade-off is the avoidance of further scandal and a breach of confidentiality for what at times can be a lack of transparency. Personal affections, fraternity, and influence can still be at play in the process. These features of the process can be ecclesiastical barriers to transparency that would not be an issue with an independent review board.

Engagement with Civil Authorities

Civil authorities can also be influenced during investigations and must be treated with impartiality. Bishops are often well-connected to the leaders in their communities. In a case involving the late Bishop Patrick Ziemann, once auxiliary bishop of Los Angeles and then-bishop of the

Diocese of Santa Rosa, he was sexually involved with a priest suspected of stealing money from a parish. The parish pastor reported the crime of the suspected priest to a police detective "...despite a phone call from Ziemann instructing him not to cooperate. Then the bishop got on the phone with [the city's] police chief and a lifelong Roman Catholic, and persuaded him to send his detective away without arresting [the priest]....
[...] It was the most embarrassing mistake of my professional career," says [the police chief], now retired. "I felt very close to Bishop Ziemann and had a lot of respect for him. He confirmed all three of my children." [The police chief] says he should have listened to his wife, who was immediately suspicious of Ziemann's motives. "That night she told me, 'You know, you're the most naïve police chief in America.'"[411]

Pascite Gregem Dei–Pope Francis

As the process of incremental change and reform moves forward, Pope Francis released an apostolic constitution dated May 23, 2021, titled *Pascite Gregem Dei* ("Shepherd of God's Flock"). In doing so, he promulgated a complete revision of book VI of the Code on Canon Law concerning penal law that began with Pope Benedict XVI and will go into effect December 8, 2021. The new book VI was launched by a press conference on June 1, 2021, during which comments were offered by Archbishop Filippo Iannone, O. Carm., president of the Pontifical Council for Legislative Texts, and Bishop Juan Ignacio Arrieta Ochoa de Chinchetru. The rework of this section of Canon Law continues to uphold the three pillars of ecclesiastical penal law, namely, in the words of Archbishop Filippo Iannone, "the restoration of the requirements of justice, the amendment of the offender, and the reparation of scandals,"[412] while discouraging a laxity in applying Church criminal law.

---

411 Ron Russell, "Bishop Bad Boy," *San Francisco Weekly* (March 19, 2003), retrieved 6/30/21, https://www.sfweekly.com/news/bishop-bad-boy/.

412 Holy See Press Office, "Press Conference to present the new Book VI of the Code of Canon Law, 01.06.2021," Intervention by Archbishop Filippo Iannone,

Below I will briefly provide observations about the promulgation and characterize some key takeaways. The effort is a sound incremental step, but still far from addressing the underlying causes of the crisis.

In the June 1, 2021, press conference Archbishop Filippo Iannone stated that the revisions, at least in part, "emerged from the disconcerting and very serious episodes of paedophilia."[413] Due to the narrow purpose of the announcement, there was no expectation that this event would be the occasion to discuss the root causes of the biggest scandal in the Church. Yet, any terms used to describe the crisis could be insightful. I would remind the reader that pedophilia explains only a portion of the behaviors in this scandal. Archbishop Iannone's exclusive use of the word *paedophilia* in this instance to characterize the crisis suggests to me one of four possibilities in the thinking of Vatican officials:

1. They have broadly and inaccurately applied this term to the full spectrum of cases in this crisis.
2. They have not yet reached a consensus on the true causes and have chosen pedophilia as the safe and noncontroversial term.
3. They internally recognize the possibility of broader pathological behaviors but don't want to publicly go on record, or they believe it is unnecessary to articulate terms beyond pedophilia because they believe penal law, if applied in the spirit it was intended, will address the matter appropriately.
4. They have intentionally mischaracterized the totality of the problem because they are in denial about the possibility of other causes.

In the final analysis, this narrowly defined and inaccurate characterization was a disappointment. In 2010 Msgr. Charles J. Scicluna, promoter of justice (prosecuting attorney) in these cases, characterized the nearly 3,000 worldwide cases between 2001–2010 that were handled at, or

---

O. Carm., retrieved 6/3/2021, https://press.vatican.va/content/salastampa/en/bollettino/pubblico/2021/06/01/210601e.html.

[413] Holy See Press Office, "Press Conference to present the new Book VI of the Code of Canon Law, 01.06.2021," Intervention by Archbishop Filippo Iannone, O. Carm.

monitored by, the Vatican. In that interview, available on the Vatican's own website, he noted that only "ten percent were cases of paedophilia in the true sense of the term; that is, based on sexual attraction towards prepubescent children."[414]

As to the content of the revision, I would summarize some key highlights as follows. The revision

- encourages bishops to use penal remedies for a host of offenses;
- encourages the imposition of penal remedies progressively and with vigilance or supervision as needed or more severely if circumstances dictate (the presumption is that incremental application of penal laws for slighter offenses may help ward off continued and more harmful behaviors);
- broadens the applicability of certain offenses to nonclerics (members of the faithful);
- rewrites or creates certain canons that acknowledge certain subtleties, nuances, and circumstances based on things learned in the years of handling the sexual abuse scandal (e.g., the role of conspirators or attenuating circumstances in the commission of the offense or in omissions, persons who neglect to report an offense, a priest guilty of sexual abuse absolving his accomplice in the confessional, etc.);
- strengthens penalties for those who misuse the temporal goods of the Church (likely deriving from such cases as the former bishop of Wheeling-Charleston, West Virginia, Michael Bransfield, and issues with Vatican finances);
- incorporates into the law provisions of past motu proprios mentioned above on the subject of clergy sexual abuse;
- provides some additional due process protections for clerics (including penalties for those guilty of perpetrating falsehoods or harming the reputation of a cleric).

---

[414] Msgr. Charles Scicluna, "Interview of Msgr. Charles Scicluna conducted by Gianni Cardinale on the Strictness of the Church in Cases of Paedophilia," Holy See, June 10, 2010, retrieved 6/8/2021, https://www.vatican.va/resources/resources_mons-scicluna-2010_en.html.

This revision of penal law will theoretically provide bishops with more tools and institutional support, and it will project to clerics that a new, more disciplined environment is afoot.

The final chapter on this crisis has yet to be written. Many Church leaders continue to demonstrate that they are prisoners in a system and unwilling to come clean on the root causes of this scandal. The lens one uses to discern the root causes of the problem is critical to the path chosen to rectify it. Church leaders can fixate on treating the offenses and symptoms, or they can honestly probe its causes. I pray that the Holy Spirit will enlighten Church leaders and provide them the courage needed to fly to, and cling to, the truth.

XVIII

Impacts on Society

I hope this book has begun to give Catholics a framework for understanding the causes of this recent tragic episode of child sexual abuse by the clergy and the responses of the Church. This perilous and painful chapter in the Church's history has affected not only Catholics but also society at large. For those of us who have not jumped ship and remain on the stormy sea, the crisis has moved Catholics, both clergy and the faithful, into several camps. Some are rightly confused and are flailing for answers. Some seek quick fixes, some are resistant to any change, some have steadily prayed for healing and reform, and still others will attempt to capitalize on this dilemma for prior and unrelated agendas. True to Her character, the Church is not a society that operates as a democratic club, relying on polls and focus groups to decide on a path forward.

Guided by the Holy Spirit, She is accountable to Scripture and Tradition, the entire deposit of faith handed down, of which She is the custodian. Fr. James Fischer, CM, once wrote that at-large "polls showing that such and such percentage favor married priests, or women priests, or community parishes that select their own leaders, should be viewed with some suspicion. It is easy for those who have little stake in the matter and no intention of making any great sacrifices to favor proposals that seem to be popular or avant-garde."[415] I can add to that trendy list the more pernicious effort to desacralize the priesthood. If there's to be an increase in the prevalence of married priests, it won't be due to polling. Moving on from stormy seas will require an openness to the Holy Spirit, ears to hear God's inspiration, and thoughtful imagination.

The Cynicism in Society

In the last century, cynicism was fueled by world wars, barbarism and carnage. It was followed by a questioning of the institutions of society and now we are contending with forces which seek to break down those institutions. These breakdowns can paralyze us and fuel fear. But in these difficult times, it is worth being reminded of the observation of German theologian Michael Schmaus who wrote: "Our concern with [Christianity] is not merely that of interested spectators, but that of people whose very existence is at stake."[416]

Faithful Catholics, convinced of the redemption wrought in Christ's death and resurrection, run the risk of becoming so self-absorbed with the clergy abuse crisis that they ignore how the scandal impacts the larger society, possibly forgetting their call to evangelize in love. This larger society, unfortunately, includes Catholics who have jumped ship. The scandal has reinforced in many the idea that faith apparently does not instruct right behavior and therefore rings hollow. Although disillusionment abounds in society and comes from many sources, this crisis has breathed new life into, or rather hardened, barriers to belief and has invigorated a whole host of "isms"—moral relativism and nihilism, atheism, religious syncretism, anti-sacerdotalism, Donatism, New Age

---

[415] James Fischer, "The Non-distinctiveness of the Catholic Priest," *The Priest* (Nov. 1987): 10-15, 15.

[416] Schmaus, Michael, *The Essence of Christianity* (Scepter Publishers, LTD: Dublin, 1961), 33.

spiritualism—all of which have been present in the culture. They are typically pursued not as quests for truth, but more often as default alternatives resulting from the blanket rejection of time-honored Christian patrimony, the "deposit of Faith."

Although Western society was indeed founded on Judeo-Christian tenets, it is certainly not a mythical world of European medieval societal uniformity and zealotry. Catholics were "living in the diaspora"[417] long before this recent scandal—a scattered but pilgrim people. The truth is that the world is not all Catholic, nor even all in Christian tradition. With tremendous implications for evangelization, society was already drastically morphing under the views of social Darwinism, secular utopianism,[418] and other forms of purely human creation.

In the second-century document known as *The Didache,* or *The Teaching of the Twelve Apostles,* there is a passage of clear eucharistic imagery: "Even as this broken bread was scattered over the hills, and was gathered together and became one, so let Thy Church be gathered together from the ends of the earth into Thy kingdom."[419] Catholics begin, then, with a recognition that in baptism they belong to the kingdom of God, the mustard seed which, "when full grown...becomes a large bush, and the [scattered] birds of the sky come and dwell in its branches."[420] It is at this very difficult moment in time that Catholics can flock to the large bush as a shelter, as a home, and as their object of hope, for "our heart is restless until it rests in You [Lord]"[421] (St. Augustine's *Confessions*).

Noteworthy is *The Didache*'s use of the word *hills* (or *mountains*, in some translations). Another image about a mountain comes to mind. The

---

[417] Karl Rahner, SJ, *The Christian Commitment* (New York: Sheed and Ward, 1963), 31–32.

[418] Rahner, *The Christian Commitment,* 37.

[419] *The Didache,* Roberts-Donaldson English Translation, cited on website Early Christian Writings, http://www.earlychristianwritings.com/text/didache-roberts.html.

[420] Matthew 13:32, *The New American Bible,* Catholic Mission Edition, St. Jerome Press (Wichita, Kansas: Devore & Sons, Inc., 1987 and 1981).

[421] St. Augustine, *The Confessions of St. Augustine* (Garden City, New York: Image Books, 1960), 43.

Gospel of Matthew recounts Jesus's words to his followers: "You are the light of the world. A city set on a mountain cannot be hidden. Just so, your light must shine before others, that they may see your good deeds and glorify your heavenly Father."[422] The themes of God's kingdom, the Eucharist, and the call to evangelization in a struggling world converge in these few images. Even today, they form the very outline for Catholics in a suffering world and amid this crisis.

In Pope St. Paul VI's 1967 encyclical letter *Populorum Progressio*, he describes this post-Christian world order when he writes, "In effect, the moral, spiritual and religious supports of the past too often give way without securing in return any guarantee of a place in the new world. In this confusion, the temptation becomes stronger to risk being swept away towards types of messianism which give promises but create illusions. The resulting dangers are patent: violent popular reactions, agitation and insurrection, and a drifting towards totalitarian ideologies."[423] Regrettably, these tendencies have emerged here in the United States.

On a more granular and individual level, Pope Benedict XVI wrote the following in meditation upon the temptation of Jesus in the desert by the Evil One (who could also quote Scripture for his purpose and cause): "Moral posturing is part and parcel of the temptation. It does not invite us directly to do evil—no, that would be far too blatant. It pretends to show us a better way, where we finally abandon our illusions and throw ourselves into the work of making the world a better place. It claims, moreover, to speak for true realism: What's real is what is right there in front of us—power and bread. By comparison, the things of God fade into unreality, into a secondary world that no one really needs."[424] Both pontiffs have aptly summarized today's reality, which is marked by a lack of faith in, a distrust of, and sometimes a denial of, God, and supreme

---

[422] Matthew 5:14,16, *The New American Bible.*

[423] Pope St. Paul VI, *"Populorum Progressio* (On the Development of Peoples)," Encyclical Letter, March 26, 1967, #11, https://www.vatican.va/content/paul-vi/en/encyclicals/documents/hf_p-vi_enc_26031967_populorum.html.

[424] Joseph Ratzinger, *Jesus of Nazareth: From the Baptism in the Jordon to the Transfiguration* (New York: Doubleday-Random House, 2007), as quoted in (San Francisco: Ignatius Press, 2008) 28–29.

confidence in man's efforts alone. Engagement with the needs of the world is but one dimension of the Gospel, the horizontal dimension. But if pursued without a communion with God—the necessary vertical dimension and the very source and strength of that engagement—it will lead to distortion and futile results. Sometimes even our religious leaders neglect this second and indispensable dimension.

I'd like to highlight the moving words describing Jesus in the Gospel of Matthew: "At the sight of the crowds, his heart was moved with pity for them because they were troubled and abandoned, like sheep without a shepherd."[425] Such was the plight of many of the three quarters of a million inhabitants in Israel who worked the land, were under Roman occupation, and were crushed by a Roman tax and a temple tax. They longed for liberation and relief, as the elite landowners lived in the cities and the Pharisees looked down upon them. Would-be messiahs occasionally appeared, as did zealots who were eager for insurrection, for the power and bread. I think Jesus would repeat those words today, nearly two thousand years later. Despite the marvel of flight, men on the moon, unparalleled increase in wealth, technology, and the prideful sophistication in advanced human "enlightenment," society is riddled with despair, unrest, intolerance, racism, poverty, human trafficking and exploitation, alcoholism, drug dependency and overdoses, and alarming rises in suicide. Life, liberty, freedom of thought, and religious practice are all oppressed.

The Spectrum of Society's Disillusionment

The Spiritual but Not Religious

Prompted often by the moral failings in the Church, and perhaps the demands of Christian life itself, some have disassociated their spiritual life from any religious tradition and have plotted a subjective journey. For these people, perhaps there is a God, but there are no real objective moral standards, and if those do exist, they cannot possibly be taken

---

[425] Matthew 9:36, *The New American Bible.*

credibly from sources such as the Church, which shows signs of institutional decay. While there is a reasonableness in their search for truth and goodness, they often form and adhere to very nebulous standards independent of any religious tradition.

Those retaining some semblance of a spiritual search—the "spiritual" but not "religious"—conclude that they will simply try to be a good person, live by the Golden Rule, and "live and let live." Conditioned by society to not judge the choices of others, the basis for any of their discernment is nothing but the shifting sand of society's values. Spirituality, then, might simply be found in meditation, communing with nature, New Age spiritualism, or exploring the teachings of world religions to find truth for the modern (post-Christian) mind. This increasingly popular spiritual journey is often private—a retreat into "being a nice person." But "being nice" is not synonymous with discerning, choosing, and acting upon the moral good with an engaging Christian love. The Christian acknowledges that God entered into a covenant with His People, culminating in Christ and His Church. Christianity is a corporate affair—not merely the sum of individuals searching for God. It is a communion with God and each other.

Modern Nihilism

What is nihilism? *Nihilism* comes from the Latin word *nihil*, meaning "nothing." It is a philosophical viewpoint with many variants, but it is often embraced as a practical atheism because of disillusionment with the limits of human knowledge and society's institutions. It also can mean that nothing exists and that reality is a construct of the mind. This form of nihilism bears a similarity to some strains in Buddhism that recognize consciousness only.

More pernicious forms of nihilism hold hints of ancient Greek skepticism—nothing can be known, and values are based on nothing but cultural conditioning, making life virtually meaningless. Nihilists claim that it is mere folly and vain ambition to pursue ideals that cannot be known with certainty. The nihilist, ignoring notions of objective truth or meaning, will attempt to reconstruct values of their own. This often results in floating with the tide and pursuing only short-term goals in opportunistic fashion without regard to a framework for individual and social responsibility.

In rejecting the shackles of institutional religion and authority, the nihilist is left with only a series of subjective decisions that are measured by subjective standards or that will become swept up and paralyzed by the external whims of society's continually changing propositions. As Dean Inge wisely observed in 1911, "If you marry the spirit of your own generation, you will be a widow in the next."[426] Under the guise of freedom, anything becomes permissible. This "freedom" then necessarily expects, nay, demands, a freedom from the consequences of those choices, ultimately to the detriment of self and society.

But if there is no solid guidepost for moral behavior, what does society turn to when discerning the moral good and avoiding anarchy? Why are some behaviors bad for society while others are not? Some claim there is only scientific truth as the basis of society's judgment. But even science does not exist in a vacuum and is subject to interpretation, which is not immune from politicization and can be used as a pretext to achieve a specific societal outcome. In an essay titled "Faith and Reason," Charles Davis observed:

> Scientific method and reasoning have their place; they do not embrace the whole of human knowledge even in the natural order. The claim that no knowledge is valid unless it is gathered by man as a detached spectator with no personal commitment, that would influence his judgment, cannot be sustained of all branches of human thought. The affective side of man has its part to play in the acquisition of truth. Again, the prejudice that everything can be expressed in clear and distinct ideas and that what is not knowable in that way is not worth knowing serves to cripple man's thinking.[427]

---

[426] William Ralph Inge, *The Diary of a Dean,* 1949, as cited on https://quoteinvestigator.com/2019/02/16/spirit/.

[427] John J. Heaney, SJ, ed., *Faith, Reason and the Gospels,* (Westminster, Maryland: The Newman Press, 1963), 15.

There may still be a few behaviors that are more or less universally accepted, even by the nihilist, as antisocial behaviors: the capital offenses of murder, sexual abuse, incest, and rape. In pointing to the 613 commandments given to Moses (including the Ten Commandments), the Jewish tradition uses one midrash that distinguishes "'laws that, had they not been revealed would have had to be invented,' [for] no society or state can exist without laws."[428] But even during the Enlightenment, those who relied solely on human reason (i.e., the Deists) to guide man and aid in inventing these laws underestimated the impact of Divine Revelation (Scripture) in the formation of Christian and societal moral norms that are essential for social order.

There is neither real freedom nor hope in nihilistic viewpoints. Real freedom is not found in the absence of constraint, but rather in empowerment to know and pursue the good. Real freedom is not an unexamined and haphazard existence. Both natural law—discernible by reason—and revealed truth give proper order to relationships with God, neighbor, self, family, and society.

Moral Relativism

Although a growing number of people in society have had little exposure to good moral influences in their lives, many have. The term *moral majority* started as the name of a formal movement in the late 1970s but became synonymous with the notion that most Americans had a knowledge of right and wrong, having been raised in the Judeo-Christian tradition and understanding its link to the country's founding documents. This group has been recast as the "silent majority," and the movement now reflects an admixture of popularism, libertarianism, and patriotism, as moral relativism is generally on the rise.

Is that somewhat amorphous group still the moral majority? Why are they now silent? How has this happened? If there has been a trajectory toward silence in this majority, scandals like the clergy sexual abuse crisis certainly haven't helped to change that trajectory. This scandal has had

---

[428] Emil L. Fackenheim, *What Is Judaism?* (New York: Collier Books, 1987), 137.

the effect of undermining a partner (the Church) in the effort to speak truth and fortify society. Satan, the Evil One, has tried through this crisis—albeit unsuccessfully—to silence Her voice.

One of the earliest disinformation campaigns against Christianity happened when Emperor Nero conveniently blamed Christians for a fire that swept through Rome (the Roman historian Tacitus, *Annals*, XV:44). For generations, it has been the concerted campaign of many in academia and other social influencers to scapegoat Christianity for several perceived ills in society: colonialism, a patriarchal society, abuse of the environment, impediments to science and reason, and suppression of human actualization. The irony in today's environment increases as their list also includes censorship and book-burning, along with the Inquisition, where "reprogramming" is alleged to have taken place. This vigorous campaign seeks to muzzle a voice that today's thought leaders view as a barrier to their agenda.

In this diaspora, moral relativism, as it exists today, rarely comes from reasoned arguments. The undiscerning, beguiled by partial truths or by supposed sincerity or passion for truth, will admire movements that develop under the guise of "positive change for the world" and "human evolution," or other "religions of the day." Although a few of these movements possess some elements of truth and strive, knowingly or otherwise, for the moral good as they see it, many of them are deeply flawed and in opposition to natural law and revelation, leading to contradictions and a culture of death. While admirable to the impressionable, sincerity and passion around a cause are not imprimaturs as to what is morally good. One can be incorrect and sincere at the same time.

Pope St. Paul VI notes that "all social action involves a doctrine [a belief or set of beliefs, and their corollaries]. The Christian cannot admit that which is based upon materialistic and atheistic philosophy, which respects neither the religious orientation of life to its final end, nor human freedom and dignity."[429] Commitment to the Gospel requires Christians

---

[429] Pope St. Paul VI, *"Populorum Progressio*, (On the Development of Peoples),"* Encyclical Letter, March 26, 1967, #39, https://www.vatican.va/content/paul-vi/en/encyclicals/documents/hf_p-vi_enc_26031967_populorum.html.

to be discerning and acknowledge that there is a hierarchy of values that begins with protecting life. Life itself is a necessary condition which alone gives meaning to the existence and exercise of all other natural rights.

Opponents of traditional moral values will also use psychological and emotional tactics to force change and keep others in allegiance to their militant orthodoxy. They will exclude through dreaded social isolation or, worse yet, they will enact violence. Those with moral convictions will be viewed as haters, intolerant, and self-righteous. They will be told that truth is just personal opinion or feelings, for everyone is entitled to their own truth. Because people are wired as social beings, no one wants to endure that cost. Because people too often rely on these external cues, and not objective truths, to regulate feelings and beliefs, they become vulnerable to a compliance with these influences. That is why those who subscribe to moral truth have become the silent majority, to the extent they even form a majority at all.

The articles of faith in this relativism will invariably lead to a long series of ironies and contradictions. The same people who accuse others of intolerance have themselves become intolerant. They rally against bullying at schools but think nothing of bullying. They see no purpose for guilt in their own lives, but they shame. They have become the self-righteous and the arbiters of truth, knowing what is best for our society. It is a militancy in the name of positive change for the world and simultaneously a distrust of God, author of truth, who can alone change hearts and perfect mankind, with the help of a Christian witness of love. Logically, what is just, what is right, what is ethical, is now settled by the power of the one who makes the laws—"might makes right"—and so anything can be morally justifiable. How do these behaviors toward fellow citizens make a nation "a more perfect union"? Instead, these behaviors rob the enterprise of rich ideas and creativity, making it poorer and ill-equipped to achieve the unity it claims to espouse. Such tactics are no more sophisticated than an older child yelling down at his younger sibling to get his way.

The totalitarian impulse will ultimately fail, as it always does. Its contradictions inevitably turn on itself over time and its tenets of orthodoxy are always in flux. More importantly, the irrepressible human needs for conversation, the exchange of ideas, music and artistic expression are deeply embedded in the human personality.

If their truth is so compelling and right, why must they use these tactics to silence the expression of a different viewpoint? Certainly, there is fringe thinking held by a few on both sides that is incurable purely from a reasoning perspective. But short of that, the fact that one's truth may not be compelling to large segments of the population should give one pause for reflection instead of the green light for suppression of others. Perhaps a goal appears noble, but one has chosen unacceptable means to achieve it? Perhaps something in the stated goal is riddled with flaws and half-truths? In short, is a "truth" not accepted by others truly because of invincible ignorance, or is it flawed in some manner?

Just as some have tried to use the government to propel an anti-Christian agenda while in power and in the name of "human advancement"—though not without backlash and resistance—so theologian Karl Rahner, SJ, astutely observed that "if [Christians]...cry out for the Government to make laws to check the decline in moral standards, we are forgetting that we live in a diaspora and that all this will do, in the long run, is generate anti-clerical feeling in people who don't want to be burdened with enforced regulations laid on them by us."[430]

Both sides end up substituting the government for the Gospel. Government cannot change minds and hearts. Government alone is not a reliable substitute for the discernment needed to achieve a more just society when Gospel values are distorted, marginalized, or entirely discarded. Every victory on either side is temporary or fleeting until the other side takes control, as both sides speak past each other on different frequencies. Nonetheless, Christians esteem and advocate for "law which molds characters and is the shield of righteousness [that which is just]."[431] Christians do so not as a special interest group among many, but as the People of the Way, for Jesus is the Way.

---

[430] Rahner, *The Christian Commitment*, 30.
[431] Pope Leo XIII, *"Inscrutabili,"* Encyclical Letter, April 21, 1878, cited from *The Great Encyclical Letters of Pope Leo XIII,* (New York: Benziger Brothers, 1903), 9.

This moral relativism will try to convince many that the Church is only fixated on human sexuality and the suppression of freedom. Though sexuality is an important aspect of the total human person as designed by God, the mark is missed in not understanding Her potent prophetic, societal message that opposes the real evil of moral relativism.[432] This concept is expressed aptly in Paul Peachey's 1981 *Chicago Studies* article, "American Cultures and Human Sexuality": "The situation in American society today is hauntingly reminiscent of Christ's parable of the swept room; older servitudes have been swept away, but models of responsible autonomy are wanting. The results are often shattering. The search for 'personal happiness,' legitimate enough in moral community, leads instead to growing narcissism (cf. Turner 1976). The decline of solidarity ties, which permit responsible moral action, spawns hedonism instead. Many a person is seduced, a marriage is terminated, a child is rejected, because 'I'm entitled to my own happiness.'"[433]

Religious Syncretism

What is religious syncretism? It can mean two things: (1) the creation of a religious tradition by a blending of various features from other religious traditions or (2) the idea that all or most religious traditions are basically saying the same thing and there is little to differentiate them. It is this latter manifestation that I will speak about here.

What might cause someone to hold this view? Below are some common reasons why people conclude that religious traditions are all saying the same thing:

- Most religious traditions speak similarly about love, peace, and forgiveness.
- One has only a shallow appreciation of their own tradition or has no tradition, therefore having no basis for comparison.

---

[432] For more on moral relativism, I recommend Edward Sri's excellent book *Who Am I to Judge?* (San Francisco: Ignatius Press, 2016).

[433] Paul Peachey, "American Cultures and Human Sexuality," *Chicago Studies* 20, no. 1 (Spring 1981): 79–99, 95.

- It could be an indictment of their own tradition. One makes the determination that their own tradition has not "fed" them, and so the priority becomes a search for a tradition that will feed them, irrespective of the tenets of that tradition.
- One has a general disillusionment with religion. Seeing no good examples, it is easier for them to lump them all together.

This honest assessment means that if Catholics (and other Christians) have left their faith tradition, as the polls suggest, then the unique Christian message, and its witness, has failed to resonate. In the case of Catholicism, not only has it failed to resonate for some, but the clergy sexual abuse scandal has, tragically, torn asunder the foundation of the faith of many. The anger and disappointment are natural and understandable.

Despite this reaction, the "power and bread" offered by society cannot fulfill the yearning that derives from the religious nature of mankind. During his testing by the Evil One, Jesus reminded the Evil One of the words in the Book of Deuteronomy (8:3) when He said, "One does not live by bread alone, but by every word that comes forth from the mouth of God."[434] The search for truth, including the purpose and the supreme good of human life, rests in an instinctual recognition of having been created by, and destined to, God. It remains among the probing stirrings in one's soul that even scandal cannot remove or abate. Although scandal may seem to have doused the fire of faith, the universal desire for happiness will prompt man to choose something to fill the hole. Like the song title "Looking for Love in All the Wrong Places"[435] implies, the search will take some away from faith, perhaps to some social cause devoid of the Gospel and to others eager to fill their void. St. Augustine "looked in all the wrong places" for many years, but through a long, discerning journey, he finally realized that his heart was not at rest until it rested in the Lord. He reached the same conclusion as the disciples,

---

[434] Matthew 4:4, *The New American Bible.*
[435] Looking for Love in All the Wrong Places, 1980, written by Wanda Mallette, Bob Morrison and Patti Ryan, and recorded by American country music singer Johnny Lee.

who said to Jesus, "Master, to whom shall we go? You have the words of everlasting life."[436]

I have heard pain in the voices of parents calling in to radio shows concerned that their sons and daughters have left the Catholic Church over this scandal and have gone elsewhere. Like St. Monica, the mother of St. Augustine, who prayed patiently for her son until he found Christ and His Church, parents should be patient and loving and be equipped to speak not only to the scandal, but to their Catholic faith.

Faith is not an emotion. It is an assent of the mind, heart, and will. It recognizes the reasonableness of belief. That reasonableness is based on the testimony and joyful witness of others. Of this, St. Paul says, "But how can they call on Him in whom they have not believed? And how can they believe in Him of whom they have not heard? And how can they hear without someone to preach?"[437] Parents can gently but confidently share their faith and how it has impacted their lives.

Parents should share the message that Christ alone saves us through His death and resurrection, offering His grace in concert with the Church He established (Matthew 16:18–19). He willed that all would be one (John 17:20). Even St. Paul, to whom people point for justification by faith, wrote his letters to established church communities and was very concerned with unity (1 Corinthians 12:13), which is "inscribed in the nature of the Church."[438] It is a unity in creed and praxis, with St. Paul stressing a shared participation (Greek *koinonia*) in the Eucharist (1 Corinthians 10:16–17), "the source and summit of the Christian life."[439]

The formation of the defined biblical canon makes it a "Catholic book" in the truest sense. The Church, the community of believers, imbued with the Holy Spirit, testified to the person and message of Christ, the Risen Lord, by memorializing it first in Her liturgy and oral preaching ("the living and abiding voice," as described by Papias, AD 60–130).

---

[436] John 6:68, *The New American Bible.*

[437] Romans 10: 14-15, *The New American Bible.*

[438] Pope St. John Paul II, *"Euntes In Mundum* (Go into All the World)," Encyclical Letter, Jan. 25, 1988, #15.

[439] Libreria Editrice Vaticana, *Catechism of the Catholic Church*, 2nd ed., (Citta del Vaticana: Libreria Editrice Vaticana, 1997), 334, #1324.

That voice of apostolic authority guided the Church in continuity before, during and after the writing of the New Testament. Through a process of discernment, the Church affirmed the books of the New Testament and the wider canon of the Old Testament precisely as an act of strengthening unity and as the measuring rod of the internal cohesion of divinely inspired written revelation. With the close of that canon, all public revelation ended. As She continues as a pilgrim community awaiting the return of Her spouse, Jesus, the Christ, that same teaching authority and praxis form a continuous tradition consistent with St. Paul's words in 2 Thessalonians 2:15, and not in the sense misinterpreted by some as "the traditions of men," as used in either Mark 7:8 or Colossians 2:8.

It is tragic whenever the unity that Christ willed has been harmed. An honest appraisal acknowledges that countless fractures in Christianity since the sixteenth century have led to confusion and cynicism, ultimately weakening the witness. All Christians must pray and work for that unity and be witnesses in charity.

Anticlericalism or Donatism

Strains of anticlericalism and antisacerdotalism also abound in today's environment. The neo-Donatist view asks, "If the Church is to be identified with St. Augustine's City of God, how can its leaders not be saintly and holy?" Shouldn't "the ministry of Christ be founded on personal holiness rather than on the impersonal, official authority of the priesthood?"[440] If the leaders are unholy, are the sacraments they administer efficacious? Is the message they preach applicable to me if it is not applicable to them? Would it not be better to have no priests rather than unholy ones? Can the governance of the Church be trusted? This growing cynicism gets expressed regularly in popular culture. An entertainer I saw live in early 2020—who was on stage as a singer, not as

---

[440] Norman F. Cantor, *Medieval History*, 2nd ed. (Toronto, Canada: MacMillan, 1969), 412.

a comedian—said, "I went to confession recently. I turned to the priest and said, 'You go first.'"[441]

The guarantee of Christ in Matthew 16:18–19 is made to the Church, the Body of Christ. The Church is built on rock, the rock of Peter: "The gates of the netherworld shall not prevail against it."[442] There was no guarantee that weeds would not mix with wheat. But Christians have the assurance that Christ will be with us until the end of time,[443] when the weeds and wheat will be separated. This is not blind trust in humanity or in religious leaders. This is confident faith in the words of Christ. The witness to the Gospel in all its dimensions cannot be diminished because of the egregious behavior of some.

From Her earliest days, the Church has dealt with the question posed by the Donatist heresy about the validity and efficacy of the sacraments if the validly ordained minister was himself not in a state of grace (perhaps in a state of lapse). God's work of grace is not impeded because of any unfortunate state of the clergy, because of Christ's promise and the Church's divine mission and intent, which is transmitted through visible sacraments. God's work will not be stopped because of the frailty of the vessel.

Citing St. Augustine of the fourth century, Bishop Wilhelm Stockums writes, "The parity between Christ and the priest in regard to the administration of the sacraments is stated in the clearest possible way also by St. Augustine: 'Peter may baptize, but this is He [Christ] that baptizes; Paul may baptize, yet it is He that baptizes; Judas may baptize, still this is He that baptizes.' By citing the name of Judas, St. Augustine meant to indicate in an impressive manner that the effect of the sacraments administered by Christ is not impaired by the moral unworthiness of the minister."[444]

This does not negate the justice demanded for those who commit crimes. The Catechism of the Church notes that—not including the

---

[441] Paul Anka, February 29, 2019, Soboba Casino & Resort, California.

[442] Matthew 16:18, *The New American Bible.*

[443] Matthew 28:20, *The New American Bible.*

[444] Wilhelm Stockums, DD, *The Priesthood* (Rockford, Illinois: TAN Books and Publishers, 1974, 1982), 48.

sacraments, in which the priest acts in the person of Christ—in "many other acts the minister leaves human traces that are not always signs of fidelity to the Gospel and consequently can harm the apostolic fruitfulness of the Church."[445]

In a recent essay by Pope Emeritus Benedict XVI, he writes,

> The timeliness of what the Apocalypse is telling us here is obvious. Today, the accusation against God is, above all, about characterizing His Church as entirely bad, and thus dissuading us from it. The idea of a better Church, created by ourselves, is in fact a proposal of the devil, with which he wants to lead us away from the living God, through a deceitful logic by which we are too easily duped. No, even today the Church is not just made up of bad fish and weeds. The Church of God also exists today, and today it is the very instrument through which God saves us.
>
> It is very important to oppose the lies and half-truths of the devil with the whole truth: Yes, there is sin in the Church and evil. But even today there is the Holy Church, which is indestructible. Today there are many people who humbly believe, suffer and love, in whom the real God, the loving God, shows Himself to us. Today God also has His witnesses (*martyres*) in the world. We just have to be vigilant in order to see and hear them.[446]

---

445 Libreria Editrice Vaticana, *Catechism of the Catholic Church*, 2nd ed., (Citta del Vaticana: Libreria Editrice Vaticana, 1997), 387, #1550.

446 Anian Christoph Wimmer, trans., "Full text of Benedict XVI essay: 'The Church and the scandal of abuse,'" Vatican City, Catholic News Agency, April 10, 2019, Section III of essay, https://www.catholicnewsagency.com/news/41013/full-text-of-benedict-xvi-essay-the-church-and-the-scandal-of-sexual-abuse https://www.catholicnewsagency.com/news/41013/full-text-of-benedict-xvi-essay-the-church-and-the-scandal-of-sexual-abuse.

A Personal Message to Catholics

Even in the face of regrettable scandal, we cannot be seeds bearing only shallow roots, easily blown away in the wind. Our duty is to pursue truth, which is not feeling-based, but rather discerned through the highest faculty of reason, illumined by Divine Revelation. In this way, our will is moved to respond in faith and charity as Christ commands. There will always be human shortcomings that are temptations to abandon faith, but Christ reminds us that "the one who perseveres to the end will be saved."[447] Christ calls His followers to a deeper, trusting, covenantal relationship with Him, an interior conversion, and the command to act consistently with that belief (*lex credendi, lex vivendi*). Put another way, "we act according to who we are and, even more fundamentally, believe ourselves to be (*agere sequitur esse/credere*)."[448] This Aristotelian–Thomistic axiom means there is a consistent connection between our being created in love by God (our ontology), our acknowledgment of this, and the moral obligations that necessarily flow from this and induce our actions.

This consistent connection necessitates that Christians deepen their faith and inform their conscience so that their actions are consistent with the demands of the Gospel. To what or to whom is the Christian to turn? Twitter, the media, a TV psychologist, or ideologies like the sexual revolution or those that often erode hope and offer a false gospel? Everyone should ask themselves, What is my credo? What is my gospel? The true liberty and genuine joy found in the good tidings of the Gospel are affirmed in the Resurrection and confirmed in us by the Holy Spirit, particularly in living out our vocation and in acts of self-giving love.

The Church and many parents bear responsibility for not handing off faith and morals effectively and not witnessing to it in love. Parents are a child's primary educators and role models. Many parents have a shallow knowledge of their faith. It has not been offered with zeal and rigor. Like undertaking calculus with no background in algebra, many adults are

---

[447] Matthew 24:13. *The New American Bible.*

[448] David Bohr, *Catholic Moral Tradition* (Huntington, Indiana: Our Sunday Visitor Books, 1990), 74.

ill-equipped to grapple with life's realities, having left instruction as a child. Even a K–12 Catholic education has left many wanting for a good understanding of their faith. Therefore, it is no surprise that when the heat of the sun bears down, the seed does not take root and grow. The Venerable Fulton J. Sheen, whose television show *Life Is Worth Living* ran on mainstream ABC from 1955 to 1957, summed up the situation thusly: "There are not over a hundred people in the United States who hate the Catholic Church. There are millions who hate what they wrongly believe to be the Catholic Church."[449] This characterization is not about denominational or parochial protectionism, but about ensuring an appreciation of the fullness of the means of grace in the Church.

For this reason, there is an urgency for the Church to understand the underlying causes of clergy sexual abuse and to make seminal changes so Her leaders, too, hear the words of Jesus, "Go and sin no more."[450]

---

[449] Fulton J. Sheen, *Radio Replies, First Volume* (Radio Replies Press Society, 1938), cited in version published by Tan Books (Rockford, Illinois: Tan Books and Publishers, Inc., 1979), IX (Preface written by Fulton J. Sheen).
[450] John 7:11, *The New American Bible.*

Conclusion

This scandal and resulting crisis has come a long way since some of the chronicled cases dating back to the 1950s. The abuse and the reports have not stopped even to this day, though it appears the cases are becoming less frequent. I attribute that to both awareness and prevention, as well as an aging clergy. The phenomenon has left wounded victims and tragedy in its wake. The harm to human dignity and faith is incalculable. As someone who was discerning a calling to the priesthood in the early stage of my life, and who saw in it a means of grace and healing for God's people, I feel pained and paralyzed as this episode in the Church's history transpires.

I have covered many of the key proximate, contextual, and aggravating factors in this *wicked problem*. Though this problem shares some parallels with human behavior found elsewhere in society, it has enough distinct characteristics to be labeled unique. If the Holy Spirit is now trying to move the Church, the message cannot be drowned out by upholding the status quo. The Church must be willing to cross the sea of turbulence with courage and faith, open to "the wind where it blows" (John 3:8). Interior reform will always be required because Christians are called to holiness, to communion with God. Yet concrete steps of institutional reform within the Church are needed as well.

Truth must be the guiding principle of reform in order for the Church to see the issue with clarity and begin to move beyond theological platitudes toward real, concrete solutions. The Church's findings and the steps taken must be not only transparent but also proactively communicated to society effectively and with clarity.

The Church must reexamine mandatory celibacy and the prevalence of homosexual clerics. She must continue to form her priests as faithful servants, affirming their consecrated service but correcting clericalism. As lay involvement continues to increase, lay formation should also guard against traits of clericalism, and their efforts should be directed toward evangelization in the world.

Parish life must be strengthened so that it truly mirrors a community of committed and formed Christians who

- are marked by a formation in the virtues,
- have a joyful eschatological hope for the Lord's return,
- are committed to the service of others strengthened by a shared participation in the Eucharist,
- are beneficiaries of orthodox catechesis that informs the Christian conscience and orients the Christians for a fraternal engagement in the world, and
- are supported in strengthening the "domestic church."

In this way, new leaders will emerge who are well-grounded and well-oriented, and the Catholic faithful as a whole will be equipped to be strong witnesses of Christ's love in the world, where confusion and pain is rampant. Chastity is not just what priests and religious "do." The "New Evangelization" acknowledges that Catholics have been sacramentalized but not catechized. Catholic schools, long praised for their academic rigor, should continually reexamine their role in forming people of sound faith and good citizenship.

May all Catholics hear Jesus's words: "You are the salt of the earth. You are the light of the world" (Matthew 5:13–14). The Lord never fails in His promises to those who trust.

From this dark period can emerge anew "a day that the Lord has made" (Psalm 118:24). Our help is in the Name of the Lord.

Appendix A:
The McCarrick Report

Despite the anticipation and media hype around the McCarrick report released by the Vatican City State on November 10, 2020, I did not feel compelled to weave its findings into the corpus of this book. Though an impressive report intended to document the rise of former cardinal Theodore McCarrick through the ecclesiastical ranks, it is really no more than an attempted explanation of the symptoms underlying the crisis, already well covered in this book. It simply documents what George Weigel, biographer of Pope St. John Paul II, called the "massive system failures."[451]

Theodore McCarrick gained notoriety because, as a cardinal and the archbishop of Washington, DC, he was among the highest-ranked clerics accused of immoral, unchaste conduct both with a minor and among adult seminarians and priests. Naturally, questions arose about how he ascended in ecclesiastical rank given the rumors swirling around his conduct, and the McCarrick report attempts to address the questions

---

[451] Al Kresta, *Kresta in the Afternoon* radio broadcast, Ave Maria Radio, December 1, 2020, Interview with George Weigel, https://avemariaradio.net/kresta-in-the-afternoon-dec-01-2020-hour-1/.

regarding who knew what and when. Given the high-profile case and the findings by the Congregation for the Doctrine of the Faith during an investigation that led to his removal from the clerical state, Pope Francis asked, in October 2018, for a review of all documentation pertaining to him. It resulted in a 449-page report prepared by the Vatican's Secretariat of State titled "Report on The Holy See's Institutional Knowledge and Decision-Making Related to Former Cardinal Theodore Edgar McCarrick (1930 to 2017)."

McCarrick was ordained as a priest of the Archdiocese of New York in May 1958 by Cardinal Spellman and given the honorary title of *monsignor* by Pope St. Paul VI in 1965. He was appointed auxiliary bishop of New York by Pope St. Paul VI and consecrated in 1977. Under Pope St. John Paul II, he continued his rise and was appointed the bishop of the newly created diocese of Metuchen in 1981, made archbishop of Newark in 1986, and then made archbishop of Washington in 2000. He was created a cardinal in 2001.

Some in the media latched onto an observation made in the report that states, "Although McCarrick admitted that his sharing of a bed with seminarians at the beach house was 'imprudent,' he insisted that he had never engaged in sexual conduct and that claims to the contrary, including the anonymous letters, constituted calumnious and/or politically motivated gossip. Though there is no direct evidence, it appears likely from the information obtained that John Paul II's past experience in Poland regarding the use of spurious allegations against bishops to degrade the standing of the Church played a role in his willingness to believe McCarrick's denials."[452]

The inference is that Pope St. John Paul II, due to his understanding of communist tactics, either intentionally overlooked any rumors and concerns about McCarrick or was readily willing to discount them due to other considerations. Though the answer may never be known with

---

[452] Secretariat of State of the Holy See, "REPORT ON THE HOLY SEE'S INSTITUTIONAL KNOWLEDGE AND DECISION-MAKING RELATED TO FORMER CARDINAL THEODORE EDGAR MCCARRICK (1930 TO 2017)," Vatican City, November 10, 2020, 9, https://www.vatican.va/resources/resources_rapporto-card-mccarrick_20201110_en.pdf.

certainty, I want to offer two points on the report's observation. First, as John Paul II's biographer, George Weigel observed in an interview with Al Kresta: "sanctity is not a guarantee of shrewd perception."[453] Second, Pope St. John Paul's alleged concern about the possibility of "spurious allegations" by enemies of the Church is not unfounded in the minds of those in leadership.

Consider the remarks in the autobiography of St. Anthony Mary Claret (1807–1870), who served for six years as archbishop of Santiago, Cuba:

> The...Communists, and Socialists know that their greatest enemies, the ones most likely to thwart their designs, are the Catholic priests. Since their errors are from the prince of darkness, it suffices for priests to present to the people the light of the Catholic doctrine in order to dissipate all the darkness caused by their erroneous tenets. Their most subtle and strategic move, therefore, has been to spread evil of the priests of the Church. They know full well that what they say of priests is only fable, calumny, and lies. But that makes a little difference. Something sticks. Their aim is to get people to lose their respect and esteem for the priests, for they know that this disrespect will immediately affect the religion and doctrine taught by the clergy.[454]

Though the mechanical details and chronology of McCarrick's ascendancy through the ecclesiastical ranks was important to document and understand, it is the defective cultural elements that serve as the oil to the machine. Four key points stand in high relief:

1. Consider Ronald Reagan's adopted tag line for international diplomacy that became synonymous with his brand: "Trust, but verify."[455] Discerning the rumors surrounding McCarrick was an

---

[453] Al Kresta, *Kresta in the Afternoon* radio broadcast, Ave Maria Radio, December 1, 2020.

[454] *The Autobiography of St. Anthony Mary Claret* (Rockford, Illinois: TAN Books and Publishers, 1985), 190.

[455] "Trust, but verify," https://en.wikipedia.org/wiki/Trust,_but_verify.

exercise in trust with little, or faulty, verifying. Though the efforts were understandably discreet, the few parties consulted were likely compromised or intimidated and did not provide accurate information. Those seeking the answers, including trusted advisors to Pope St. John Paul II, naively believed McCarrick's own words and the information generated by asking four bishops to respond to a questionnaire would be adequate to get a complete picture. The investigation should have been more robust.

2. Despite persistent rumors about McCarrick, they were too easily explained away in the absence of formal accusations. Their hesitation to probe or act in the absence of such formal or legal accusations against McCarrick meant that vital time was lost in identifying and addressing the behavior. The expression "where there is smoke, there is fire" did not seem to rule the day.

3. People with knowledge lacked the courage and understanding to come forward to report what they knew. This is a serious cultural problem, and there must be consequences for failure to come forward.

4. It appears that sexual activity among "consenting adults" by celibate clergy drew far less attention than it should have. It should have been a clarion call that something else was at play. The narrow focus on abuse of minors cannot blind leaders to signs of severe moral weakness in other areas.

The McCarrick situation makes for a remarkable case study. The focus must be on lessons learned along with implementing concrete steps from this learning. Ultimately, the case should not be viewed in a vacuum; it is a symptom of the deeper culture addressed in this book.

Appendix B: Chronology of Some Key Steps Taken by the Church

In fairness, it is important that I document for the reader the steps taken by the Church in response to this crisis, in addition to the changes in Canon Law described in chapter XVII.

1990s   Human formation in the seminary was more universally adopted. It is a "training in self-understanding and the development of emotional and psychological competence for a life of celibate chastity"[456] in conformity with Pope St. John Paul II's instruction #50 in *Pastores dabo vobis*.

1992   The United States Conference of Catholic Bishops adopted five principles to guide dioceses across the nation in the handling of these cases. Unfortunately, the principles were not uniformly followed.[457]

---

[456] John Jay College Research Team, "The Causes and Context of Sexual Abuse of Minors by Catholic Priests in the United States, 1950–2010", (Study Report, May 2011), 5, http://votf.org/johnjay/John_Jay_Causes_and_Context_Report.pdf.

[457] John Jay College Research Team, "The Causes and Context ," 4.

1993   The Proposed Guidelines on the Assessment of Clergy and Religious for Assignment was approved by the USCCB on November 18. Because clerics and members of religious orders get transferred for work between dioceses, this policy creates a "consistent approach"[458] that stresses that all dioceses and religious orders are "partners in responsibility for the common good."[459] As such, the policy creates an assessment to confirm "the suitability of the person for the assignment," to make sure "the individual candidate will not cause some harm to a member of the Church or to the entire Church community."[460]

2002   "The Promise to Protect, Pledge to Heal: Charter for the Protection of Children and Young People," also known as the Dallas Charter, was approved (and amended in 2011 and 2018).

        A. National responsibilities.

           The charter created a national infrastructure to assist the Church in the protection of young people and the vulnerable by

              1. creating a National Review Board "to assist in the assessment of diocesan/eparchial compliance with the Charter"[461]

---

[458] United States Conference of Catholic Bishops, "Proposed Guidelines on the Assessment of Clergy and Religious for Assignment," USCCB (website), Nov. 18, 1993, 2, https://www.usccb.org/sites/default/files/issues-and-action/child-and-youth-protection/resources/upload/1993-Suitability-Guidelines.pdf.

[459] "Proposed Guidelines on the Assessment of Clergy and Religious for Assignment," USCCB (website), Nov. 18, 1993, 1.

[460] "Proposed Guidelines on the Assessment of Clergy and Religious for Assignment," USCCB (website), Nov. 18, 1993, 1.

[461] United States Conference of Catholic Bishops, "Promise to Protect, Pledge to Heal: Charter for the Protection of Children and Young People," 6, USCCB (website), last revision: June 2018, https://www.usccb.org/test/upload/Charter-for-the-Protection-of-Children-and-Young-People-2018-final(1).pdf.

2. creating the Secretariat of Child and Youth Protection to serve as a national resource for dioceses and eparchies

3. commissioning a study that resulted in two requests for proposals both awarded to the John Jay School of Criminal Justice: the scope report (2004) and the cause and context report (2011); the cause and context report notes, "No other institution has undertaken a public study of sexual abuse and, as a result, there are no other comparable data to those collected and reported by the Catholic Church. Other organizations should follow suit and examine the extent of sexual abuse within their groups"[462]

4. suggesting and implementing mandated safe environment programs and training to be conducted cooperatively with parents, civil authorities, educators, and community organizations

5. producing an annual report on the progress made in implementing this charter, based on an annual audit process

B. Responsibilities on the local diocesan and eparchial levels.

1. Pastoral outreach to victims. Emphasis is placed on the pastoral outreach "to victims/survivors and their families" to demonstrate "a sincere commitment to their spiritual and emotional well-being," to include provisions for "counseling, spiritual assistance, support groups, and other social services agreed upon by the victim and diocese/eparchy."[463]

---

[462] John Jay College Research Team, "The Causes and Context," 5.
[463] USCCB, *Promise to Protect, Pledge to Heal*, Art. 1, pg. 9.

2. Policies and procedures. Each diocese and eparchy are to "have policies and procedures in place to respond promptly to any allegation where there is reason to believe that sexual abuse of a minor has occurred."[464] A "competent person or persons" are to be assigned to coordinate assistance for the victim's pastoral care.

3. A review board. Each diocese and eparchy are to have a "review board that functions as a confidential consultative body to the bishop/eparch."[465] The majority of the board is to consist of laypersons not in the employ of the diocese or the eparch. The board will advise on the assessment of allegations and in the determination of a cleric's suitability for ministry. They will also regularly review policies and procedures and can review related matters retrospectively and prospectively on all aspects of responses in connection with these cases. An example of a case where the board's recommendations were overridden in a diocese was provided in chapter X of this book.

4. Only consensual settlement agreements. Dioceses and eparchies are not to enter into settlements that bind the parties to confidentiality unless the victim or survivor requests confidentiality and this request is noted in the text of the agreement.

5. Cooperation with civil authorities with concurrent jurisdiction. Dioceses are to report allegations to the public authorities, comply with all applicable civil laws on reporting, and cooperate in civil investigations in accord with the law of jurisdiction. This applies to alleged victims

---

[464] USCCB, *Promise to Protect, Pledge to Heal*, Art. 2, pg. 9.
[465] USCCB, *Promise to Protect, Pledge to Heal*, Art. 2, pg. 9.

even if they are no longer a minor at the time of reporting.

6. Removal from ministry of those credibly accused. If the cleric or offender has admitted to the act or it has been established, the offending priest or deacon is to be permanently removed from ministry and, if warranted, dismissed from the clerical state. The offending cleric can be offered therapeutic professional assistance, both for the purpose of prevention and for his own healing and well-being, but he shall not continue in ministry.

7. Due process for clerics. A cleric who is accused of the sexual abuse of a minor is to be accorded the presumption of innocence during the investigation of the allegation, and all appropriate steps are to be taken to protect his reputation. I have covered some concerns on this matter in chapter XVII on Canon Law.

8. Clear and well-publicized diocesan policies. Dioceses and eparchies are to post on their websites clear policies for ministerial behavior and appropriate boundaries for clerics, paid personnel, and volunteers regarding contact with minors. They are to be open and transparent in communicating with the public about any clergy sexual abuse of minors, with due deference to the privacy and reputation of those involved. They are to have a clear and easily available means of reporting abuse along with a list of credibly accused clerics. Some dioceses now participate in an independently run compensation fund for victims.[466]

---

[466] United States Conference of Catholic Bishops, "Promise to Protect, Pledge to Heal: Charter for the Protection of Children and Young People," USCCB

Appendix C: Section 50
of *Pastores dabo vobis*

The following is the text of Paragraph 50 of Pope St. John Paul II's March 25, 1992 Post-Synodal Apostolic Exhortation *Pastores dabo vobis,* (On the Formation of Priests in the Circumstances of the Present Day). It serves as the standard in the formation of candidates for the priesthood in their embrace of celibacy.

> 50. The spiritual formation of one who is called to live celibacy should pay particular attention to preparing the future priest so that he may know, appreciate, love and live celibacy according to its true nature and according to its real purposes, that is, for evangelical, spiritual and pastoral motives. The virtue of chastity is a premise for this preparation and is its content. It colors all human relations and leads "to experiencing

(website), last revision: June 2018, https://www.usccb.org/test/upload/Charter-for-the-Protection-of-Children-and-Young-People-2018-final(1).pdf.

and showing...a sincere, human, fraternal and personal love, one that is capable of sacrifice, following Christ's example, a love for all and for each person."(151)

The celibacy of priests brings with it certain characteristics thanks to which they "renounce marriage for the sake of the kingdom of heaven (cf. Mt. 19:12) and hold fast to their Lord with that undivided love which is profoundly in harmony with the new covenant; they bear witness to the resurrection in a future life (cf. Lk. 20:36) and obtain the most useful assistance toward the constant exercise of that perfect charity by which they can become all things to all men in their priestly ministry."(152) And so priestly celibacy should not be considered just as a legal norm or as a totally external condition for admission to ordination, but rather as a value that is profoundly connected with ordination, whereby a man takes on the likeness of Jesus Christ, the good shepherd and spouse of the Church, and therefore as a choice of a greater and undivided love for Christ and his Church, as a full and joyful availability in his heart for the pastoral ministry. Celibacy is to be considered as a special grace, as a gift, for "not all men can receive this saying, but only those to whom it is given" (Mt. 1911). Certainly it is a grace which does not dispense with, but counts most definitely on, a conscious and free response on the part of the receiver. This charism of the Spirit also brings with it the grace for the receiver to remain faithful to it for all his life and be able to carry out generously and joyfully its concomitant commitments. Formation in priestly celibacy should also include helping people to be aware of the "precious gift of God,"(153) which will lead to prayer and to vigilance in guarding the gift from anything which could put it under threat.

Through his celibate life, the priest will be able to fulfill better his ministry on behalf of the People of God. In particular, as he witnesses to the evangelical value of virginity, he will be able to aid Christian spouses to live fully the "great sacrament" of the love of Christ the bridegroom for his spouse the Church, just as his own faithfulness to celibacy will help them to be faithful to each other as husband and wife.(154)

The importance of a careful preparation for priestly celibacy, especially in the social and cultural situations that we see today, led the synod fathers to make a series of requests which have a permanent value, as the wisdom of our mother the Church confirms. I authoritatively set them down again as criteria to be followed in formation for chastity in celibacy: "Let the bishops together with the rectors and spiritual directors of the seminaries establish principles, offer criteria and give assistance for discernment in this matter. Of the greatest importance for formation for chastity in celibacy are the bishop's concern and fraternal life among priests. In the seminary, that is, in the program of formation, celibacy should be presented clearly, without any ambiguities and in a positive fashion. The seminarian should have a sufficient degree of psychological and sexual maturity as well as an assiduous and authentic life of prayer, and he should put himself under the direction of a spiritual father. The spiritual director should help the seminarian so that he himself reaches a mature and free decision, which is built on esteem for priestly friendship and self - discipline, as well as on the acceptance of solitude and on a physically and psychologically sound personal state. Therefore, seminarians should have a good knowledge of the teaching of the Second Vatican Council, of the encyclical Sacerdotalis Coelibatus and the Instruction for Formation in Priestly Celibacy published by the Congregation for Catholic Education in 1974. In order that the seminarian may be able to embrace priestly celibacy for the kingdom of heaven with a free decision, he needs to know the Christian and truly human nature and purpose of sexuality in marriage and in celibacy. It is necessary also to instruct and educate the lay faithful regarding the evangelical, spiritual and pastoral reasons proper to priestly celibacy so that they will help priests with their friendship, understanding and cooperation."(155)[467]

---

[467] Pope St. John Paul II, Pastores dabo vobis, Post-Synodal Apostolic Exhortation, On the Formation of Priests in the Circumstances of the Present Day, #50, https://www.vatican.va/content/john-paul-ii/en/apost_exhortations/documents/hf_jp-ii_exh_25031992_pastores-dabo-vobis.html.

Appendix D: Historical and Current Underpinnings of Clerical Continence

Historical Rationale

Joseph A. Komonchak, in his 1981 *Chicago Studies* article, "Celibacy and Tradition," lays out the principal historical reasons for clerical continence, as follows:

> A brief consideration of their arguments may help us form a judgment about the disputes among scholars as to the motives and factors that influenced the development of the legislation. The several documents in which Pope Siricius, Innocent I, and Leo I imposed the law of clerical continence are built upon the following foundations:

1. The Scriptures. The popes appeal to both Testaments in defense of their law. Besides a vague reference to Adam's transgression, they refer to Lev. 20:7 ("Be holy, even as I, the Lord your God,

am holy"), and to the practice of Old Testament priests of separating from their wives when engaged in the ministry. All of the New Testament texts come from the Pauline literature: the distinction between life in the Spirit and life in the flesh (Rm. 8: 8–9, 13:14, 1 Cor. 15:50); the discussion of marriage and celibacy in 1 Cor. 7:5, 7:29; the Church "without spot or wrinkle" (Eph. 5:27); Tit. 1:15: ("For the pure all things are pure, but for the defiled and unbelieving nothing is pure"). The regulation that the clergyman must be "the husband of one wife" (1 Tim. 3:2) is interpreted to forbid digamy and not to permit sexual relations after ordination.

2. Tradition. The first decretal of Siricius maintains that "the Fathers" require the clergy to keep "bodily continence." Scholars do not agree on the interpretation of this general reference.

3. Pagan practice. Siricius twice refers to the practice of continence by pagan priests: "When idolaters perform their impieties and sacrifice to demons, they impose continence from women on themselves…, and do you ask me if a priest of the true God, about to offer spiritual sacrifices, must constantly be pure or if, wholly given over to the flesh, he may attend to the cares of the flesh?"

4. Reason. Siricius also claims that "sound reason" requires continence, but does not appear to give the reason.

5. Ministerial responsibilities. Two of these are adduced; daily celebration of the sacraments and the need to give guidance and example to virgins and to widows.

6. Ecclesiology. If the Church is to be "without spot or blemish" when Christ returns, it must shine with the "splendor of chastity."

7. Ritual purity. This appears to be the chief motive in these documents; it is the one most often cited and it provides the link among all other reasons. It is neatly stated by Siricius: "If intercourse is a defilement (*si commixtio pollutio est*), it goes without saying that a priest must remain ready to perform his heavenly duty, so that he does not find himself unworthy when he must plead for the sins of others.…That is why, my dear friends, the mystery of God must not be entrusted to men of this sort, defiled

278

and unbelieving (Tit. 1:15), in whom the body's holiness has been polluted by filth and incontinence." The argument is a fortiori: If pagan priests, Levitical priests, if Christian laypeople must abstain from sexual activity when engaged in prayer, how much more must priests of the new and spiritual Covenant![468]

Current Rationale

In laying out the current rationale, Fr. Martin W. Pable, OFM Cap., provides a good summary of Pope Paul VI's Encyclical Letter on this subject. Pable writes,

> he [Paul VI] groups the reasons under three headings: Christological, ecclesiological, and eschatological:
>
> 1. Christological: The existential fact that Jesus Himself lived in a state of celibacy, "which signified His total dedication to the service of God and men." In doing so, He opened to mankind a new way of holiness "in which the human creature adheres wholly and directly to the Lord, and is concerned only with Him and His affairs."
> 2. Ecclesiological: Priestly celibacy is first of all symbolic. It manifests, Pope Paul says, "the virginal love of Christ for the Church." Celibacy is supposed to be a sign of disinterested, unselfish love. At the same time, it is presumed to be a stimulus to that kind of love. The notion of "availability to all of God's people" is another element here. Because the celibate priest is not bound by marriage or family ties, he is more free to be of service to all.
> 3. Eschatological: Based on the New Testament notion that "in the resurrection they neither marry nor are given to marriage" (Mt. 22:30), the Church sees celibacy as a sign of the world to come, where sexual relationships will be transcended and "God will

---

[468] Joseph A. Komonchak, "Celibacy and Tradition," *Chicago Studies* 20, no. 1 (Spring 1981): 5–17, 7–8.

be all in all" (1 Cor. 15:28). As Pope Paul puts it, "In the world of man, so deeply involved in earthly concerns and too enslaved by the desires of the flesh, the precious divine gift of perfect continence for the kingdom of heaven stands out precisely as a singular sign of the blessings of heaven" (Encyclical Letter on Priestly Celibacy, 34).[469]

---

[469] Martin W. Pable, "Priesthood and Celibacy", *Chicago Studies* 20, no. 1 (Spring 1981): 61.

Appendix E: Flow Chart: Response to the Sexual Abuse of Minors

The Crime/Offense/Delict is alleged to have occurred

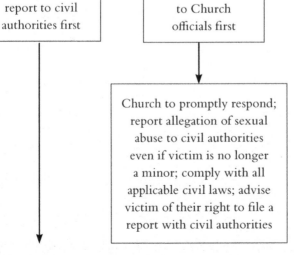

Alleged perpetrator: a cleric, religious, employee, or volunteer

Alleged victim: a minor at the time of the offense; need not be a minor at the time of reporting

Reporting: (A) By whom and (B) To whom

(A) Perpetrator turns himself in; self-reports

(A) Victim reports

(A) Any third-party reports based on observation or suspicion; clerics and religious and mandatory reporters must report promptly to their bishop, unless he is the accused offender

(B) May report to civil authorities first

(B) May report to Church officials first

(B) May report to both, concurrently

Church to promptly respond; report allegation of sexual abuse to civil authorities even if victim is no longer a minor; comply with all applicable civil laws; advise victim of their right to file a report with civil authorities

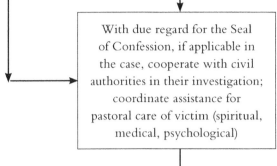

With due regard for the Seal of Confession, if applicable in the case, cooperate with civil authorities in their investigation; coordinate assistance for pastoral care of victim (spiritual, medical, psychological)

If the accused is the local ordinary, the report goes to the Holy See and the region's Metropolitan

Case intake: concurrent with any civil investigation, commence an investigation process in accord with Canon Law; determine which delict and statute of limitations applies

If the Metropolitan is the accused, or the See is vacant, report goes to Holy See and most senior suffragan bishop of region

Accused cleric is to enjoy the presumption of innocence; take appropriate steps to protect his reputation; cleric will be advised to retain the assistance of civil and canonical counsel; cleric may be asked to voluntarily comply with a medical and/or psychological evaluation; the bishop may rely on advice from a qualified review board as needed; if offense is admitted to, or sufficiently established after investigation ("some semblance of truth"), bishop is to indicate this to the CDF and determine the appropriate tribunal of first instance; cleric is not to continue in ministry, pending disposition of case; diocese to be open and transparent in communicating to the public with due respect to privacy and reputation of those involved

If a papal legate is the accused, report goes to the Vatican Secretariat of State

If the facts do not warrant a full judicial process, but other circumstances raise concern, the bishop may impose medicinal remedies

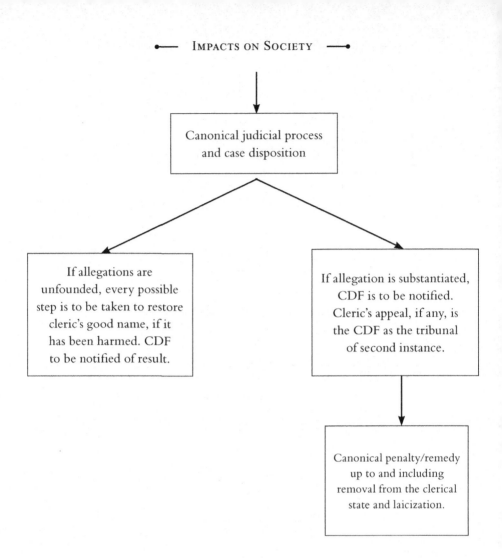

Made in the USA
Coppell, TX
22 July 2022